SERMONS.

Ever - yours, & Christ's,
L. L. Hamline

WORKS

OF

REV. LEONIDAS L. HAMLINE, D. D.,

Late one of the Bishops of the Methodist Episcopal Church.

EDITED BY

REV. F. G. HIBBARD, D. D.

SERMONS.

CINCINNATI:
HITCHCOCK AND WALDEN.
NEW YORK:
CARLTON AND LANAHAN.
1869.

CONTENTS.

PAGE.

INTRODUCTION, ... 9

I.

THE DUTY OF BELIEVING AND CONFESSING, . 29

II.

CHRISTIAN ANGER, ... 53

III.

THE SEEN AND THE UNSEEN, ... 72

IV.

WHAT IS MAN? 92

V.

THE SENTENCE AGAINST UNBELIEF, ... 106

VI.

FRIENDSHIP WITH CHRIST, ... 118

VII.

PAGE.

GOD THE RIGHTEOUS JUDGE, ... 133

VIII.

THE WAGES OF SIN, ... 150

IX.

THE GIFT OF GOD, ... 165

X.

THE SUFFERINGS OF CHRIST, ... 179

XI.

DELIGHT IN THE HOUSE OF GOD, ... 195

XII.

DEPRAVITY OF THE HEART—First Discourse, . . 213

XIII.

DEPRAVITY OF THE HEART—Second Discourse, . 228

XIV.

THE WISDOM OF GOD, ... 250

XV.

THE GOODNESS OF GOD, ... 264

XVI.

CHRISTIAN BAPTISM—First Discourse, ... 276

XVII.

PAGE.

CHRISTIAN BAPTISM—Second Discourse, ... 308

XVIII.

THE SOUL AND THE WORLD, ... 337

XIX.

JESUS REVILED, ... 354

XX.

THE SABBATH OF THE WORLD, ... 366

XXI.

THE IMMUTABILITY OF CHRIST, ... 382

XXII.

CHRISTIAN PATRIOTISM, ... 396

XXIII.

THE INCARNATION, ... 414

INTRODUCTION.

ON a graceful swell of the prairie, beside one of the great ways that thread the rapidly growing West, and near the wondrous central city of commerce, lies another equally growing city, into which the slow procession often moves with measured tread and solemn mien. Here, the pomp, and noise, and rivalry of commercial life are not known. It is Rose Hill Cemetery. Let us enter its "Gates of Peace." We pass along its silent avenues, musing on dread partings and buried hopes, till, turning from where wealth seeks, by costly monuments, to give utterance to the heart's affection and disguise the terrors of the tomb, we seek a less frequented, but not less beautiful spot. Here let us pause. Filial affection has prepared the place, sweet flowers shed their incense here, and angel watchers guard the sacred dust. Here, too, conjugal love in sorrow renews a union which death can not sever. Before us is a simple, well-adjusted mound of earth, with its plain slab of gray syenite, brought from "old Scotia's" hills of rich minerals, as the last offering of filial reverence, bearing the inscription, "LEONIDAS L. HAMLINE." The inscription is as the sleeper, whose house it marks, willed it. We search the monument in vain for any further disclosure—no titles, no history of the labors, honors, triumphs of three-score and ten years. Stranger, if you would learn his peerage you must go to living sources, and read other monuments, whose inscriptions are more indelible, and whose memorial perishes not.

And fitting it is that his name should stand alone upon his tomb, without date or circumstance of explanation. What to him are all these trifles? to him of whom one said—himself the prince of orators*—"I have never seen such dignity in human form before;" and another, "I count myself to have heard the two men who possess the greatest power to fix and retain all the reasoning faculties of men, Rufus Choate and Bishop Hamline;" to him, upon whose lips hung listening thousands, and whose voice swept the chords of the human heart, and awoke the depths of human sensibility? "A burning and a shining light" was he, and the Church was willing for a season (alas! that that season was so brief) to rejoice in his light. We stood by that simple grave, while the multitudes were thronging the thoroughfares to the adjacent city to hear now this, now that orator, and our heart sadly exclaimed, "Alas! the orator, the Chrysostom, the *golden mouthed*, lies here!" Mysterious was the providence that suffered his sun to go down at noon. In the meridian splendor of his intellectual powers, in the fullness of his labors and usefulness, in the height of his honors and the maturity of his Christian graces, when he had humbly laid all upon the altar of the Cross, and, like his Master, had become "clad with zeal like a cloak," his physical infirmities gathered like the hurrying clouds of a coming tempest, and the nightfall of his long and terrible sufferings suddenly dropped upon him. But his light is not wholly quenched to us though his sun has set. The horizon still sends

* Henry Clay.

back the reflected luster of his example, and the "lesser light" of his pen shall stand at least as a bright star in the firmament, with others of the illustrious dead.

It is not our purpose to sketch a monograph, and yet, from the nature of the case, we can not wholly avoid it. We call attention to the man, not for the ends of biography, but to explain the character and value of his writings, and the motive in offering them to the world. Ours is a delicate office, embarrassed on every hand. For who can reproduce the great original? The regrets of the world at the death of a great and good man, naturally enough, prompt to the effort to restore him to society in some form—if possible in some characteristic production of his own mind—that his influence may be perpetuated to other generations. There are men whom death can not destroy. They are representative men—men for all ages—"who being dead, yet speak," and their voice will be heard in all time, and "their words unto the ends of the world." Their influence on other generations is scarcely less than on their own living age. They live in monument, in story, or in song, or, most of all, by their own genius through their own writings. The Church has her great men—great in goodness and gentleness, and not less than the greatest in the fires of true genius. She has become rich in her literature—the accumulation of all ages, the gathered offerings of every variety of mental type, in every department of sacred lore. The influence of this literature upon the world is like the prophet's salt cast into the fountain; like the branch of Moses in the waters of Marah. It is the influence of men speaking from the soul of philosophy and the heart of Christianity, and their thoughts are the common property of the race. Such men are the conservators of society. Their writings are the genetic growth of the history of philosophy and religion. In the Church, their example and their writings are the chief human means of conserving sound doctrine and wholesome practice. If ever the Church becomes the "pillar and ground of the truth," it is chiefly, so far as the human element is concerned, through the working of such minds. Like Peter, they become the "rock" on which the Church is built—not "Simon the son of Jonas," but Peter, the enlightened believer, the bold confessor, the able defender, and the dauntless martyr. The writings of such men supply, in the offensive war of the Church, the heavy artillery; in the defensive, the impregnable bulwark. They are a legacy of priceless worth, which they have

> "Like the prophet, ere his flight began,
> Dropped on the world—a sacred gift to man."

What is it we mean by the term "standard writers," but writers who have penetrated the essential truth—the absolute philosophy of things—the "mind of the spirit," and who have, like Solomon, "given good heed and sought out and set in order," and have "sought to find out acceptable words," so that that which should be written should be "words of truth?"

As a branch of the great Christian family the Methodist Church has had no lack of such men. Nay, in all the life-forms of Christianity, the ages have produced no equal fruit, in this regard, in any equal time. Her literature has not been the mere product of leisure and culture, but has sprung from the workings of her inner life. She has not aspired to the supremacy of letters, but to lead men to Jesus. With letters and philosophy at her command, she has used them for the higher ends of her great commission, and has assumed to "know nothing among men but Jesus and him crucified." This was the example set her by her fathers, and in adhering firmly to this she will fulfill her calling.

Here, then, is the true position for her great men. Models of Christian meekness, gentleness and humility, while "not a whit behind the chiefest" of the literati of their age, they are called, not to teach philosophy and letters, but the truth "as it is in Jesus." With a thorough conception of the workings of philosophy, both on the cultivated and popular mind, they see the dangers of their age, and the fearful driftings of the human thought away from God, and are the better prepared to set up beacon fires along the coast, even should they fail "to make all men see what is the agreement of the mystery, which from the beginning of the world hath been hid in God"—which is "Christ in you the hope of glory."

It is from the stand-point of these suggestions that we are to contemplate the works of Bishop Hamline. Himself gifted by nature with an order of intellect equal to any calling, he knew no treasure too dear to offer upon the altar of God, and aspired to no honors which he could not lay at his Master's feet. With a gift of eloquence of the highest order—the eloquence at once of the reason and the sensibility, of argument and of love, of thought and of diction—it was Christ and not the speaker that attracted the auditors. All minds were like his own, filled with his theme; every thing forgotten in the high mental absorption in the desire to save souls. Literally he fell a martyr to his burning zeal. Perhaps few men, since Isaiah's time, could more fitly say, "The Spirit of the Lord God is upon me, because he hath sent me to preach." This was his great calling, and few among the "stars" of the Redeemer's "right hand" have been more fitted for the work. His style was chaste and elegant, showing familiarity with the English classics, and the

Latin cultus. It was, however, his own. His intellect was not imitative. He copied no one; but while his lofty spirit disdained dependence, he always showed deference to authority, without being enslaved by it. It was the habit of his mind to contemplate every dogma in the light of first principles, and first lay bare its metaphysical foundations. But in these soundings below the depth of common vision, he never lost his perspicuity. In all his manuscripts I have not found an ambiguous or obscure sentence. He was an admirable debater, and knew, what is too seldom known, how to conduct a close argument courteously. His forensic discipline came to his aid here, and to the pith and point of his diction his synthetic power added the rarer quality of comprehensiveness. His terseness was never harsh, and if his logic was severe, and his imagination had feathered and even barbed the arrow, yet it was never poisoned. It was the error, not the deluded victim of it, against which he aimed the shaft, and while "the law of truth was in his mouth," the "law of kindness, also, was in his tongue." Against certain errorists only, he sometimes rose to the terrors of his commission in the stern denunciation of the Baptist. Perhaps the best ideal that could be given of his eloquence, and of his own ideal model of that divine art, is given by himself in his admirable address on that subject, found among his published addresses.

It is not easy to do justice to his character without exaggeration on the one hand, or disparagement on the other. His individuality is so marked that, after all comparisons, he must stand alone. He possessed the enthusiasm, but not the frenzy, of Whitefield and Chalmers. He was more terse and pointed than Robert Hall, with less polish, and with an imagination and an order of intellect of superior adaptations to the ends of oratory. If the reader has ever compared the pictures of Wesley, Fletcher, and Whitefield, in their characteristic pulpit attitudes, he will obtain some idea of the place we would assign to Bishop Hamline. Between the transport of the last, and the calm earnestness of the first, there is the chastened rapture of the second, which speaks, and breathes, and glows through his animated form, but never breaks from the restraints of the reflective reason. It is in this middle realm we would place our author. His debating talent is unsurpassed, and while his acuteness "divides asunder the soul and spirit, the joints and marrow," his amenity never forsakes him. He could well afford to be affable and self-possessed, resting in the calm consciousness of his power, but more than all, in his exalted conviction that he was pleading the cause of God. His periods every-where bear the stamp of a classic mind, but the reader is not oppressed with the elaborate finish of Hall, or the smooth and faultless monotony of Blair. There is no rushing to conclusions before the mind is logically prepared for them, and there is no torturing suspense as in the interminable periods of Chalmers. He never sacrifices the moral effect of the thought to the finish or ornament of the sentence. The arts of oratory he never affected, as we so often meet in the French masters; but in the majesty of his person, the simple ease and dignity of his manner, the earnest and unstudied eloquence of his delivery, he gave the true ideal of pulpit oratory. The flow of his utterances was like the swell of the river current, more deep than rapid, yet moving on without interruption or commotion, always majestic, often quickened, like hurrying waters impatient of restraint, but never like the wild rush of the cataract. In this he contrasted with Olin. Hamline was impassioned, never boisterous—Olin was vehement; Hamline was earnest—Olin impetuous; Hamline was like the even, though often rapid flow of a beautiful stream, bearing its buoyant burden safely and gracefully onward—Olin was like the torrent, or the whirlwind, hurrying all before it. With him the hurricane was inevitable, but he rode upon it in majesty, and, like the spirit of the storm, directed all its forces. Hamline never suffered the storm to arise, but checked it midway, and if the sweep and force of his eloquence were less, the auditors were left more self-controlled, and the practical ends not less salutary. It is beautiful to know that in their lives, Hamline, with characteristic humility, though not a whit behind, yields the palm to his great compeer. "What a man!" says he; "his eloquence is all out of the ordinary course, yet he has no eccentricity, only greatness. Could I preach as he does, I would almost desire never to stop. He will leave no proper memorial of his greatness. He can write, but then his thoughts lie on the paper, like the cinders around the volcano, affording no conception of the scenes of the eruption." At another time after hearing him, he said: "It was one of the grandest exhibitions of intellect I ever witnessed, and as pious as it was majestic. I doubt not that Dr. Olin is the greatest man on the continent; *simple* as *great*." Eloquence, like beauty, is difficult to define, having no absolute uniformity of type. The legal studies of Bishop Hamline had imparted great discipline of mind, and a precision and simplicity of language which never forsook him in the highest flights of his imagination, or the intensest glow of his feelings. The structure of his mind forbade excess, which his exquisite taste eliminated with spontaneous facility.

In his attitude he was erect without stiffness, at ease without negligence. Slightly above the middle size, his physique was full, not corpulent; in his walk, his step short and elastic; in the pulpit, his motions ready and natural, never redundant. With the rising inspiration of his theme, his dark, clear eye gathered new luster and emitted the fire of his thought, his countenance became suffused with the internal glow of his soul, and his whole person was animate with the genius of his subject. "His elocution," says Dr. Lowrey, "was perfect. His voice—how could the Creator have improved it? like the key-note of well-composed music—just right. Soft, mellow, full, rich in its grave accents, clear and insinuating in its higher inflections, tenderly impassioned and melting in its minor and sympathetic tones, it possessed the power of self-adjustment to every word, syllable, and sound of his sentences. I heard him speak twenty years ago, and to-day many of his words, and his mode of uttering them, live in my mind with all the vividness that belongs to the memories of yesterday. This I attribute largely to the enchanting effect of his elocution." His imagination was not gorgeous, not copious; his taste, no less than his "godly sincerity," would have excluded all excess and dazzle. He was not a poet, but an orator, and his imagination described and illustrated rather than invented, and diffused an exquisite tinge of beauty over all his utterances. "His tea-table and parlor talk," says the writer last quoted, "was always ready for the press; pruned, punctuated, emphasized, and eliminated of all redundancies." This was due to the easy play of his imagination, no less than the cultivated habit of his mind.

Terrible was the stroke which brought him low, and forced him to quit the field as a leader of the Lord's hosts, but in the ruins of his body his restless spirit was still active for Christ. While residing at Schenectady, after his retirement from the Episcopacy, among many other labors and devices to bring souls to Christ, he on one occasion enlisted a visiting brother, Rev. Henry Cox, to hold meetings every afternoon and evening for a week in a grove near by. At the last meeting, after sermon, writes Dr. Carhart, "the Bishop arose, and though scarcely able to stand without assistance, made an application of the sermon, and an appeal to the people, such as I have never heard equaled. The Holy Ghost fell on us; weeping was heard in every direction in the vast assembly; sobs and cries for mercy followed; and as the speaker continued, and even before the invitation was given, penitents crowded around the rude altar, and the whole assembly, rising to their feet, seemed drawn toward the speaker, and to melt like wax before the fire. When the invitation was given to those seeking Christ to come forward, it seemed to me that the whole audience moved simultaneously, while some actually ran and threw themselves prostrate upon the ground and shouted, 'God be merciful to me a sinner!' The memory of that scene can never be effaced from my mind."

It was herein that his great strength lay. He had power with God, and hence power with men. Whether we follow him as editor of the Western Christian Advocate, or afterward as editor of the Ladies' Repository, or as a preacher, or a correspondent, or a Bishop, or a polemic, or in the privacy of social life, we find him ever true to his one calling and profession, to bring souls to Christ. His sermons and sketches are uniformly evangelical and spiritual. A hasty view might almost account them monotonous for their ever-ready recurrence to the spiritual and practical, but a closer attention will discover the suggestiveness of his illustrations, the openings of collateral and connecting trains of thought, the sympathy he takes in general knowledge and philosophy, and, what is more rarely found, the depth and originality of his insight.

It was his purpose, upon retiring from the cares of public life, to devote his leisure hours, as his infirmities might allow, to the preparation of a volume of sermons, and some other writings, upon which, in his earlier life, he had bestowed thought. The public expectation had been excited, through the periodical press, to look for this, and no living minister would have been hailed through the medium of the press with a heartier welcome. But even this last hope was doomed to disappointment. Such was the wreck of his nervous system, that Nature refused her office to serve the ever-active spirit, and the Church has lost thereby much that would have stimulated her faith and piety, and that would have adorned and dignified her literature. During his episcopal labors he had little leisure to write, and with difficulty sustained himself against his physical infirmities by all the rest and personal care which his duties allowed. He had attended the General Conference of 1844, at which he was elected Bishop, in compliance with the earnest demand of his delegation, against the equally strong remonstrance of his counseling physicians. His literary productions, therefore, mostly date anterior to that period. Not being able to write to his own satisfaction, he revised but little. Indeed, it was even more difficult to please himself than satisfy his friends. He generally wrote and preached from the inspiration of an occasion, with living souls before him, and an immediate result in prospect. This awoke the fire of his genius, and the vigor of his mental powers, and style and thought, by a self-adjusting intuition, shaped to the high standard of his own mental culture; nay, from the moral height of his argument he forgot all criticism, and his zeal disdained this restraint. But in the cool hours of reflective reason, and the "critically dull" labor of authorship and revision, he seldom reached his ideal. "It is surprising to me," said he, to the writer last quoted, "with what facility some men write books. I do n't think I could write a book, for the reason I could never satisfy myself; I should have to write it over twenty times." But this opinion of himself was the natural result of his profound and unaffected humility on the one hand, and his high ideal of excellence on the other. It was beautiful to observe his great humility. Knowing the acuteness of his mind on abstract themes, the writer of this once sought his opinion on a theological point, involving at once metaphysical distinctions and principles of law and government. He replied with some apparent surprise, "Why, brother, I am no theologian. I was a poor, wicked lawyer when the Lord converted me, and I consecrated what knowledge I had to him, in bringing sinners to Christ." This was his highest profession, the ultimate aim of his ambition. At another time he said, while in conversation upon the missionary work, and the honor of bringing souls to Christ: "I would rather be Brainerd, wrapped in my bearskin, and spitting blood upon the snow, than to be Gabriel." When called to the ministry, like Paul, "immediately he conferred not with flesh and blood." With a competency of this world's goods, a beautiful home and family, a thriving profession, and a prospect of political preferment, he had enough to tempt a selfish mind to decline the call. As an advocate at law—the point of highest honor in the profession—no man of his years excelled him. His talents here were indisputably of the first order, and he only needed time to make his history among the legal magnates of the country. A seat in the Senate chamber of Congress was already in prospect, and would, though unsought by him, probably have resulted at the next elections. He had become not only a promise, but already a power in society, and was universally popular. The nobility of his soul was born in him—it was nature, not accident—and he aspired, even before conversion, to the noble, the generous, and the true. But his call to preach suddenly reversed the current of his life. From the height of worldly hopes and promises, he at once accepted a license to preach, and, after a year of local labor, took an appointment on a circuit with the venerable Jacob Young.* From his spiritual death he seemed to spring, fully armed, into the battle-field. To him it was a new world. All was real as eternity. After ten years' experience he writes, in reply to political friends, from the General Conference of Baltimore, (1840:) "As to politics, tell your worthy nephew I scarcely think of them once a week. I am myself a candidate, but it is for *eternal life.*

* The following, from the Autobiography of Rev. Jacob Young, is too characteristic to omit. He says of Hamline, when he came to his circuit to labor as a junior colleague, after his first year's experience as a local preacher: "While I was preaching, a genteel-looking stranger stepped into the church. His person, costume, and polite manner of entering the house, showed plainly that he was a gentleman of high order. He attracted the attention of the congregation to such an extent, that they could not keep silent till I was done preaching. They soon began to whisper, 'Who is that? Who is that?' Some said it was a Mr. Greatrake, a Baptist preacher, from Pittsburg, who had come down there to neutralize Alexander Campbell, they verily believed; only they thought he was too fine a looking man to be Greatrake. Others said it was Judge Smith, of that district. They concluded they would certainly find out when preaching was over; when, to their utter astonishment, the stranger remained to class meeting. We had a noisy time in class. When I came round to him, he rose and spoke like one who understood himself and was filled with the Holy Spirit." After this humble labor a plan of the circuit was formed, when each preacher took his part of the field. "Hamline went on, making his own appointments, and preaching as he went. Before he had finished his second round there was a general revival on the circuit. All classes flocked out to hear him—even the Seceders. The Radicals and Campbellites became silent. Brother Hamline went on preaching, visiting, and meeting class, as though he knew nothing of such a people; at the same time he took uncommon pains to preach the pure Gospel. His sermons were

I aspire to a throne, but I must have one which will not perish. I labor to secure my election to a sphere high above all thought of earthly minds. I would rather be frozen up at the north pole in a globe of ice, and be doomed to exist there in agony a century, than to be an *hour* exposed to lose forever *heaven* and *God* and *all*. How, then, can I stay to be a politician?"

The period of his chief literary labors did not exceed thirteen years—from 1831 to 1844—a period crowded with events and "labors more abundant" in the active ministry. His writings are always the product of a practical necessity. Aside from the calls of his vocation, he carried on no independent literary pursuits, and had no plan or purpose of authorship. A few sermons were made

theological, experimental, and practical; strengthened by sound logic, and ornamented with pure rhetoric.

"Awhile after this, the Campbellites had a meeting in Wellsburg, and they were talking freely about their Church. One of the leading members rose to his feet and said: 'We have no Church; Hamline has preached us out of existence, and yet he has never said any thing about us.' A conversation took place between Mr. Campbell and Mr. Hamline at a funeral. One of our pious friends died in the vicinity, Mr. Hamline was called upon to preach a funeral sermon, and Mr. Campbell was one of his hearers. After the sermon was over, they walked to the grave together. Mr. Campbell professed to be highly pleased and edified with the sermon. He observed to Mr. Hamline: 'I believe the doctrine you preached to-day.' Mr. Hamline replied: 'You surprise me, sir; for if I understand your doctrine, I was preaching against it.' 'It is very likely you misunderstood me,' said Mr. Campbell; 'for I am very often misunderstood, but I can assure you that I believe the doctrine you preached to-day.'" The leading topic of the sermon was the absolute necessity of regeneration by the Holy Ghost. When he left the circuit, says our author, "he left many spiritual children behind him, and though twenty-five years have passed, many pious persons still retain a grateful recollection of the man, his eminent abilities, ardent zeal, and successful labors." "We were certainly united in heart. Nestor never loved Ulysses any better than I loved Hamline; and Ulysses was never more attentive to Nestor than Hamline was to me."—*Autobiography, pp.* 410–417.

ready for the press by his own hand, but his manuscripts remained almost entirely unedited. Many of his sermons and sketches were written for special uses. His admirable discourse on "The Witnesses," of which unfortunately we have only the plan, was prepared with special reference to a skeptical friend of the legal profession, in his earlier ministry. His sermons on "Depravity" were to arrest the attention of Unitarian members of his congregation, and are models of close argument and eloquent appeal. Many of his sermons were aimed at the special forms of infidelity and indifferentism among the people he served. This applies to his editorial, no less than his pulpit labors. One can not read his writings without feeling a living sympathy with their sentiments. They are the workings of an earnest mind, in a real world, and grapple sturdily with the great practical duties and destinies of our race. He comes not to us with abstract or erudite questions to discuss; in scholarly pretensions many surpass him. It was not his profession. A Macknight or a Warburton might bring to the pulpit more lore, and a John Foster might, for a sermon, present an elaborate "essay with a text at top," but with Hamline preaching and writing had a direct aim at present effect. The salvation of the soul was his ever-present object. Like a true soldier, he carries into the field only the armor for use, but his arsenal stores are never exhausted, and always accessible. His, indeed, was a camp life, and his writings smell of the battle. His proper sphere is the life, not the lore of Christianity. His realm is philosophy rather than erudition. No man was more profoundly versed, than he, in the knowledge of mind, whether considered metaphysically or morally. His sounding line reached the depths of certain knowledge here, and the familiar ease with which he spoke of its mystic workings, whether as a philosopher or a theologian, was like the "voice of one that can play well on an instrument." In the departments technically termed theology, anthropology, and soteriology, he had few superiors.

As a logician, he was scholarly and adroit, but upright and courteous. His mind was naturally logical and orderly in its processes, as it was acute and discriminating in its perceptions. In his writings, ever and anon, his knowledge of law comes to his aid, and discovers itself in defining issues, stating points, (in which he never had a superior,) conducting the argument, precision of language, illustrations, meeting objections, estimating evidence, and indeed almost every-where. The value of this study is not easily estimated by the student in divinity. Philology is scarcely more a key to exegesis than is the knowledge of the principles of law and government, and the course of practice in human courts, to the divine moral government. It is so because, by the institution of God, and by his oft-repeated declaration, all just human government, in its essential principles and judicial forms, is but a transcript of the divine. The advantage of contemplating one branch of science from the stand-point of a cognate branch, is seen in other departments. The nervous organism of the body stands related to the mind, through the senses, and is necessarily brought in to explain many points in mixed metaphysics and psychology, and it is hence that the study of physiology has modernly become so indispensably necessary to metaphysical science. But the study of law is related to the science of mind in another way, not metaphysically but ethically, and sheds great light upon the relations of mind to God, as a subject of his government, and an object of his redeeming love. Sin brings man into penal relations to law; atonement is a provision for rescuing him from that condition, and restoring his lapsed powers. The whole scheme of redemption is of the nature of a juridico-moral process. Here opens a realm of thought unknown to the human mind till Revelation dispels the darkness. God, man, Christ; sin, law, justice, mercy, justification, sanctification—glorious themes! "Angels desire to look into them." Man's relation to law, his desert as a sinner, God's methods of judgment, of mercy, remedial agencies, the sphere of the Church and ministry, the written Word and the ordinances, all arose to view in new and overwhelming visions, when once our author felt the scales of unbelief fall from his eyes, and especially when, entering the higher degree of Christian life, he received the "baptism of the Holy Ghost." It is impossible to fail to see that he reasons, perceives, feels, and speaks as a jurist. The principles of law and evidence, without being named or paraded in form, are unconsciously applied from the spontaneity of habit, and the reader is forced to receive his conclusions, or deny the truth and justice on which human government and society rest. What the learned Dr. Greenleaf has done in defense of the credibility of the Gospel history, in his admirable "Examination of the Testimony of the Four Evangelists," as a subject of fact, Bishop Hamline has not inconsiderably accomplished for theology, as a mixed science of fact and philosophy. By the former, facts have been "brought to the tests to which other evidence is subjected in human tribunals;" by the latter, doctrines have been scanned and principles discussed under the same scrutiny, and with the same application which courts of equity would give to analogous truths. We can only regret, if it be lawful to regret any thing under the reign of Divine Providence, that the lamented author was not permitted to finish what he had so hopefully begun.

The value of a writing is not wholly dependent on its literary finish. This is its dress; the material value is the thought. Like the diamond, its beauty is inherent, though enhanced by skillful cutting. Style is the mere cutting of thought, and it is meet that beautiful things should be placed in beautiful forms and settings. The style of our author is an improving model for our youth, and will bear comparison with any writer in our Church; I may add, with the better class of English and American authors. Yet, it is not for this secondary value that his works are offered to the public, nor do we challenge criticism at every point, but wish it ever borne in mind that his works are strictly posthumous, published not by his order or expressed wish, but on the judgment of friends,* in which the editor must bear a share of responsibility, and at the solicitation of many. In this we but follow current and long-established example.

In the works of Bishop Hamline the Methodist Church and family have one more able witness, not only of the cardinal truths of Christianity, but of the peculiar characteristics of Methodistic doctrine and policy. Should that Church ever decline in piety so as to ignore her characteristic tenets, or should her enemies rally and, as in

* In addition to numerous other calls of a more private character, for the publication of Bishop Hamline's works, the following is from the last General Conference, (1868.) On the twentieth day of the session, Dr. A. Lowrey offered the following preamble and resolution, which were adopted:

"*Whereas*, We learn that the manuscript theological, literary, and religious works of Rev. L. L. Hamline, D. D., late Bishop in the Methodist Episcopal Church, have been placed in the hands of Rev. Dr. Hibbard, to be edited for publication, and are now nearly ready for the press; therefore,

"*Resolved*, That from the known piety, genius, and high culture of the lamented author, we commend the purpose to publish his literary remains under judicious editorship, believing that they would be valuable to the Church."

earlier times, assail her doctrines or endeavor to impeach her orthodoxy, the works now offered to the Church and public will be a swift witness against her in the former case, or a wall of defense in the latter. It is well for any Church to have such guards thrown around her standards, and such admonitions to contend earnestly for the faith once delivered to the saints. These great way-marks of the generations are not to be viewed merely as monuments of men that have lived, but as guides to men that are yet to live, and the lapse of ages will but increase their living power.

F. G. H.

SERMONS.

THE DUTY OF BELIEVING AND CONFESSING.

"*With the heart man believeth unto righteousness, and with the mouth confession is made unto salvation.*" Romans x, 10.

IT is true, as Christ has said, that "Wisdon is justified of her children." Those doctrines of the Christian revelation which annoy the unregenerate, become as "marrow and fatness" to them who are born of God. The believer can bear witness. Perhaps, before conversion, nothing perplexed him more than faith; whereas, after conversion, nothing filled him with greater admiration. Then he could realize the force of those words, "Believe on the Lord Jesus Christ, and thou shalt be saved;" "He that believeth on the Son hath everlasting life."

Confession, as well as faith, is to many a "stone of stumbling." Christians attach an importance to both, which, in the view of unbelievers, is wholly unaccountable. Unsanctified reason is confounded that righteousness should be wrapped up in faith, and salvation be made to hinge on confession. Yet God has so ordained. And if these connections are mysterious and even repulsive to the unbelieving, they are simple as well as grateful to him who enjoys their saving benefits: "The secret of the Lord is with them that fear him, and he will show them his covenant."

The text presents for discussion FAITH and CONFESSION, with the *Scriptural relations or dependencies of each.*

I. FAITH—that faith which is "unto righteousness"—is, in the language of the text, believing "with the heart." In other words, it is such a belief in divine revelation as involves not only a conviction of its truth, but a hearty delight in it. As thus defined, it is,

1. *Simple belief.* This is an office of the mind. It is the mere perception of truth as such, regardless of its bearing on our interests or affections. Applied to Christianity, it is crediting the Scriptures as a divine revelation, with all the truths which their just interpretation inculcates; and especially those Gospel statements which may be aptly called the *test truths* of the system, one of which is named in the context: "If thou shalt confess with thy mouth the Lord Jesus, and shalt believe in thine heart that God hath *raised him from the dead,* thou shalt be saved." Not that crediting this isolated fact would save a man, but that the confession of this offensive feature of the Gospel, in the face of persecution, implied a full Christian faith. But, according to the text, saving faith is more than this simple belief. It is,

2. Believing "*with the heart.*" It is gust as well

as vision. It not only credits, but relishes the truths of revelation. It is not only convinced, for instance, that Christ is risen from the dead, but, like Mary at the sepulcher, is *joyfully* convinced; and, in the surprise of rapt affection, cries out with Thomas, "My Lord and my God!" Let us dwell a moment on this feature of saving faith.

Propositions addressed to men's understandings produce a great variety of inward states in the mind; among others, belief and unbelief; and, in the affections, gratification and regret. How various the effects produced by a series of reports made to an avaricious merchant concerning one of his ships at sea—as, first, that she is lost with crew and cargo; which, believed, inflicts pain. Second, that she outrode the storm, and is safe, which, *dis*believed, produces equal disappointment. But at last the ship comes in, and the commander in person reports her safety and successes. This is credited with joy.

The first is an example of speculative faith like his who credits Christianity, but feels that it is a sentence of condemnation to him. Of such there are thousands. They are not the absolutely stupid who scarcely take the pains to believe or disbelieve; but are persons of more serious convictions, whose faith disturbs their consciences—who, moved by the Spirit, concede the truth of Christianity with some solicitude, but find their tastes and views of interest at war with their convictions. Their belief *without the heart* is an important element of faith; but, of itself, it can neither comfort nor save. It belongs in common to anxious sinners, undone reprobates, and fallen angels—"Thou believest there is one God; thou doest well. The devils also believe and tremble."

It may be questioned if the second example applies to our theme. Yet there are men who say they wish to believe the Bible, if they could find reasonable proofs of its divine inspiration. "Wish to believe and can not!" It is possible. For we learn that men may "resist the Holy Ghost"—may resist till they are forsaken to blindness of mind, are given "over to believe a lie." Then light becomes darkness, and darkness light unto them. They who "would believe the Bible if they could," should look, alarmed, into their own religious history, and consider if they have not armed themselves against believing. They who first "*turn* away their ears from hearing truth," may at last "*be* turned unto fables." If we struggle for years to disbelieve the Gospel, no wonder that, God-forsaken, we at last make it out.

The third example illustrates saving faith, which, as stated, is the joyful belief of Gospel truth, which credits Christian doctrine as the testimony of God, and exults over it as good news from heaven—such faith as the Psalmist had: "Thy word is very pure; therefore thy servant loveth it;" "I rejoice at thy Word as one that findeth great spoil."

3. This faith has *spiritual limits.* As a speculation, it credits *all* Bible truth; as an affection, it relishes or delights in all. The believing heart is docile. It first seeks to know, and then "receives with meekness the ingrafted word." There is an easy faith, which, not content with the old, sets

itself to frame a new Bible. It expurgates and adds. It fondly canonizes one series of texts and sharpens criticism against another series. It is a bold operator. It leans with composure over the Bible; moves and cuts, light-fingered, through and through its pages; and in its progress makes and unmakes worlds, quenches and kindles hells, or changes the date and venue of these small things at pleasure!

True faith is quite another thing. It will not have a syllable added or blotted in God's book. It abhors all expurgations. It will not tolerate tradition as a supplement to Scripture. Its language is, "The Bible, the *whole* Bible, and *nothing but* the Bible!" He who has this faith can say, "I love thy commandments above gold; yea, above fine gold." "How sweet is thy word unto my taste! yea, sweeter than honey to my mouth."

4. This faith embraces *self-application.* What it credits it also appropriates to its legitimate end; otherwise it could not be a *hearty* faith. How can we cordially embrace the averments while we decline the Gospel uses of God's truth? Does not the same authority which attests to us the truth assure to us also its uses and its efficacy? Take the promise, "Believe on the Lord Jesus Christ, and thou shalt be saved." Here are three particulars. The first is faith: "*Believe.*" The second is the *object* of faith: "*On the Lord Jesus Christ.*" The third is the *efficacy* of faith: "*And thou shalt be saved.*" Must not faith in this promise embrace each of these particulars? If it leave out the second—"Jesus Christ"—can it be a hearty faith? No more can it be hearty if it leave

out the third particular, "Thou shalt be saved." To doubt the *efficacy* of the promise as much dishonors God as to doubt its *whole truth*, seeing both are vouched for by the very same authority.

But cordially to believe each particular of this promise is so to believe it as to secure or to *experience* its efficacy, because the only authorized method to obtain the virtue of it is to "believe it with the heart." Observe, however, we say cordially, or "with the heart," as this qualification is the safeguard of the doctrine. For faith which thus involves the affections is divinely wrought—is "of the operation of God."

It follows, then, in regard to thus believing with the heart that it is a state of salvation—not of *finished* salvation, but of "*righteousness*," which prepares for, and is an element of it. This is no more than to say that faith in this promise is such a state as God has pledged shall be the adjunct of faith. And here we are brought to

II. THE SCRIPTURAL RELATION OF FAITH AND RIGHTEOUSNESS.

Righteousness, in the text, has its evangelical import, and means that freedom from guilt which follows pardon, and that moral purity which flows from "sanctification of the Spirit." Faith in Christ is the condition on which these are received. The text declares, "With the heart man believes unto [both these branches of] righteousness." Not that faith justifies by its intrinsic merit, or sanctifies by its inherent power. The words are, "Believeth *unto* righteousness." The merit is in Christ. The righteousness is not *in*, but *through* faith, which derives to the soul a gracious dispensation of God's pardoning and purifying love. But as faith, and faith alone, can reach this righteousness, it is known in Scripture as "the righteousness of faith."

As to pardon, the Bible teaches us, "By Him all that believe are justified from all things, from which they could not be justified by the law of Moses." "But to him that worketh not, but believeth on him that justifieth the ungodly, his faith is counted for righteousness." "Therefore we conclude that a man is justified by faith without the deeds of the law." In regard to purity the apostle says, "And put no difference between us and them, *purifying their hearts by faith.*" "That they may receive forgiveness of sins, and inheritance among all them that are *sanctified through faith* that is in me." These, with many other texts, clearly show that both pardon and sanctification are received through faith. We may add, each blessing is enjoyed whenever the promises which specifically pledge the one or the other are believed *with the heart.*

It should be stated that the words, "man believeth unto righteousness," have not only an inclusive, but an *exclusive* force. Besides proclaiming the efficacy of faith, they enforce the inefficacy of all other things, except as other things involve or infer faith. This is plain from the connection. The preceding verses array the righteousness of the law, as to its saving efficacy against the righteousness of faith, and condemn the Jews for going about to establish the former, called "their own righteousness," instead of submitting themselves to the latter, called "the righteousness of God." In this connection the text clearly and forcibly denies that righteousness can be attained by any means but faith. God chooses none to salvation, but "through sanctification of the Spirit, and *belief of the truth.*"

None, then, can devise a substitute for faith which has not a concurrent, but an exclusive jurisdiction, so to speak, over the grace which saves. All merit is in Christ. All ways of seizing it are one; namely, faith. We can acquire no merit by any amount of effort or penance on our part. The holiest saints that live, or *ever* lived, are so far behind all works of deserving, that they have no plea for *self*-security, to say nothing of those rich supererogations which are cheaply set over to the credit of the needy, whose recanted heresies do not yield to the ordinary remedies. *All* are needy, and all are guilty. "All have sinned," says the apostle, "and come short of the glory of God." All, then, must fly to the cross. Looking to be saved in other ways is to reproach that very cross; for "if righteousness come by the law, then is Christ dead in vain."

As to our guilt, so far from being *removed*, not a grain's weight can it be *lightened* by the sorest grief for sin; by reformations the most exact; by self-denials the most rigid; by penances the most abject, painful, and protracted. Should we commence all these in early childhood, and pursue them unremittingly till death, so far from saving, without faith they would involve us in growing guilt and ruin; and the law which we "thought to be unto life," we should find "to be unto death." All such struggles after life by the law would proclaim our disparaging views of the Gospel; for, like Judaism, it would be going about to establish our own righteousness instead of submitting to the righteousness of God. From these self-righteous deeds and self-denials, we must turn to naked trust in Christ; or the Gospel, so full of mercy, will denounce, in thunder-tones, "By the deeds of the law shall no flesh be justified;" "He that believeth not shall be damned."

To this wholesome doctrine there is nothing to object. Other things than faith may seem to be made conditions of salvation; but they are all so related to faith as to make the latter really the condition. Sometimes salvation seems to hinge on repentance; as, "Except ye repent, ye shall all likewise perish;" but repentance is connected with faith as its forerunner. So of prayer: the context says, "Whosoever shall call on the name of the Lord shall be saved; but," it is added, "how shall they call on him, in whom they have not believed?" showing that prayer *involves* faith. James would seem to teach that we are saved by works; but he only means that faith, without works, is simple belief, and not belief "with the heart." His doctrine is, that, unless our deeds indicate our faith, our faith is defective, and can not save our souls. And here we pass to another branch of the subject; namely,

III. Confession, which is also named in the text as a condition of salvation; but which, as we shall see when it comes in place, has this efficacy simply as the cherisher and exemplifier of faith. Let us now glance at the *nature*, the *matter*, and the *mode* of confession.

1. Its *nature* is not determined by the meaning of the word, which denotes assent to imputations on our conduct, or the voluntary exposure of our evil thoughts or deeds. This is a frequent meaning of it in the Bible. The Israelites thus confessed, under the reproofs of faithful prophets; and thus we are told to "confess our faults one to another."

The confession named in the text is not of crime, but rather of religious grace and virtue; namely, faith in Christ. Yet it is confession; for it is, by some, denounced as crime. Moreover, ancient forms of martyrdom often challenged recantation with the promise of escape; and to avow faith in Christ, under such appalling circumstances, might well be called "confession." But this avowal was confession, whether with or without challenge; and so it is to this day. If without, it is sometimes called *profession;* and that from Scripture warrant. Thomas confessed, when he cried, "My Lord and my God!" as well as Stephen, who testified before enraged foes. And if the attending trials make it a "confession," there are crosses besides martyrdom. Derision and reproach can wound as well as wild beasts; and when the former assail us at the sacred fireside, they may well claim for us the honors of confession.

But, if challenge were necessary, we have it from God himself, who commands us to "be ready always to give an answer to every man that asketh a reason of the hope that is in us, with meekness and fear." If not the foes, the friends of Christ will want the reason of our hope; and shall we not be as ready to meet the requirements of Christian love, as the martyrs were to endure the demands of stern and wrathful persecution?

2. As to the *matter* of confession, the context seems to limit it to Christ's resurrection: "If thou confess, and believe in thine heart that *God hath raised him from the dead.*" To understand this we must regard the *spirit* of it. Certain acts, in given circumstances, prove sincere piety, when, in different circumstances, they would prove nothing at all. Look at Daniel. Kneeling for prayer by his window, displayed, in the circumstances, heroic zeal for God; but take away the king's decree and den of lions, and suppose his prayers offered up in the city of Jerusalem, where the most profane Jew observed the custom, and this act of Daniel loses all its force. Another example is the conduct of the three "Hebrew Worthies." Not to worship idols on Mount Zion was common to all classes, whether pious or profane. But, in Babylon, where nations bowed down in submission to royal edicts enforced by the terrors of a burning, fiery furnace, for three captive strangers to resist, and hurl defiance at the monarch in the name of Israel's God, was periling every earthly interest, and afforded the strongest proof of sanctity and zeal.

In the light of these examples how evident it is, that confessing one offensive feature of Christianity may involve a full confession of the system! What that feature is must be determined by the state of public sentiment. In one age or region it may depend on "caste;" in another, on the practice of polygamy; and, in a third, on false histories or "traditions," which cherish national vanity or profane superstitions, and are in conflict with the doctrines or chronologies of Scripture.

In Paul's day the resurrection was peculiarly offensive, and concentered on itself the sum total of the odium which fell upon Christianity. Christ was slain as a deceiver. Except by his disciples he was abhorred above mankind. His resurrection would not only draw after it his Godhead, but would infer upon his crucifiers unexampled guilt. It was therefore *the* question of the times—the point of desperate conflict between Christ's friends and foes. When persecution raged, it was directed to that point, and met by the specific testimony of the unresisting martyrs—a testimony cheerfully sealed in their own blood. Surely this was a plenary confession, involving faith in Christ's Godhead, atonement, and offices, in the inward work of the Spirit, in every doctrine of his Word, and in his promises, even to that "exceeding precious" one, "*He that loseth his life for my sake shall find it.*"

Thus the brief form of confession in the context was made all-comprehensive by those existing circumstances which, whenever they return, will stamp that form with its original force and meaning. But to confess Christ's resurrection in the midst of present Christendom, would scarcely pledge a man to decent orthodoxy, and might leave him suspected of the grossest infidelity. Of course true confession must be made more explicit. When popular sentiment moves men not to deny, but acknowledge Christ, as the true God and risen Savior, if the disciple would bear the cross of true confession, he must go some steps beyond that unoffensive summary, to those features which now come under the ban of public prejudice. Maintaining these with the firmness of a martyr, he will show that he is not ashamed of Christ or of his Word; for Religion has still unwelcome features, and always will have to unsanctified minds. Moreover, she will be subject to that milder persecution which, when it does not bind and burn, will turn its victim over to contempt and ridicule.

An ingenious writer hints that religious persecution has passed through several stages, answering to the progress of Divine Revelation. Its first aim was God the Father, in that Divine unity which stood opposed to idolatry and polytheism, and in defense of which so many prophets gave their lives. Next it assailed God the Son; first in his own sacred person, and then in that great "cloud of witnesses" who "loved not their lives unto the death." Now it wars against God the Holy Ghost, by deriding his gracious work upon the souls of men.

Is there no ground for these distinctions? What doctrinal test can now separate the true Christian from an orthodox, guilty world? The unity of God was a badge to the Jew, but none to Christ's disciple, for all Jewry held it; and to Christ's very crucifiers it might have been said, "Ye believe there is one God—the devils also believe." The resurrection was, in turn, a badge to the apostles, but it can be none to us; for now to the worst blasphemer it may be said, "Thou believest Christ is risen—devils also believe." These ancient tests are obsolete in Christendom, unless sometimes arrayed against a haggard infidelity which lingers here and there in low and vulgar haunts.

What, then, is now required? Confessions of Christ in the work of the Holy Spirit—that Comforter which he sent to "take of the things of Christ, and show them unto us"—confessions from living witnesses that the Spirit reproves, regenerates, and "sanctifies wholly," through faith in Jesus Christ. The Jews testified of God's works in their day; the apostles, of his miraculous deeds in the commencement of Christianity; and what belongs to us? We can recount no plagues like those which smote Egypt, nor delivering miracles like those of the exodus. Yet God has not withdrawn his presence from our world. He "works a work" in our day. "It shall come to pass in the last days, saith God, that I will pour out of my Spirit upon all flesh." This he now does, as we have seen and known, convincing and regenerating—"sprinkling clean water upon" us that we may "be clean." And of the plagues of sin within us, worse than the plagues of Egypt—of the rod, not of Aaron, but of Christ smiting our rocky hearts and causing the waters of repentance and then of joy to gush forth—we too are witnesses.

Outward miracles in our day almost cease to be disputed. Other matters are now drawn into the issues which separate and antagonize the Church and the world. Christ's Messiahship is yielded; but the

Spirit's gracious work is denied and derided. Not the advent, but its *aim*, provokes man's enmity; and this has become the issue which must next be settled, not merely with the world, but with formal Christianity. This in turn is *the* question—the point at which persecution aims, with such annoying subtilties as her malice may employ when she dares not use force; and, as faithful witnesses, we must shape our testimony to her present modes of assault. Of what avail is testimony which does not touch existing issues?

3. The text prescribes the *mode* of confession; and the mistakes committed on this point show how important it is that the question should be settled by Divine authority.

(1.) Some say, "My position in the Church testifies." Not so. For to this day "they are not all Israel who are of Israel." The visible Church is not mainly composed of Christians. It may be that nineteen-twentieths of her members know nothing of vital religion; and even her Protestant branches are fields in which the tares and wheat "grow together until the harvest." Membership in such a Church will not be received as an explicit avowal of saving faith in Christ. A Church is condemned as heartless and Christless for general silence on the subject of experimental religion; and if an unwitnessing *Church* fall under such reproach, an unwitnessing member of it can surely fare no better. And what if Church membership were a profession of Christian "hope?" are we not commanded to "give a *reason* of that hope?"

(2.) Others say, "Let your *life* testify." Testify what? If well ordered, it may testify the purity of your morals, and the innocency of your social dispositions. It may prove you honest, industrious, and neighborly; but all these you may be without regeneration or the love of God. How shall it be known *why* you are honest—whether grace or nature, the love of Christ or the love of praise, makes you so? Your life testify? Absurd! As well might the blameless conduct of a witness at the bar be offered in reply to fifty cross questions.

(3.) The mode is fixed by God's authority. "With the *mouth* confession is made unto salvation;" that is, in words spoken or written—for in different circumstances they are equal. This has been the usual mode from the beginning. When Noah built the ark, he mingled his testimony with his daily toil, warning a wicked generation of its impending doom. Those "holy men of old," the patriarchs and prophets, "*spake* as they were moved by the Holy Ghost;" some of them enjoying his infallible guidance. The Psalmist wished to "*declare*" what God had done for his soul. He prays, "O Lord, open thou my *lips*, and my *mouth* shall show forth thy praise." In harmony with the text, which connects faith and confession, he says, "I believed, and therefore have I spoken." The New Testament saints followed this example; for the apostle says, "We also believe, and therefore *speak*." Stephen testified with his expiring breath, and Paul records his experience in its remarkable details, visions, power, and all—not leaving out his call to preach, nor even his visit to the third heavens. It seems he was wont to relate all in his sermons, and that before kings; not standing on his own apostolic dignity, nor anxious about the violations of courtly etiquette.

We ought to join the Church; else we reject God's sacraments, and choose the world before God's people. Like persons brought into court, we are summoned into the Church to be qualified as witnesses by sacramental oaths. In the Church we should behave with the utmost circumspection, so that, our veracity unquestioned, we may testify with the utmost effect. But all this does not fulfill the demand of the summons. Having the position and the qualifications of a witness, we must next give our testimony, and not stand in the Church like "mutes" before the court.

IV. It remains to notice the *relations or dependencies of confession.* The text ascribes salvation to it. But the Scriptures teach, as we have seen, that faith is the only real or efficacious *condition* of being saved, as Christ's merit through the Spirit is the only efficacious *cause.* Let us consider, then, more carefully the shapings of the text.

"With the heart man believeth unto righteousness, and with the mouth confession is made unto salvation," may seem to institute a sort of double proportion; namely, "*as faith is to righteousness, so is confession to salvation.*" But we must be guarded in our understanding of "*so is,*" not receiving it in its precise technical force, or we shall do violence to Scripture. Its force is to define the *certainty of results*, but not the *principle which works those results.*

It may be difficult to illustrate this distinction, which, metaphysical as it may be in aspect, is vital both in theology and in experience, as every thing is which affects our views of faith. If a man should say to his neighbor, "The fountain by yonder hill supplies water to the vale, and these minute streams revive the withered herbage," two relations — connecting the fountain with the vale, and the streams with the herbage — would be expressed; but two other relations — connecting the fountain with the streams, and the fountain with the herbage — would be implied; and these last, being familiar to our experience, would impress us as forcibly as though they were expressed. So in the text, the relations of faith to righteousness, and of confession to salvation, are expressed; but the relation of faith to confession and to salvation is not expressed. Faith, as a *condition*, bears the same relation to these which the fountain bears to the streams and the refreshed herbage: it gathers into the soul, from Christ the hidden source, the life-waters of salvation; but confession, as an outward act of faith, renders these life-waters refreshing and beneficent.

In the light of this illustration we may perceive in how different a sense confession and faith are conditions of salvation. Faith is the *real* or efficacious condition; yet, as confession must interpose, like the streams, to attain the end of faith, it is ordinarily as indispensable as faith itself. Even the thief upon the cross not only believed but confessed, suddenly as he was hurried into the presence of his Judge.

But what service does confession render which

makes it indispensable? It cherishes and exemplifies our Christian graces.

1. It cherishes them, as light and air do the plants which must perish without their influence.

(1.) Confession promotes *humility.* Tracing our pardon and purification to Christ is conceding our own guilt, pollution, and helplessness. To claim Christ as a Savior, is to proclaim self a sinner. This is a cross against which pride rallies, and which, borne, lays pride in the dust. Confession glories in the cross, which is glorying in self-abasement, yea, in self-crucifixion, as Paul did when the Pharisee was dead in him: "God forbid that I should glory save in the cross of our Lord Jesus Christ, by whom I am crucified to the world." What he once thought of that in which his humility now gloried, is familiar to us all.. When Peter stood in the judgment-hall and warmed himself, confession would not only have humbled, but would have *saved* him.

(2.) Confession aids *self-consecration,* by dissolving our connection with the world, and breaking up our union with the creatures. It says, not of the friends, but of the enemies of religion, "Let us break their bands asunder, and cast away their cords from us." It yields a public pledge to Christ and his Church, and fortifies religious purpose by compelling its worst foes, such as earthly policy and the sense of shame, to become its aids and allies. If the Christian would multiply the cords which bind his sacrifice to the altar, let him often proclaim his purpose to keep it there. God will employ our confessions to lead us out of the world into his closer fellowship. What we feebly bind on earth he will be pleased to bind in heaven, writing on our hearts, "*I will receive you.*"

(3.) Confession strengthens *faith itself.* Like filial piety, it nourishes its parent. It is to faith like those braces which the juices of the stalk throw out for self-support. Its influence may partly depend on the laws of mind; for such is our mental constitution that avowal fortifies and almost creates conviction. In this way skepticism has been wrought into atheism; for men have become confirmed in infidelity by lightly vindicating it in conversation. And if against evidence a man can talk himself into the belief of fatal error, how much more may he deepen the impressions of truth, when he has reason and conscience on his side to enforce his own avowals? Doubtless, on natural principles, confession strengthens faith.

And so it does evangelically or by the Holy Spirit, under whose gracious culture the renovated heart is like a vine which becomes more fruitful for its pluckings. God will work faith in them who use it for his glory, by standing up in its strength as his unflinching witnesses: "Whoso offereth praise glorifieth me; and to him that ordereth his conversation aright will I show the salvation of God."

2. Confession is the *representative* of faith. It is true that good works execute the same office: "Show me thy faith without thy works, and I will show thee my faith by my works." Thus the apostle. But important as works are to confirm our testimony, they fail in some respects to represent our Christian graces. They are sometimes unseasonable. Confession is quick, works are slow. That requires a

moment; these consume months or years. The thief upon the cross had time *merely* to confess, which, in his circumstances, was "the cup of cold water;" for though his faith could only cast one look at Christ, its confiding exclamation so kindled the Savior's pity that it blazed into trains of light and guided him to paradise.

Works can only give a bird's-eye view of faith. They can not report the minute changes of experience—the trials and assaults, the conflicts, wounds, and triumphs, of the Christian warfare. But confession can map out every turn in the pilgrim's course to Canaan; and, for warning and encouragement to those who follow after, can describe each help and hinderance he meets with in the way. If works lay down the heads of our experience, confession fills up the skeleton.

And we must not forget that confession is itself one of the most important works of faith. It is the *genesis* of them all, and its omission betrays a want of earnestness in religion, a state of heart unfruitful of all good works. He whose zeal does not confess, will limp and lag in other duties. The power which can not turn her wheels will never move the steamer. As a general rule, the grace which has force enough to act, will move its subject to proclaim God's saving mercies. "I have believed, and therefore have I spoken," was the experience of early times. And so under the Gospel: "We also believe, and therefore speak." Here the word "therefore" involves a vital principle; namely, *faith speaks.* Its very instinct is to vent itself in words. Its birth is usually not in silence, but with the voice of groans; and when the work is finished, and Sabbath calms and raptures now first betide the soul, no wonder if over the new creation there is a "shouting aloud for joy." May not the dying penitent, new-born of the Spirit, be roused by that which moves the sons of God in paradise? "There is joy in heaven over *one* sinner that repenteth."

There is a still-born faith, which should be always silent, for it would be misrepresented by a show of roused affections. What has no inward ardors demands no outward signs. There is a way of *thinking* which men call faith. As it touches not the heart, both heart and lip are still. It moves, like surgery through a hospital, around the Savior's cross, but with a colder speculation regards the suffering victim.

The faith which speaks is different. To its renewed affections the cross is a home-tragedy, where science is a mockery, but the yielding heart dissolves amid the groans and death-throes of the atoning Son of God. He who has this faith, believing "*with the heart*," may sometimes find himself in untoward moods for silence. His musings may kindle fires not easily controlled, which, bursting the barriers of his own false discretion, will remind him of that saying, "If these should hold their peace, the very stones would cry out." The glorious things revealed, the ardors of his divinely wrought conviction, and the new creations "unto righteousness," which take his being captive, may render silence inconvenient. Thus it seemed to be with David, in the sixty-sixth Psalm. While his song premeditated joyful offerings in the tabernacle, he felt such sudden overflows of rapture as could not brook the delays and moderations of his plan; and he seemed disposed to hurry up a love-feast in the palace: "Come and hear, all ye that fear God, and I will declare what he hath done for my soul."

How vital, then, is the connection between confession and salvation! Without faith we can not be saved. And confession, as we have seen, must cherish and prove our faith. And, above all, if our faith be of the heart as well as of the intellect, it *will* speak, even as the breath comes and goes by the urgencies of nature. Then let us beware of silence. If it has already grieved the Holy Spirit, till confession is no longer easy and spontaneous as it was at our conversion, let us proceed to enact, as a duty, that which should have been a privilege, and thus recover what is lost. If it is still a privilege, let us not "sell our birthright." Let us be faithful witnesses, and keep back nothing. The text is broad, and covers all experience—not select portions of it which involve no cross, because they invite no reproach. Our confession must be of *God's grace*, whatever it hath wrought in its regenerating, comforting, and sanctifying forms; or, unlike the Psalmist, we hide God's "righteousness within our hearts," and "withhold his loving-kindness and his truth from the great congregation." We do not "talk of *all* his wondrous works."

It is true that circumstances should be regarded in performing this great duty. To confess perfect love in a large and mixed assembly would be unseasonable; but to do it in a love-feast would be highly proper; for there, unless the Discipline has been grossly violated, it will not be "casting pearls before swine." Rising in such a place to relate God's dealings with us, we should feel that we are as witnesses sworn "to tell the truth, the *whole* truth, and nothing but the truth;" or to "declare *what* he hath done for our souls." This will edify both ourselves and those who hear. The Psalmist not only looked for self-relief, but expected to minister comfort to others. "My soul shall make her boast in the Lord; the *humble shall hear thereof and be glad.*" "From you," says the apostle, "sounded out the word of the Lord; and in every place your faith to God-ward is spread abroad, so that *we need not to speak any thing.*" This at least borders on declaring that even the necessity of apostolic ministrations was waived by the confessions of the Thessalonian converts. Nor is it strange; for what argument can have the force of simple testimony?

We may say, then, confession "is twice blessed;" is blessed in him that speaks and him that hears. It is a "stream that maketh glad" on every side. Not only does its outflow refresh the house of God, but with a reflex force it returns on the confessor, and sets all inward grace in motion, which occasion the Holy Spirit seizes to enlarge and fill the channels of his inward life, and sweetly multiply the volume of his graces. May God so enrich us with his abounding grace that, as Paul prayed for Philemon, "*the communication of our faith may become effectual by the acknowledging of every good thing which is in us in Christ Jesus!*"

II.

CHRISTIAN ANGER.

"*Be ye angry, and sin not.*" Ephesians iv, 26.

ANGER is commonly reckoned among the vices; and so seldom, since the fall, is it worthy of a different classification, that the inspired writings mostly fall in with the usage. Hence it is written, "Let all bitterness, and wrath, and *anger*, be put away from you." Yet the text represents anger as of possible innocence and propriety, not only prescribing it a limit, but also affording it a license; from which the inference is legitimate, that the passion is not evil in itself, but becomes so by the unwarranted forms, or occasions of it.

If this is questioned, we have only to observe how oppositely the vices are treated in this same chapter, wherein theft and falsehood are unconditionally forbidden, no possible form of either being allowed. And in addition to these hints, we must remember, that while theft and falsehood are prohibited in the decalogue, anger is not embraced in the preceptive summary. Connect with these considerations the fact that our Savior was angry and yet immaculate, and we are compelled to believe that there are harmless and praiseworthy forms of this passion.

But while innocent anger is possible, we shall all agree that it is difficult. In its best ordered forms it conducts us into the neighborhood of sin—into a region full of dangers. The qualifications of unoffending anger are so many and so vital, as amount almost to a prohibition; which we shall easily perceive as we proceed to discuss the question, "*How can we be angry and not sin?*"

Engrossing the principal points of the inquiry, we propose that Christian anger (by which we mean such anger as Christ experienced and warrants) has just PROVOCATIONS, MEASURES, MANIFESTATIONS, and PERIODS. Let us consider each.

I. CHRISTIAN ANGER HAS JUST PROVOCATIONS. To assure ourselves of a sufficient provocation, we should inquire,

1. *If the reputed offender has done wrong.* This may prove a perplexing question. Blinded by interest, we can not safely trust ourselves to decide it. What we call wrong may happen to be right; the other party may vindicate it—may urge against us cross-complaints, and set forth himself as the aggrieved person. Differences of opinion, in such cases, may be expected, and it will be safe to learn the views of disinterested observers, and, if they decide against us, abide their verdict. But if the wrong be clearly and confessedly on the other side, we must proceed to inquire,

2. *Whether that wrong was intended.* If not, though it may put us to inconvenience and awaken our regrets, it should not provoke our anger. Let us view it as a trial of Providence, and study how it may

subserve a gracious end, by schooling our hearts to meekness—that most difficult attainment. Our Christian graces need a discipline of this sort to strengthen and mature them. And while the trial presses on us, shall we indulge the very tempers which it was sent to mortify? It is unreasonable to be angry at an inadvertent trespasser. A sailor will sometimes curse the winds, and the currents, and the tides, when they happen to be adverse; and shall we, Christians, do worse, by indulging a heat of evil temper at the erring *fellow-mortal,* who, by mere mistake, has wounded us? This were unworthy of our *nature,* vicious as it is, and were an utter reproach to *grace.* But if the wrong seem intended, we must wait to inquire,

3. *If that intention can be proven.* Nothing can warrant anger but the most conclusive evidence that occasions do exist. And if the *wrong* be indisputable, malice must not be presumed, lest the charity which "thinketh no evil" should be wounded. Grant that malice is probable in the eye of impartial observation, yet that probability should wait for proof, instead of which there may come up counter-proofs, dispelling our suspicions, and opening to our love a way of peace and fellowship. There is an argument for this delay in the proverbial carelessness of kind and easy tempers, which often inflict a wound when they propose to heal one.

If anger thus delay, we are sure to lose nothing. Let the wrong prove to have been malicious, that very delay will show that our passion is not blind, but blends with a fixed and righteous principle far more formidable than any fretful impulse of our nature.

The proof here spoken of must be not only of a wrong, but of malice in the actor. And if this be made out, we must inquire,

4. *If the trespasser has repented.* Repentance can not atone for sin, or repair a wrong committed; but it shows a will for both, if they were possible. Christ forgives believing penitents without impossible restitution, having himself atoned to justice in their behalf. Shall we spurn whom Christ forgives, receives, and loves? As we prize the hope of pardon, we must not, dare not do it. Do we not pray, "forgive our debts, as we forgive our debtors?" What is the force of such a prayer to them who spurn the penitent offender against their peace or dignity? The repentance of our enemy must finish off our anger, or we, in turn, become malicious.

And we must be forward to perceive the tokens of his penitence. Our charity must watch with fond desire for that moral state in him, over which angels will rejoice. We must not regret, like Satan, to see repentance in our foe. We must not cavil, like him who said, "Can any good thing come out of Nazareth?" Let us, vile and guilty, expecting heaven by gracious acquittals which will cost the blood of Christ, be sure to pardon a fellow-servant who lies in prostrate penitence at our Redeemer's feet. But suppose the offender betrays an after-malice: we must then inquire,

5. *Whether we have used due means to bring him to repentance.* This we are solemnly bound to do. And what *are* due means is not left to our discretion, but laid down with great precision in the Word of God:

"If thy brother offend against thee, go and tell him his fault." Hereafter this and cognate Scriptures will be more fully considered. It is enough to say at present, that this visit to the offender must go before all anger. The errand may be ungrateful, but Jehovah has imposed it. And the precept is one of mercy toward both parties, promising to "save souls from death, and hide a multitude of sins." The message is peace-making, and the obedient messenger may well be "called the child of God." To mediate peace in matters which do not involve ourselves, is well pleasing to the Almighty; but to do it under wrongs inflicted by him whose guilty passions we would pacify, is sublimely meek and Christ-like. It brings honor to religion. Its utility is past reckoning. Under this Gospel regimen, more than half the quarrels of mankind might be healed, and seldom should we see budding mischiefs ripen into cruel enmities.

And if this measure fail, others must be resorted to before we can innocently assume the final ground: "Let him be unto thee as a heathen man and a publican." If a man of the world offend against us, to visit him and urge our claim to restitution or concession, will show a spirit of forbearance adapted to commend the religion which we love.

Finally: if these prescribed means move not the heart to penitence, a sufficient provocation to anger may be assumed. But with this just occasion, we must see that our anger be not sinful,

II. In its measures.

Nothing should provoke us to a burning, blinding

passion. Sinless anger is a deliberate, clear-sighted, strong displacency. In regard to its degrees, we must observe the following cautions:

1. *It must be so moderated as not to hurt ourselves.* In its usual forms, it is a violent, peace-disturbing passion, and, unrestrained, makes the bosom a volcano. When its fires begin to kindle, we may well warn the soul as the apostle did the jailer, "Do thyself no harm." There have been instances in which the hangman's rope was not more fatal than this passion; for the wrath of the immortal was more than the mortal could endure. But far short of such excesses, less suddenly, but not less surely, the passion is soul-killing. Religion, especially in its higher life, withers under its blight; and must wither, because the gracious agency which sustains it, at first withstood, is finally withdrawn. Will the peaceful dove rest amidst the battle fires? No more will the Holy Spirit dwell in bosoms convulsed by raging passions. The heavenly Guest must have a peaceful home. Let us be sure, then, so to moderate our anger as not to drive the Holy Spirit from our hearts. Then it will not wound us. Like some other passions, sinful until cleansed, let it be crucified with Christ, and with Christ rise again, and then, untouched by the hand which nature would put forth to it, it will be always heaven-ascending, lifting us upward toward the ever-blessed God. Each sanctified emotion tends to this result, deepening our devotion, kindling in us warmer love for man, and for our Maker. Anger which does it not is sinful, and brings a snare.

2. *Anger in just measures does not injure others.*

To retaliate is always sinful. God reserves that office to himself: "Vengeance is mine; I will repay, saith the Lord." Shall we usurp his rod of punishments? Then he will smite the smiter. Whatever may provoke us, let us observe the mandate, "Neither render evil for evil unto any man." How exceedingly comprehensive is this precept! Here *all* methods of revenge are reprobated. Neither openly nor covertly—by violence, nor by the subtilty of sly insinuation—may we molest a foe, except for absolute self-defense.

Some men's anger approaches madness. It unfits them for society, and makes their going abroad unsafe. Enraged, they do not always distinguish friends from foes. Their hurricane of passion pours its vengeance upon all, and plunges the offending and the harmless in one common doom. Yet less to be dreaded are they still than a noiseless class of enemies, who, like the coiled serpent in your unsuspected pathway, make sure but silent work of it. There are ways of mischief-doing, which employ no bowie-knife. A sharpened tongue can butcher. The eye can blink—the lip can curl—making a wound deeper and more painful than lead or steel can give. All these methods of revenge we must forever eschew. Could we conceal them from Omniscience, the question of right would still, or *ought* to, press upon our conscience. We must, then, guard our anger with most industrious vigilance, and pray as well as guard. It is difficult for anger to do or say nothing wantonly to molest a persecutor. Our unsanctified nature can not compass it. As to the world, its very *friendship* is less kind. O, what a world it is, through the revengeful, treacherous conduct of mankind! What oceans of misery are supplied by countless streams from that one fountain!

The first thought of revenge, from whatever provocation, should alarm us; for it is of hell's injection. If the spark be quenched at once, all is safe. But for this, the conception must instantly warn us to the closet, where, in pleadings for our foe, all imbittered feelings shall be sweetened into charity. The conclusion is, that whenever our displeasure would inflict evil on an enemy, it is *sinful in its measure.*

3. *Anger, in just degrees, will do good to its object.* It blends with a benevolence so fervent and diffusive, that *not to injure* can not satisfy it. Some men abstain from injuring a foe, yet feed on his distresses, inflicted by other hands. They will not throw down his fence, and waste his harvests, but neither will they repair a breach, and eject the roving herd. They will not fire his dwelling, nor mourn if others fire it. They are not murderers, but cannibals. Others slay—they eat. Is it sinless? "This wisdom cometh not from above; but is earthly, sensual, devilish." It has the cruelty without the courage of mature, infernal malice. When Christ was angry, "being grieved for the hardness of their hearts," did his passion crave to feast itself on his erring creature's sufferings? Nay; his bowels yearned to bless them. Such must be our anger. It must fulfill that blessed precept, "Do good to them that hate you, and pray for them which persecute you."

As to the measures of our anger, then, it must be so moderated as not *to hurt ourselves,* injure *others*, or restrain our *kind offices* toward the *subjects of it.*

III. Christian anger has just manifestations.

Here are two things which we will separately notice.

1. *Our anger must be manifested.* Concealment alone will make it sinful. This should not be forgotten. Some take concealment to be a virtue, because it veils a wrong from the public eye which might otherwise become an element of social discord. But have they forgotten that our Savior forbids concealment, or at least enjoins a limited disclosure? "If thy brother offend against thee, go and show him his fault." This language creates a solemn obligation. It binds the injured man to go and state to the offender the occasions of his displacency or anger. And lest grief or pride should prevent him, the precept is varied thus: "If thou bring thy gift to the altar, and there rememberest that thy brother hath aught against thee, leave there thy gift before the altar and go thy way: first be reconciled to thy brother, and then come and offer thy gift." These two precepts cover the whole ground, and leave no license to either party for delay. Whether more or less to blame, or not at all, is equal, so far as this interview for peace is concerned. If both instantly obey, the parties may meet in the public highway, so intent on making up the difference, that the "sun will not go down upon their wrath."

"Reconciliation" involves a statement of the offense and its occasions. To secure so good an end, we are commanded to withhold the sacrifice and adjourn religious rites. In the spirit of this precept, should not the very closet be forsaken through our haste to pacify, lest our devotions become offensive unto God?

These directions of our Lord were probably the basis of that language in the Discipline, "Tell every one under your care what you think wrong in his conduct and temper, else it will fester in your heart; make all haste to cast the fire out of your bosom."

"It will fester in your heart"—that is a true philosophy. And to conceal our disgust toward a personal adversary will produce the same effect, and kindle unholy flames within us. The only way to cast the fire out of our bosoms is to declare our displacency to him who has provoked it.

2. *But this manifestation of anger must be just.* We must keep in mind the object of our interview, namely, reconciliation; or, that we may "gain our brother." "Go and be reconciled," says Jesus. We must go, then, with winning words, and prosecute our errand with meek but manly gentleness. We must convince the trespasser that we are not implacably offended, and that we claim, as grounds of peace, no more than he can well afford to yield. Toward a brother in the Church, the Scriptural mode of manifesting anger, though adverted to already, will be noticed more at length.

(1.) "Go and tell him his fault." Tell *him*—the offender. It is a common error to tell others, but not him. And who can fail to see that this is a "war-measure?" If we whisper the wrong to others, it will soon fly abroad, and the whole town may know it before it reaches the wrong-doer. And when the floating proverb comes to him, through the circles of social gossip, it must provoke resentment and foreclose the way to peace. It leaves him no hope so to explain, concede, or vindicate, as to screen the parties from public reprehension and reproach. Yield him the advantage of knowing, before his neighbors do, the nature of your grievances, so that, without their intermeddling, he may make you restitution.

(2.) Tell him his fault "*between thee and him alone.*" Throw in his way no avoidable embarrassments, or you set him on an effort at self-vindication. Strengthen the motive to concession by tendering him a confidential interview, which ought to win his gratitude and move the hardness of his nature toward an endeavor after peace.

(3.) Should this fail, "*take with you one or two witnesses,*" and with their aid repeat the effort. They will testify your zeal for peace, and, if discreetly chosen, their persuasive mediation may contribute much toward the healing of the breach. If still unsuccessful,

(4.) "*Tell it to the Church.*" Summon the offender before her tribunals, and there let him answer to your complaints. If he refuse submission to the order of the Church, or slight the decision of her courts, rendered according to her usages or canons,

(5.) "Let him be unto thee as a heathen man and a publican." Decline to hold communion with him as a Christian, and no longer recognize him in that endearing fellowship. This is the severest form of Christian anger. It warrants neither hatred nor revenge; for either would be sinful toward a heathen man or publican. But it authorizes a display of strong and spirited displacency. To meet the offender with flushed cheek, and repel him in a rage, may not befit the meekness of true Christian dignity. But reproof can be administered by formal, slight obeisances. And we not only may, but *must* (for the phrase is mandatory) withhold from him the tokens of fraternal and complacent love. To say nothing of ourselves, this is due to the Church, whose honor is involved in the obstinate misbehavior of her refractory member.

If not a member of the Church, can we pursue a better course than that comprising the first three steps herein laid down? We can not take it before the Church, whose jurisdiction reaches only to her members. But if we may, in part, let us adopt the counsels of our Lord, rather than the devices of an erring human intellect. Christ's precept is, doubtless, based on reason, or adapted to the human constitution, and should, therefore, be obeyed. If we gain no more by this course than salutary restraints on our own rising passions, it were a vital benefit. But, possibly, our ungodly enemy may see that our religion is not powerless, but holds in check the impetuous rage of nature, and subdues the soul to Christ; which may commend it to his notice, and move him to seek its renovating grace.

Thus must Christian anger have just manifestations; or, exhibit itself in forms prescribed by Holy Writ. This is especially binding between members of the Church, and, as far as circumstances will permit, should be carried out in the Christian's dealings toward men of the world, who know, or may know, what the Gospel requires of us.

IV. CHRISTIAN ANGER MUST HAVE JUST PERIODS. The heat of it must be quenched, though the principle of it may continue, if need be, through life. But we will notice more particularly the risings and the quietings of it.

1. *As to the risings of anger, we must carefully regard the injunction, "slow to wrath."* It is unsafe to leap suddenly to the summit-level of this passion; for by such a daring movement the soul must gather an impetus which will carry it too high. Better try an inclined plane, and ascend with careful observation, learning where to stop, and preserving enough of self-possession to make a stand. To get angry as here proposed, is a deliberate procedure. Waiting to muster the provocations, adjust the measures, and mete out the manifestations, must, of course, prevent haste. And if it seem a slow business to men of choleric inclination, they should consider that these necessary haltings guaranty the very thing enjoined by our blessed Lord. But this deliberation is important, aside from the principle of obedience. It will save ourselves and others many and great mortifications. A temper which kindles into flashes almost without a touch, is a perpetual self-annoyance. It is like burning at the stake. The victim of this irascibility should be pitied. His soul hath a cutaneous disorder, which fills and defiles it with uneasy inflammations. Or it hath St. Vitus' dance, and for its own sake should hurry after a cure.

Others, also, are annoyed. It is a spreading, as

well as an uncomfortable sickness, touching with unclean contagions the undiseased around us. One petulant spirit in a community of thousands, will contrive to work half the number into a state of fretful discords. It is a drawback on one's bliss to fall into a street, or ward, beset by such a nuisance. One can bear sights and smells of every disagreeable sort better than proximity to such a moving shell of mischief, overcharged with mortal mixture of missile and combustible, and ready, you know not when, for unprovoked explosions. For these, and many more reasons, how needful the Scriptural caution, "slow to wrath!"

2. *As anger must be slow in its beginning, so must it be quick in its decline.* "Let not the sun go down upon your wrath." That is, hasten to remove the occasions, or quench the fervor of your displeasure. Delay here is perilous, and instant resort to prayer and the means of reconciliation is your only safety. A just displacency, such as we have already described, may last as long as the offender is relentless, but the fervid heat of displacency will be as fire in your bosom, and must be instantly cast out. The "*wrath*" of anger must not stay with us. It is wrong in itself, and leads to overt acts of wrong. Long continued, it will turn to a deep and burning malice. Would you sleep in contact with a battery, whose strong galvanic force distorts the very limbs and features? Make haste to pacify thy enemy. Quench these lightnings of the soul. Cast the fire out of your bosom. Before the sun go down, seek and find that "peace which passeth all understanding," then go and take thy rest.

That is sinless anger, whose risings and whose quietings agree with these divine warnings.

Having pointed out the qualifications of Christian anger, it may be profitable to observe,

1. *That such anger is rare.* In this all will agree, even though they should affirm that all other forms of this passion are innocent. Of the anger here described, where shall we find examples? They may be more frequent than volcanoes, and may create less surprise. But shall we, on this account, lower the standard of Christian affection? We are aware it may be urged, that "unless we resent injuries a proud world will trample on us." Doubtless it will. But did it not trample on Christ and his Apostles? Happy for the bleeding cause of Christ, when its adherents shall "have no fellowship with the unfruitful works of darkness, but *rather reprove them!*" Happy for the cause, when Christians shall pursue a course so unlike the world, that the world will find in their non-conformity a provocation to trample on them as it did on saints of old!

2. *Sinful anger is very common.* This, we presume, will not be disputed. For what a world of rage this has been, from the days of Cain until now! War is the grand feature of its history. If all the resentments and wrongs of six thousand years could be snatched from their oblivion and wrought into living chronicles, who but demons could endure the mere recital of them? This is, indeed, an angry world. Yet if the Church were placable, it would afford a shade of relief to this dark picture. But is she? As a general rule, even among professing Christians, is

not anger a resentful passion, rather than a Christ-like indignation? Her members often forbear revenge; but, alas! it is often more from a dread of retribution than from the restraints of holy charity. Perhaps revenge *is* sought—not tragically, but in the subtile whispers of detraction, poured into the willing ears of connivers at the mischief. Forgiveness, full and free, is little practiced in the Church, except for selfish ends. Many seem to forgive; but it is often the suppression of a curse, not the hearty pouring forth of blessings, as it should be, to merit that designation.

3. *Sinful anger is a great evil.* It is injurious to the soul. To this how many backsliders owe their fall, and how many reprobate apostates their ruin! Their history warns us of Satan's devices. Well may the Apostle add, in close connection with the text, "neither give place to the devil;" for whoever surrenders himself to the dominion of resentful passion, moves Satan to take the plenary *seizin* of his heart.

The Church also suffers. How deep her wounds inflicted by the rancorous altercations of her children! Schools of theology have waged against each other wars of wordy wrath, and from the heated dialects of their ambitious strife have found their way to each other's bosoms, and finished with bloody steel, or martyring fires, what was commenced in polemical disputations.

4. *We should watch against anger in our own hearts.* This especially becomes us in the midst of strong provocations. It is assumed by many, and may be true, that we have now strong provocations, and

should be filled with "holy indignation." If the provocations do exist, we need to exercise an answering care and caution. In quiet seas, trust a careless helmsman; but on a lee-shore, under the pressure of a storm, take care who is at the helm.

Let it be granted that this is a day of rebuke—that men's passions are let loose, and threaten to lay waste and destroy, do we not need a calm and guarded temper to meet so dread a crisis? It may be safer to stop short, than to reach the utmost limits of Christian anger. It is said there is a call for "holy indignation." It may be there is a louder call for holy caution, lest our indignation become *unholy*. And have we not experimented in holy indignation? Let us turn awhile to holy self-abasement, and get into the dust. Prayer may help us where indignation fails; and prayer is out of the neighborhood of danger; while they who use that weapon, "indignation," are like men battling on the brink of a precipice in a dark and stormy midnight.

Let all men be angry, as Christ was, on suitable occasions. But is there not, just now, too strong a tendency in this direction? It is *easy to be angry*. It may come of existing provocations; but we must not forget that Satan is wont to *go*, and *stay*, and *mix* with all things; and why not, then, with these very provocations? When in Job's day, the sons of God would present themselves before the Lord, he must needs go along, though the errand seemed forbidding. He went, too, with a bold parable, and sued out a bold commission. May not that evil spirit whose work was then so subtile and so formidable, contrive to seize on these many provocations, and use them to our disadvantage and discomfiture? "What I say unto you, I say unto all, WATCH!" is the warning of our Lord.

5. *Sanctified anger is always safe.* On the words, "Looking round about on them with anger, being grieved for the hardness of their hearts," Mr. Wesley says, "Angry at the sin, grieved at the sinner—the true standard of Christian anger. But who can separate anger at the sin from anger at the sinner? None but a true believer in Christ." To do it with assurance, we need mature grace. Feeble faith brings too small a measure of the Spirit. If any sinful taint remains in our affections, will it not show itself in anger? If so, we may not hope to be angry without sin, unless we are "crucified with Christ." He who has the *mind* of Christ—who can say, "I live; yet not I, but Christ liveth in me," may, like Him whose life then reigns over a crucified nature, be "angry at the sin, and grieved at the sinner."

May He circumcise our hearts to this end! May "the very God of peace sanctify us wholly," and teach us what changes his almighty power can work in our very worst passions! Let the whole Church plead for this as the voice of one man. And let each of her members look to Christ, and be "healed of whatsoever disease he has." Look thyself, O reader! look to the ALMIGHTY SAVIOR! Look to him as ready to save—ready to "save to the uttermost." "Say not in thine heart who shall ascend into heaven." The Purifier is near at hand, and not far off. Already his arm is revealed. "Believe the report," precious soul, believe now and be saved; believe, and thou shalt be blessed indeed. "Now unto him that is able to do *exceeding abundantly*, above all that we ask or think, according to the power that worketh in us; unto him be glory in the Church, by Christ Jesus, throughout all ages, world without end. Amen."

III.

THE SEEN AND THE UNSEEN.

"*While we look not at the things which are seen, but at the things which are not seen.*" 2 Cor. iv, 18.

TO look at a thing sometimes means to contemplate it as an object of desire and pursuit. In this sense things spiritual and invisible may become objects of mental vision, and may absorb the attention of the soul.

The text asserts it as a fact in Christian experience that the minds of the pious are engaged in the pursuit of an invisible good, to the neglect of those multiplied objects which are soliciting us through the senses.

"While we look not at the things which are seen, but at the things which are not seen." The text also announces facts which justify this habit of a pious mind: "for the things which are seen are *temporal*, but the things which are not seen are *eternal*."

We invite you to consider:

I. THE DIFFERENCE OF THINGS VISIBLE AND INVISIBLE.

II. THE DIFFERENT AFFECTIONS WE SHOULD BESTOW UPON THEM.

I. *The difference of things visible and invisible.*

The text affirms that the things visible are "*temporal.*" And here there is certainly a vein of true philosophy, which any one may perceive without the assistance of revelation. The visible and temporal are considered as *one.* And how just is this view of them may be seen by a slight observation. Cast around and consider the changes which are passing upon all your eyes can behold.

Human life consists of stages, each of which rejects many former attributes, and develops those which are new and strange. From the budding of life until, matured, it wastes and vanishes into a spiritual invisible form, this is its character. You see, first, weeping infancy rousing the sympathies of the maternal bosom by its appealing helplessness. Look again, and infancy has given place to childhood, tripping around in all the levity of laughing innocence, waiting like the swelling bud, to spread its beauties to the light of another morning sun. That sun arises, and the graces of youth at once supplant the dimpled sweetness of childhood. The opened bud reveals the full-blown flower. Beauty is penciled on every leaf of this interesting chapter of human life. There are a form and mien such as your fancy sketches when you dream of Eden and its spotless bowers, and its tenants fashioned in the likeness of God. But it is not merely a grace of form and a dignity of mien which enchant you. These are coroneted with the commingled beauties of the diamond and the rose. A voice, too, sweeter than the tones of the lute, pour upon the soul entrancing melodies, and wakes within it the joys of time or eternity, of earth or heaven.

We gaze and listen, and almost exclaim, "This specimen of God's infinite skill was made never to fade or perish."

"Age of strength, age of beauty, thou shalt remain surely forever!" Alas! we are mistaken. These graces are to fade like the rainbow from the cloud, and leave nothing but night behind, unless the sun of righteousness arise and diffuse abroad its light and glory. Smitten by disease or withered by age, they shall fly like the shadowy figures of a dream when one awaketh. Yes, child of vanity,

> "The roseate flush that dyes thy cheek,
> All bright with beauty's glow,
> Just like the radiant crimson streaks
> Of sunset o'er the snow,"

shall fade forever. Age, like night, is hastening on to blot with its shadows the fairy scene.

Thus the sweetness of childhood and the graces of youth are supplanted by gray, withering age. Death and the grave follow after, and leave not a wreck behind.

The *works* of man, as well as man himself, are temporal. Among his works we rank many of the productions of mind. The mind itself is invisible and eternal. It will take to itself immortal graces, and bear them to the skies; or it will be clothed in moral corruption and wear the polluted garment in the abodes of shame and everlasting dishonor. And alas! how many reject the ornaments of piety suited to the society of heaven, and exhaust all the energies of their lives in seeking immortal ruin and disgrace!

But to pass this by. Many of the sciences which owe their introduction to the inventive powers of man, have assumed almost as many forms as fable assigned to the renowned Proteus. Since men began to examine the phenomena of nature and speculate upon abstract principles, how many theories have followed each other in succession as rapid as the ocean waves! Each in its day was honored by an infant baptism, and consecrated by the name of truth. Each had its sanguine advocates laughing at the folly of its predecessors, and demonstrating the errors of their systems, as we, in turn, now do theirs. We, indeed, have improved much by adopting the method of induction in our search for truth. Yet a thousand things which we admire will appear to rising generations monstrous absurdities. Our grandchildren will laugh at the rudeness of many of our inventions, the infancy of our sciences, and the blunders of our boasted philosophy on many points where Ignorance now sets her bounds to investigation and speculation has boldly usurped the domain of facts. And thus, all science and all philosophy, not founded in eternal truth, shall at length be buried in one common grave, with none to lament or eulogize them. Even the provisional forms of the Church shall meet a like doom. "For whether there be prophecies, they shall fail; whether there be tongues, they shall cease; whether there be knowledge, it shall vanish away."

The *productions of taste* and of *art* are among the visible temporal things. The decorations of civilized life, all that can gratify the unholy mind, and much that ministers pleasure to the sanctified, such as the enchanting productions of the chisel and the pencil, the palace of royalty and the temple of devotion, which display the skill of architecture; in fine, all that fancy has conceived and skill has fashioned, as rare, or useful, or ornamental—all will perish like the foliage of Autumn beneath the chilling blast. We think we are building for eternity, and gathering together for endless ages. We purchase and alienate by the proud words "to him and his heirs *forever*." But the very terms are a libel upon the human understanding, and a reproach to Divine Providence. Look back upon the past and take from its history an impressive reproof of all this folly.

Where are now those splendid proofs of Grecian genius which once surprised and delighted half the world? Where are the breathing statues and architectural glories which sprung up, as by enchantment, at the bidding of her sons? Time laid his hand upon them, and they dissolved like vernal snows. They appear like the waves of the sea—specimens of beauty transformed to frightful ruins, which the solitary traveler *weeps to behold.* And will our works defy the power which has wrought this magnificent destruction upon the inimitable productions of ancient Greece? No. Our monuments of national achievements, the aspiring to hear of our skill and enterprise, the embellishments of all our rising cities and flourishing empires, of our temples, capitols, and monumental columns; our artificial rivers, fraught with life and freighted with commerce; our railroads, which make us swifter than the birds of heaven; all these are perishable, and like the hovel of the slothful poor, would soon "drop through" but for the unceasing care of industry and skill, and must ultimately be swept by the current of time into the ocean of oblivion.

Again, *riches* are temporal. Nothing is more coveted by the corrupt heart, and scarcely any thing is so uncertain and insecure. Although avarice is craving as the grave, the passion is perhaps the most unwarrantable of all the corrupt passions of mankind. But few in comparison obtain riches; those who obtain them have seldom the faculty to enjoy them; and had they this faculty it would be a curse, because it must soon be left to famish by the loss of all which gratified it. "Riches take to themselves wings and fly away." This is the *rule*—not an exception. And be assured that God, who uttered this rule, will commission the vindictive agents of his providence to execute it. He does execute it. Riches are transferred from hand to hand, from family to family, just like dresses fitted for the stage, and worn by any actor when suited to his part. What striking examples are now placed before us! Hundreds of your citizens, in a distant metropolis, retire from their costly treasures of merchandise, calculating on the gains of to-morrow, and the splendid acquisitions of many a coming year. They dream, and mountains rise before them composed of silver and crowned with gold, and labeled, too, with their own fair names. But hark! Ten thousand cries of horror suddenly burst upon the midnight silence. Starting from their dreams, they rush forth and behold their vast possessions perish in the flames. They meet the morning in beggary, and the pity of their country or the magnanimity of their friends interposes to snatch them from despair.

The laws of inheritance in civilized Europe, interpose a violent check to this change of property from family to family. But the laws of society can not abrogate the laws of Heaven. In the land of our fathers, the descendants of the ancient thanes are now among the peasantry, ditching the fields and manuring the soil. And the children of their ancient villeins who cringed before their ancestors, now surround the throne of majesty, and look down upon them from the eminence of peerage as a race of *servile* blood and name. Such revolutions will continue to occur. Fortune (forgive the word)—Fortune despises to be the *slave* of any man. She is the mistress, not the servant. She is jealous of her station. Whoever presumes that he has her in his power, either by affection or coercion, will soon find her asserting her prerogative against both her friends and her foes. She is indeed like a wheel in unceasing revolution. The rich and the poor occupy the zenith and the nadir of that wheel; but its revolution will cast the former from his height and bear the latter from his depth, and in their children they will both resume their former station. Let not the rich despise the poor, but rather be ready to bow to them in turn. Nor do you who are poor envy the rich, for to-morrow they will be the objects of your pity.

Fame, like wealth, is unstable and perishing. Thousands outlive their own popularity and become as conspicuous in their disgrace as they were once in honorable reputation. How few are the names transmitted to us by the poet's song and the historian's pen! And how many of these names are associated with all that is base and execrable! How many of them have acquired from posterity a fame which consigns them to perpetual disgrace and damns them to everlasting infamy! I mistake—not everlasting; the records of their disgrace must perish; for the name of the wicked shall rot. There can be no lasting records of human deeds but such as are composed by the divine skill and preserved by Almighty power. Tablets of brass and marble will decay. Triumphal arches and towering columns will waste into dishonored dust. Fame is like vapor suspended in the air. It assumes, and yields, and reassumes a thousand forms, and then at last vanishes forever. To this vapory, flitting show none can impart a stable form as a permanent charm. It is a "fashion of this world which passeth away."

Power and *dominion* show the same changeful destiny. They are pursued with passionate avidity, as though, once acquired, they were indefeasible. But, alas! empires rise and fall, flourish and decay. Revolution sports with the thrones of princes and the dynasties of empires, as winds and waves with a feather or an insect. Scepters pass from hand to hand. Thrones are demolished and dynasty succeeds dynasty so rapidly that the records of revolution must be made with stenographic haste, and a thousand scribes must labor at the chronicle.

Have you studied the fate of ancient empires? They were among the most magnificent of human policies, both as to the extent and the vigor of their compacts. Their foundations were supposed to be immovable forever. But where are their boasted strength and glory? Where are Babylon, and Persia, and Macedon, and Rome? Where stands in stately magnificence that image which amused the prophet's fancy, and entertained his hours of repose? Where are its feet of iron and clay? its thighs of brass, and its breast and arms of silver, and its head of gold? The storm from the mountain has smitten it into fragments, and its precious elements are scattered by the wind like the chaff of the *Summer thrashing-floor.*

And in modern times the world is in the same restless state. Look over the great waters and recollect the changes of half a century. A hurricane from heaven has swept through the forest of European states and policies, uprooting the ancient oak and towering cedar, and scattering disorder and desolation around. What systems of policy have been subverted! What customs and usages gradually grown into the authority of law have utterly perished! What armed hosts have been slaughtered by hostile weapons and hostile elements, until the rivers have flowed with blood, and the bones of the dead have bleached the fattened soil or have been gathered in mountain piles upon the embattled plain, as a monument to prove that man is demonized before his time. These revolutions, with the bloody strifes which wrought them, painfully illustrate the affecting truth that the things seen are temporal.

Last of all, *the very globe,* with its islands, and seas, and continents, and oceans, is appointed to destruction. It has long been the stage on which reptiles, beasts, men, devils, angels, and the supreme eternal God, have enacted various parts which will now soon close, and then the curtain will fall, and the stage will disappear forever.

The earth reveals to the observant eye a thousand marks of physical revolution, probably by the agency of diluvian waters and volcanic fires. One more violent change awaits it—a radical and final change. We know not exactly how it will be effected, nor in what renovated form the world will finally and forever exist. It may be hurled from its orbit and located in a remote region of the universe. It may be transformed into a state of beauty surpassing all that our minds can conceive, and become the paradise of the redeemed. Where Jesus wept, and bled and died, he may reign with his *saints* forever. It may, like the sun, become a conflagrated world, and be ordained as the burning prison of men reprobate and damned. And where the sinner scorned and crucified Jesus, he may sigh and weep forever, "but not in mercy's sight." Lastly, it may be blotted from the map of being, and no place be found for it. Either of these hypotheses is perfectly consistent with the attributes of God's holy providence, though suggested by no providential facts within our knowledge, on a scale equally grand and terrific. But we need no analogies or precedents to sustain our faith. We have God's irrevocable Word, and there we rest. Noah had no example of such a catastrophe as the threatened deluge; but the Word of God became his sure, as it was his sole reliance. But we have some apparent provision for an event, which God's Word announces as sure. The elements of renovation or destruction seem to be stowed in the bowels of the earth. Its secret dungeons appear to be magazines of fire. The atmosphere contains a combustible element circling us around as an omnipotent friend, to soothe, and cherish, and bless. Water, which covers three-fifths of the earth's surface, is itself composed of two substances, one a most highly inflammable gas, and the other a supporter of combustion. Let God speak in anger, and in a moment these elements, now so friendly, whether emboweled in the earth, or overspreading its surface, or circling round it, will blend in furious rage to destroy, and will convert the dust and waters and atmosphere into a mass of blazing terror. "The world and the works that are therein shall be burned up."

Such, my brethren, is to be the consummation of this system of change. This temporal is all that our eyes can behold. This visible universe is not a *state* of things. It is the *birth* and *death* of things. It scarcely embraces life, but consists of origin and destruction, without a space between the two extremes. And is there nothing permanent, then? Must man's immortality, which has been considered his greatest blessing, prove to be his greatest curse? What evil can equal this: to possess inalienable, deathless affections, with the prospect of losing every object suited to absorb and entertain those affections? Unless there are some deathless objects, subject to our acquisition and enjoyment, we need not inquire for another hell. Here is hell enough. But, blessed be

God! there is beyond this perishing world another, superior state, where the mutable shall yield to the stable, and change shall be succeeded by the unalterable. Yes, there is a world to which we haste, in which there is neither birth nor death; neither beginning, decline, nor end. It is a *state* of exquisite misery or vital joy and rapture. That world is revealed to our faith, as this is to our grosser senses. And now we will consider for a moment,

II. *What affections we should bestow upon these two classes of objects—the visible and invisible, or the temporal and eternal.*

Unless there be a mistake both in the Christian precept and practice, the visible and temporal are to be disregarded; and the invisible, eternal are to be noticed and pursued; yea, in some measure, possessed and enjoyed, even in this life. Do you ask why? We will state reasons which shall accord as strictly with sound philosophy as with the doctrines of revelation. But here let us observe that the invisible and eternal, much more than the visible and temporal, embrace every object craved by the human affections in their uncorrupt or sanctified state.

Has the soul an affection for personal charms? They abound in the spirits of the just made perfect; they adorn the first-born sons of light; they crown the "glorious person" of Him who is full of grace and truth!

Has the soul an affection for wisdom, or does it admire the graces of mind? All classes of celestial beings blend inevitable grace of person with the most attractive glories of mind. In heaven dwells

Wisdom itself, Jesus Christ, who designed and skillfully drafted the plan of this magnificent universe.

Has the soul an affection for honor? It can acquire honor by honoring God. Honor may be found in heaven in rich abundance. The names of the sanctified will be inscribed in the book of life. On their foreheads Jesus will write his new name, and the name of the city of God. And the songs of heavenly millions will celebrate their victories and triumphs.

Has the soul an affection for power or dominion? The redeemed will sit down with Jesus in his throne, and will reign with him forever and ever. Has the soul an affection for scenes of splendor? Does it delight to dwell in the midst of magnificence? In the city called the "New Jerusalem," the "*City of God*," Jesus, the Divine Architect, is erecting and embellishing many mansions, so that each may have "a building of God, a house not made with hands, eternal in the heavens."

Does the soul delight in social fellowships? In loving and being loved, trusting and being trusted—in the intercommunications of giving and receiving knowledge, of becoming at once the recipient and the almoner of social bliss? All this is found in heaven. There the structure of society is perfect; the relations of moral and social beings pure, harmonious, and faultless. Blessed place! The true, the final, the only home of the soul! The fellowship of kindred souls flows from the fellowship of God. They are one, as the Father and the Son are one.

Has the soul an affection for the beautiful? This

natural taste and desire, as old and as imperishable as mind, is fully gratified. We have already spoken of the persons of the redeemed. But the scenery itself of heaven is transcendently beautiful, not only in the charms of moral loveliness, but of external order, variety, grace, and symmetry. What in art, or conception, can excel the beauty of that glorious city, the "New Jerusalem?" What in nature can compare with the "river of life," "clear as crystal," flowing from under the throne of God, fringed with "trees of life" on either side? And there are "fountains of living waters," and there shall be "no night there," and the blessed inhabitants "shall hunger no more, neither thirst any more; neither shall the sun light on them, nor any heat. For the Lamb, which is in the midst of the throne, shall feed them, and shall lead them unto living fountains of waters; and God shall wipe away all tears from their eyes."

But why attempt to enumerate? The invisible and eternal comprehend every thing which the soul of man may innocently admire, pursue, and enjoy. God has not endowed us with faculties to disappoint their gratification. When he commands us not to love the world, but set our affections on things above, he is careful to reveal from above every object which can entertain and absorb these affections. Do not for a moment suppose that Paul and his brethren had become unhappy by ceasing to look at the things which are seen. No: they were divinely happy in looking at the things which are not seen.

But to justify this habit of pious minds, consider that our affections are immortal. We must live, admire, and love forever. And such is our constitution, that the loss of that which we admire or love inflicts upon the soul the severest misery of which it is susceptible. Let the affections be wholly surrendered to an object, until love becomes a habit of the soul. Then separate the soul from that object, and you rend it by the violence. You give it a wound too deep to be healed. It bleeds its lingering life away. How many a parent, or a widow's heart, languishes in sorrow through slowly wasting years, for the loved ones departed, sustained only by the soothing hopes of heaven! But these alleviated sorrows of a pure soul bear no comparison to those occasioned by the loss of eternal things essential to the soul's blessedness. The misguided soul, mistaking the things which are seen and perishable for the true objects of its certain happiness, ventures all upon the fatal choice, and loses all hopelessly and forever.

This is not poetry, or fiction; it is simple, affecting truth. Who can not point to an example? The miser loved his gold: his gold perished, and he refused to live. The ambitious man loved fame: fame forsook him, and he forsook the world. The mother idolized the child: it died, and she died upon its grave. The wife, forgetting God, worshiped the creature; and when she was bereft of the earthly object of her adoration, devoted herself as the companion of the dead. The man of earth and earthly pleasure outlives the period of sensual enjoyment, and dies cursing the power that robs him of his delights. His appetites remain; but the chosen objects of their gratification perish forever. The philosopher and the man of science, in the pride of his profession, having stopped short of God and things eternal; having searched for every thing but God in the works of God; having sought and welcomed truth only in its mutable and temporary form of manifestation; having stopped at secondary laws, and refused the heart's adoration of the invisible Contriver, and Creator, and Lord, will find at last that such "knowledge will vanish away," and the latent desires of the soul for things eternal will awaken into life when there shall be found no means for their gratification. Man, in his pride and haughtiness, having laughed at the terrors of the battle, and mocked the rage of a thousand storms, has perished like the oak which despised the whirlwind, but drooped from the excision of a branch, or fell before the ax of the feeble woodman, or perished by the sear of age; but his immortal nature, quickened in its vigor to reason, to desire, and to feel, still puts forth its powers in search of congenial things to satiate its immortal cravings. Of all that the soul has treasured up in its affections—of all its "much good, laid up for many years"—nothing will remain for its enjoyment but what has been treasured up in God.

Then, how *dare* we love the world? How dare we treasure up in the soul, and embrace in our deathless affections, what must soon be *snatched* away, and leave the heart torn asunder, to bleed in deathless agony? Sinner, you are preparing for this bitter doom. Devoting your affections to perishing objects is only sharpening the weapons of death, to kill, not the immortal soul, but its mortal joys, which you have preferred to those which are immortal! Cruel wretch, more cruel to thyself than murder to its victim, because cruel to thy poor soul! Only bethink thyself, that soon death will rob thy heart of all its valued treasures and joys. You can hold on but a moment longer to the attractive objects which now sway your heart, and minister to your deceitful delights. All you behold and admire is temporal, and soon you will behold it no more. The beauty, and melody, and sweets which now pour in upon the soul a reflection so pleasant and enchanting, will find no avenue of entrance when the eye, and ear, and palate are senseless as the clod and marble which form your sepulcher, and tell the world that you are gone. But though your pleasures will die, you must live. You must live a life of distinct perception, of vigorous action, of vehement affection, of exquisite sensibility. You must so live that every faculty, formed at first for enjoyment, but now susceptible only of suffering, will be more wakeful and vigorous than ever. You must live a life which death can not assail and destroy—a life inalienable as the throne of God; and, alas! a life separate from every object you have learned to love and enjoy—such as the rich man began to live when he lifted up his eyes in torment, and found, instead of his palace, stowed with all the world could give, a hell in which one drop of water was a luxury never to be enjoyed. O who can conceive this misery! To be forced from the region of all our joys; to find the soul violently cast from its anchorage, and driven as a wreck upon the shores of eternity; its treasures lost without insurance or recovery, and nothing in the compass of eternity which it has ever learned to value or enjoy! But stop! It is a hell too terrible for description. The imagination shudders at the view, and, like the frightened dove to its home-like covert, returns to more inviting scenes.

But, beloved saints, who look not at the things which are seen, but at the things which are not seen, we rejoice to signify to you from the Bible the happiness which shall follow the cultivation of devout affections. The Christian forms his habits not for time, but for eternity. The objects of his pious affections cluster around the throne of God. He cares not for this fleeting world, only as the traveler cares for the craft or the bridge by which he passes to his happy home. Happy soul! whose relish is formed for the pleasures of heaven, whose pantings have been after the living God and the everlasting Son of his love! Happy soul! which has remained a stranger on earth, insensible to its dangerous attractions, blind to its beauty, deaf to its song, and careless both of its frowns and flatteries!

He who has thus used the world can bid it a cheerful and smiling adieu. It has only been his temporary footstool; and, finding it beset with snares, and ambushed by many a lurking foe, he had longed to spurn it beneath his feet, and cast away its unfriendly cords. It had been his observatory; and, from amidst chilling winds, and sleety showers, and sickening odors, he had gazed and gazed at the celestial glories above. In his right hand he held the Bible as a telescope, and applied it steadily to the eye of faith; with his left he beckoned for a chariot of fire, to bear him through the heavens, and drop him at the foot of the everlasting throne.

Death is the arrival of the chariot, and he glories at its approach. He shouts as he takes his passage and soars upward on his departure. He goes to the home after which he had longed, the home which contains the treasures of his soul and the friends of his heart.

Now, do you not perceive a sound philosophy, as well as piety, in the language of religion? Is it not as wise as it is dutiful to withhold the heart from the world, and send forth our affections toward God and toward heaven? Is it not as foolish as it is sinful to restrain the affections from God, permit them to embrace what is perishing, and perish with it? Would you not pity the child which, born to a fortune and a throne, should exchange it all for toys and childhood delicacies, and treasure them for the use of a thousand years? in the purchase of ten thousand suits of apparel fitted to its infant person, all to become useless after the lapse of a few years? This is a faint representation of that folly which relinquishes eternal, in order to secure and enjoy temporal things. The child is unwise, but the sinner is mad. The one wastes a little glittering dust, which the winds would soon disperse, held by however firm a grasp; the other devotes his immortal affections, made to expatiate in the fullness of God, and to be charmed with the raptures of eternity, to the base and beastly objects of sensual gratification. The one profanes an honorable earthly rank; the other damns an immortal soul! Let me entreat you, O sinner, to recall your heart from this vain world. Suffer it no longer to bow down to the dust. A tempest from heaven will soon scatter its present treasures like Autumn leaves, and leave you barren and cheerless. Then how will the heart turn inwardly upon its own vacancy, in the bitterness of its anguish, when every green thing has faded, and every idol shattered, and every hope extinguished; "and thou mourn at the last, when thy flesh and thy body are consumed, and say, How have I hated instruction, and my heart despised reproof!" How then shall every affection of your being, formed at first for God, become armed as with a scorpion's sting; or, as the fierce sirocco, scorch the soul they were intended to gladden and refresh! From such a hell there is but one way of escape. Turn your hearts from this perishing world to Jesus, who is the Life and the Truth. Reason, no less than religion, calls you to look not at the things which are seen. "Rise, shake thyself" from the dust of earth, and "seek the things which are above, where Christ sitteth on the right hand of God."

IV.

WHAT IS MAN?

"*When I consider thy heavens, the work of thy fingers, the moon and the stars which thou hast ordained, what is man?*" *etc.* Psalm viii, 3–9.

DAVID was a philosopher and a devout man. He loved to range the fields of nature, and he loved to recite the praises of nature's God. This Psalm is a record of his philosophical meditations, and his devotional exercises, on a particular occasion. It was night. He had probably wandered forth where he could silently repose under the wide-spreading heavens, and raise his eyes and his thoughts, in quiet vision and calm contemplation, to loftier regions. He saw the heavens appareled in the modest effulgence of night to display the intelligence and omnipotence of Him who had fashioned the firmament, had decked it with beauty, and had given motion to its revolving worlds. After soaring high in vision and in thought above all earthly scenes, he suddenly comes back again to man and mortality. He descends to himself, and with a spirit of anxious curiosity queries concerning his own relative consequence.

His body seems like a fragment of the visible creation, separate by peculiar composition and organization, and hasting through the process of disease and corruption, to resume its original form, and rejoin the general mass of nature. He seems to balance this form of clay against those unnumbered and unmeasured worlds; then shrinking from the comparison with self-abasement, he exclaims, "What is man?"

The modern deist would have stopped here, and in the pride and vainglory of a superficial and most false philosophy, would have said, "Man! He is but the creature of a moment; too insignificant to be noticed by Him who stationed the suns, and who moves the inferior bodies of heaven. Man! He rises to-day from the dust, and to-morrow lies down again in the grave. There his mysterious frame is resolved into the elements to be recompounded in other forms; the watery particles to stream in showers or rivulets; the earthy to enrich the soil or vegetate in plants; the airy portions to wanton in the breeze; the ardent to rise and flit in the sun, or to descend into the earth and warm its heart, or flow in its pulse, or press in volcano from its bursting veins."

Such is the vile philosophy of the infidel. But the philosophy of David was nobler and divine. It looked beyond the surface of things and penetrated deep into the regions of truth. For a moment he had contemplated man in the grossness of his material nature as the creature of sense; but again he views him in the elevation of his superior nature and in the promise of an immortal destiny, and then exclaims, in language worthy of himself and of God, "What is man? Thou hast made him a little lower than the angels; thou hast crowned him with glory and honor; thou hast made him to have dominion over the works of thine hands; thou hast put all things under his feet." Let us pursue these meditations of wisdom and devotion by observing,

I. That the text presents man as holding a conspicuous place in the considerations of the Divine Mind, as sharing in its holy sympathies.

We need not argue in this assembly the truth of such an assumption. We address those who are neither so ignorant of religious doctrine nor so profligate in religious sentiment as to require proof or illustration of this point. We can agree in this common faith, that God has distinguished man with attentions bestowed upon no other order of creatures of whose condition we are advised. Not that His providence is more beneficent toward men than toward angels; but angels are holy, and are made happy by the rewards of obedience. The kindness of God toward them, therefore, does not exhibit so intense and untiring an interest as does the pursuit of rebel man for the merciful purpose of restoring him to God and to heaven.

When we contemplate the Almighty God in the attitude of seeking a victim for our sins; in the attitude of selecting his Son for sacrifice; in the attitude of directing the sword of justice at that sufferer, and finally as giving his Spirit to reform the soul, and restore the departed innocence and honor and blessedness of man, we must confess that the richest treasures of the Divinity are poured out upon his sinful race. The Scriptures, therefore, speak of God as having "loved the world," as having "magnified man," and as having "set his heart upon him." It will be admitted, therefore, that man holds a high place in the considerations of the Divine Mind, and shares in its holy sympathies.

We observe,

II. That the Psalmist, in the text, asks for the reasons of these Divine attentions to man. And what we propose in this discourse is to reply to this interrogation. And, in reply, we say,

1. *Man is an intelligent being.* We will notice the indications of his intelligence in a rising series from its lowest to its highest and its noblest efforts.

(1.) His intelligence is certified by his knowledge of his own existence. Man knows that he is; and this knowledge is more than the blind sensualism—we could hardly call it consciousness—of the brute. True, his body, and the motions of his body, are objects which he perceives, and the states and changes of his mind are subjects of his own consciousness; still his inward and outward senses are only employed as instruments to gather up the materials of instruction. By the exercise of reason, man's knowledge of his own existence is discriminating, and unlike the blind instinct of the brute.

Man distinguishes between existence and non-existence; between life, vegetable and animal; life, animal and rational; life, rational and moral; and notices the incidents and the issues of each form and mode of being. His knowledge is not confined to the present, but views the past and regards the future. By memory, he takes cognizance of all behind him;

by vision, of all around, and by expectation, of all before him. His mind blends, then, their estates so as to give him a conscious identity, and enable him to know that he existed yesterday, lives to-day, and shall remain to-morrow the same *unchanged* being. Thus, man's intelligence is indicated by his knowledge of his own existence.

(2.) By man's intelligence he is acquainted with other beings. He knows that he is not alone in creation. He beholds beings above him and below him in ranks of gradational existence; and these, with their relations to him, to one another, to the grand system of the universe, and the Great Author of all, open new and vast and ennobling fields of study. What order of beings below man improves by its contrast with other orders? But here reason displays its divine origin and its native superiority.

(3.) The intelligence of man qualifies him for *society.* He looks with a deep and sympathetic interest upon the forms of kindred life around him. His mind is formed for society.

When man communes with man, it is the contact of minds, the *communion* of souls, the mingling of spirits. It is interchange of thoughts, sentiments, affections, joys, raptures, and sorrows. Thus the intelligence of man *qualifies him for society.*

(4.) The intelligence of man capacitates him for enjoyment. All the knowledge, all the objects and occasions of knowledge, or of enjoyment, whether from secret or sensible sources, are made through his intelligence the materials of a refined and elevated pleasure to which the merely sensational nature can not attain. Thus the intelligence of man capacitates him for enjoyment.

(5.) The intelligence of man enables him to refer his origin to its proper cause, and trace his happiness to *its proper source.* He knows he is not from eternity, and, therefore, is not self-existent. He knows that each member of his race is as dependent as all or any others; they could not *begin to be* without a Creator; and what is true of him is equally true of every other dependent existence—all must have a Creator. For an indefinite series of dependent beings could not originate or sustain itself easier than any one alone. Back of all, and above all, there must be a causing Power. And as this Cause must be adequate to the effect, it must itself be intelligent, free, eternal, possessing all the attributes of an infinite and eternal and intelligent personality. Thus the intelligence of man enables him to refer his origin to its proper cause.

(6.) The intelligence of man enables him to discover his relation and obligation to the Author of his being and bliss. He knows that between the cause and its effect there is an inseparable connection, and by induction he ascends from the effect to the cause—from the creature to the Creator. He knows, also, the evidences of that Divine Revelation which gives certainty and authority to the deductions of his reason. And having ascertained the Creator, and his relation to him, the ethical idea of obligation forces itself upon the mind. Thus is our proposition proved.

2. *Man is a free agent.* The term agent is a

derivative of classic origin, and implies actor or doer. Negatively,

(1.) Free agency is not moral agency.

(2.) Free agency is not independent agency. An independent agent is one who can perpetuate his own being. If man has this power, he must be either *self-existent,* or he must have received it as an endowment from his Creator.

Is man self-existent? If so, he either existed from *eternity* or he is self-created. Neither. Therefore he does not possess underived power to *preserve* his own being.

Is man endowed with the power of independent agency by his Creator? *No.* But (3) free agency does consist of the power of voluntary action. It implies volition and motion—*choice* and *deed correspondent.* "Choose you this day whom you will serve," exemplifies free agency. But choice always looks two ways, for it not only *seeks* but *avoids.* It implies *election* and *refusal* by the agent; for there can be no choice without preference, and no preference except among two or more objects. The ground of many divines and philosophers is untenable, namely, that free agency is doing voluntarily whatever we do, but implies no power to do otherwise. They say that man in all cases acts freely, but yet could not act differently. They think man can neither originate nor control his volitions, being, in this respect, under the power of motives. How, then, can we be sure in any given case, that we shall act as we think to do, unless we be sure that setting about it we can originate volitions, which are the only springs of action? We can and do originate volitions every waking hour. Two books lie before you, a novel and a Bible. About to take and open one of them, do you doubt your power to take either? You can not do it without volition. If not conscious of the power to put forth this volition, instinct and not reason is the law by which you do it. We affirm that man can both originate and control his own volitions, and that this power is essential to free agency.

It is asked, How can man originate or control them? We answer, We are not concerned how it is; the *fact* is certain, and we are not concerned about the *mode*. Do we doubt man's ability to originate and control his thoughts, because we can not perfectly analyze mind and demonstrate all its modes of action? We conclude, then, that a free agent can originate and control his volitions.

3. *Man is a moral agent.* We have said that *moral* agency is not essential to free agency. This is true. On the other hand we can not say that *free* agency is not essential to *moral* agency. Nor is this without a parallel. A man may be a sinner without being a murderer, but he can not be a murderer without being a sinner. A free agent acts voluntarily. A moral agent not only acts voluntarily, but he acts with moral discernment, in view of a moral law, and under a weight of moral obligation and accountability.

"Moral good or evil," says Locke, "is the conformity or disagreement of our actions to some law, whereby good or evil is drawn upon us from the will of the law-maker." It is certain, then, that man could not discern the moral complexion of actions but by a knowledge of that law which constitutes and declares them good or evil. Man, therefore, acts in view of a moral law. But to perfect his character as a moral agent, man acts under a weight of moral obligation. We have endeavored to exhibit the ground of our obligations to God in the relations we sustain to him as our Creator.

4. *Man is a sinner.* A sinner is one who, with moral discernment in view of a moral law, and under moral responsibilities, does voluntarily violate his obligations. Such a violation is the transgression of the law prescribed by the Creator to his creature. The Scriptures abundantly testify that this sinful character pertains to our race universally. "All have sinned and come short of the glory of God." "There is not a just man on earth," etc. Such is the testimony of God. "Now, therefore, if we say we have not sinned, we make *Him* a liar, and his word is not in us." Thus man stands revealed, and seems to combine in himself all that is lovely and all that is hateful; all that is noble and ignoble in rational being. Free in his sphere as God; bold and sagacious to reason upon the moral fitness and unfitness of actions; his eye fixed upon the law of his God, and his conscience acknowledging its equity; he casts off its restraints, rejects its impositions, and spurns the authority of him who prescribed it—of him who will *vindicate* it though that vindication should demand the annihilation of the universe. *Thus man is a sinner.*

5. *Man is a redeemed sinner.* God has purchased

him for the gratification of his own holy mind, that he may, if possible, repossess him of his lost purity, and blessedness and glory. In this act the Deity made an immense sacrifice—a sacrifice which can never be estimated by the human mind, because it regarded not only the principles of the Divine government and the profoundest laws of our own being, but the adorable mysteries of the Divine subsistence, and the boundless affections of the Divine mind in its chief and choicest fellowships. But although we are incapable of valuing the sacrifice in its full extent, we can know enough concerning it to be overwhelmed with amazement. In attempting our restoration from sin and hell, the first act of the Godhead was to exhibit its filial member as a largess in this behalf. Who would fail to infer the great value of the human soul, the extreme difficulty of its redemption, the mercy unfathomable of the Creator from such a provision—the gift to man of his "only begotten Son?"

6. *Man is immortal and accountable.* He is immortal, for the Scriptures declare it. Such is man, and much more. But does not this view of him, obscure as it is, present him in an attitude of fearful elevation? Does it not exhibit him as the choicest specimen of the Creator's skill? The heavens *declare* the glory of God, but man was made to be the very image of that glory. They unfold their magnificent drapery for a season, and then perish like the useless scroll. But man was made to be immortal, and was made to be the image of God's eternity. They shine in unconscious beauty, and glow with unconscious ardors, and repose in unconscious harmony under the

eye of God. Man lives to see and know, to rejoice in society and love, and to sweeten his existence by a consciousness of the Divine approbation secured to him forever. What high advantages for enjoyment are placed within his reach! He takes tribute of joy from the past by recollections, from the present by possession, and from the future by hope. He demands subsidies from nature, and nature does not deny them. When the ray-glit lights the dawn, and evening blushes in the west, every receding or approaching shadow bears him gifts of homage and happiness. Planets roll, the stars are revealed in radiance, the moon unfolds her vestal drapery, and the sun walks forth in his strength, all to cheer and to honor man.

Think not, then, that the magnificence of the heavens can compare, but by way of contrast, with the superior glory of man. Intelligence disabused is the criterion of station, and forms the true dignity of being. We can attach no essential importance to the matter which surrounds us. It moves when moved, and is motionless when suffered, without any vital principle or property. But let it become the seat of intelligence, and we view it with veneration. Matter becomes of essential value and interest when it enshrines a spirit of immortal grace, and is used by that spirit as a pencil to portray the glory of its origin and character and destiny.

Let us cease to wonder, then, that God should be mindful of *man*—that he should forget all worlds, and systems of worlds, rather than to forget the image of his Godhead. Let us cease to wonder that his attentions are unremitted, and anxious, and enduring. Let us keep in mind that God made us to be companions of his Deity; that he prepared us for this high calling by fashioning us in his likeness. Let us meditate upon the resemblance we bore him when he loved to walk in Eden with our parents. Let us reflect upon our loss, and ruin, and danger. We have lost our holiness, and are in danger of hell. But we retain our immortality, our intelligence, our freedom. At this very moment your actions are as unconstrained as the actions of Omnipotence. At this very moment you, in your sphere, perceive truth and error as with the eyes of Omniscience. Yes, at this very moment let your future eternity be placed beside the future eternity of God, and they shall be equal to each other. At this very moment you have in every thing the image of God, except his holiness and righteousness.

When we survey man in all his intellectual glory, we can not cease to admire him. We delight to behold him putting forth his strength, to fly through earth and heaven, and search out the works of God. We are ready to believe that such energy of soul must be the handmaid of all that should enter into combination with vigorous and enterprising thought. We can scarcely realize that a spirit, apparently so free and aspiring, is repressed with overwhelming guilt, and is in danger of everlasting shame. Yet this is, in fact, the case. If man is angel in endowments, he is brute or devil in the perversion of them. O, what a spectacle is this! An immortal spirit made to live and rejoice with God, formed in God's image, and about to inhabit God's eternity, madly laboring to deface that image, and to treasure up for that eternity immeasurable woe! Every thing in, and concerning him, only serves to increase the painful interest with which a serious mind surveys this scene. If man had not been made like God, it would have been different. If, when he fell, he had entirely lost that likeness, it would have been different. If he could now efface all the features of that image, it would be different. If, after some millions of ages, he could be annihilated, it would, even then, be different. If, after passing half eternity in hell, he could escape and come forth renewed in all the freshness of that image, it would be different.

But he was made in God's likeness, and retains many of its striking glories, since the fall. Think of this! He is not able fully to destroy the features of the Godhead. Think of this! He never will, never can be annihilated, and, if finally lost, never will escape hell and come forth with that abused resemblance of his Creator. The sinner will carry all, all his noble powers of soul along with him to hell. And the more noble his gifts on earth, the more cursed will be his estate in hell.

Now, look for a moment over this broad world. Behold millions, such as we have described, just stepping into hell. What are planets, and suns, and systems, and systems of systems spread through all the spaces of God's universe, compared with such a scene?

We observe in conclusion:

This subject teaches us the value of redemption. The glory and blessedness that man has lost by sin he may regain through the blood of the Redeemer. Jesus now conveys to us instructions, entreaties, and promises, and affords the offer of spiritual influences by the Holy Ghost, to create us anew in the image of God. Jesus is now here, for he is ever found where sinners are, except in hell. He is now revealed before us in the attitude of suffering, imploring solicitude; waiting, watching, weeping to find access to our hearts, and build up the ruins of our fallen nature. We need his mercy—we perish without his aid. Come, then, let us rise, ere we perish, and fly to Him for help?

Let us every one say, "I rest no more in sin. I walk no more with Satan. I *trifle* no more with my poor, ruined, suffering, sinking soul." Then let us plead beneath the cross, that streaming mercy may wash away our stains and restore us once more to the bosom of our Father, God. Jesus will hear our cry. He will enter our desolate hearts by his Spirit, and breathe health, and beauty, and rapture, through all the dreary wastes of the soul.

O sinner, listen! For Zion that bringeth good tidings, bears to you this day the offer of a Savior. He is mighty to redeem. "The Spirit of the Lord God is upon him; He is anointed to bind up the broken-hearted; to proclaim liberty to the captive, and the opening of the prison to them that are bound."

O, thou suffering Son of God! Approach, behold this people! Open to them the fountain of thy mercy, and wash them in its crimson flood. "For thou wast slain and hast redeemed us to God by thy blood!" Alleluia! Amen!

V.

THE SENTENCE AGAINST UNBELIEF.

"*He that believeth not shall be damned.*" Mark xvi, 16.

IF this announcement had been made by some angel from the skies, it were well that we should pause and consider. But it is the voice of One who hath the power and the office to judge, acquit, or condemn, both angels and men. And shall we contemn his authority, or trifle with his word? Shall we arm the law with terror against the hour of judgment? Let us rather hail with welcome the light of warning, and timely escape the threatened danger. That we may better understand these solemn words of Christ, let us attend to the several points of inquiry involved. What is unbelief? What is it to be damned? How and why are they so intimately connected?

I. WHAT IS UNBELIEF? It is not so much our business to define the word, as to illustrate the principle. This we do by tracing its operations and effects. To change the abstract for the concrete form, then, we ask, Who is the unbeliever? He is an unbeliever whose feelings and actions accord not with the commands, example, and spirit of Jesus Christ. The object of Christian faith is Christ—his commands, doctrine, promises, example, and spirit; and the office of faith is to produce conformity to these. Faith is a natural law of action in man. Men act in conformity to what they believe, in matters of interest, pleasure, honor, or obligation; in matters secular or spiritual. The opposite to this is the exception, not the rule. We assume, therefore, that where the conduct and character do not accord with the commands and moral example of Jesus Christ, it is for want of that faith in the Gospel truths which is the spring and fountain of all obedience. Were it necessary, this were easily proved by a process as simple and as conclusive as science can propose. Every-where in Scripture the evil character of the wicked is assigned to this evil cause; as opposites, obedience and righteousness, are the fruit of faith. "Abraham *believed* God, and it was counted to him for righteousness." But of the disobedient Israelites God says, "How long will this people provoke me? and how long will it be ere they *believe?*" "The people of Nineveh *believed* God, and proclaimed a fast," and repented, and were saved from the threatened judgment. But the Hebrew people "could not enter into Canaan, because of their *unbelief*," and God "swore in his wrath they should not enter his rest." But why cite examples? If any truth can be discovered by Revelation, or by argument, it is clear that unbelief and disobedience stand related as cause and effect, and that, therefore, transgressors do not believe. They may admit the truth of Revelation in the abstract. They may not deny its historical evidences, or its inspired authority. But somewhere in the chain of causes which govern their practical life you will find a belief in some error which directly antagonizes the Word of God, and has the practical effect to suspend obedience in whole or in part, in the habit of life, or in exceptional cases, in the overt act, or in the spirit. The universal law of human action is, that men will be governed by what they really believe. The sinner believes that except he repents, he will surely perish, but he believes a future day will be more convenient, and, therefore, delays. He is not governed by a universal skepticism in all revelation, but a specific distrust of that class of commands which makes "to-day" the time to "hear His voice, and harden not the heart," and warns against a boasting reliance on "to-morrow." The Christian believes he must be holy in order to see God, but adopts some theory of holiness, as to time, method, or measure, which suspends the full enjoyment or compliance to-day. Thus the law of God is made void through unbelief.

But, to proceed still further, to particulars, we say he is an unbeliever whose conduct does not evince a *universal* regard for the law and example of the Savior. Partial virtue is no evidence of faith, but partial vice is conclusive evidence of unbelief. And, for this reason, it is convenient for men to omit some sins which do not suit their taste or condition. One can refrain from drunkenness, because he has no relish for alcohol; another can refrain from swearing, because he despises vulgarity; another can refrain from prodigality, because avarice is the reigning vice and passion of his soul.

Now, it is easily perceived, that in these cases, faith in God is not the root from which such virtues spring. Faith is a medicine which, applied to the soul, heals the part diseased, and to ascertain whether it is operating, we must examine the state of our wounded members. Or, in other words, we must inquire whether a firm persuasion of God's justice and mercy, as revealed in His Word, and by his Spirit, sways the whole soul, rules all the heart, and brings, not some, but all the tastes and appetites of the soul into subjection before God.

In wicked men, one vice may triumph over another, and expel it from the outward life, but it is only to establish the dominion of sin in another form. It is a change of tyrants, but the tyranny remains. No sin can cure the heart of the love of sin. No commutation of sinful appetites can subdue the dominion or lessen the malignity of sin. But faith vanquishes every vice, and presents the subordinated spirit of Jesus, inviting him to enter and reign there. Inthroned in that heart, the Savior gives his law, and the subject spirit obeys. The Savior commands the believer to arise and follow him, and the believer follows him, forsaking all. Into his life he weaves deeds of devotion, and charity, and holiness of the same moral texture as those which were wrought by his blessed Lord. This man is worthy of the name of a believer. He shows his faith by his works. He whose fruit is different, deserves a different name. He whose fruit is corrupt, who habitually practices any sin, performs any act which Christ forbids, or omits any duty which Christ enjoins, is an unbeliever.

He discredits Jesus in his precepts, in his authority, in his royalty, and is an unbeliever and an infidel in the sight of Heaven. One act of disobedience, woven into the habit of life, is sufficient to give character to the whole life. One sin may class you in the category of unbelievers. It may suffice as a standard of rebellion under which the claims of the just Sovereign may be successfully contested. It may suffice to show the heart corrupt. "A good tree can not bring forth evil fruit." "By their fruits ye shall know them."

But further, if we could suppose it possible that any man could practice all the precepts of Christ which concern the life and conduct, and yet be destitute of the spirit of Christ, then we must still pronounce him an unbeliever. For he is an unbeliever whose feelings do not ascend with the spirit of Christ. The spirit and conduct of Jesus were the result of his knowledge and approbation of truth; and no intelligent being, whether finite or infinite, can discern and approve of truth, but it will create or occasion the same spirit and conduct as in him. Whenever truth is approvingly received into the understanding it works its own appropriate effects, and breathes its own native spirit there. It is this which "sanctifies" and "makes us free." Want of clear discernment of spiritual things, or want of hearty acceptance of truth when perceived, will mar and defeat the intended result; but otherwise "we are changed into the same image, from glory to glory, even as by the Spirit of the Lord."

Christ discerned and credited the truth that sin is

an evil—the source of all evil in the universe. He believed that man was suffering that evil. He believed that redemption was possible and infinitely desirable, both for God's glory and man's happiness. He believed that his own incarnation was the proper mode to effect it. He believed that means of grace, and the gift of the Spirit, were necessary as the instrumental and efficient causes of moral regeneration. Now, how evident is it that the clear cognition and hearty approval of these truths were essential to the benevolent scope of the Savior's feelings and actions by which our redemption was actually accomplished! All along through his life of marvelous activity and suffering he was sustained by his confidence in this plan of redemption which the wisdom and counsels of the Godhead had projected. This was founded in eternal truth, and none other could be given. If God could deny or reject truth, then he could, by the same law, become not only inconsistent, but malicious, and more to be dreaded than all other beings in the universe. If Christ had discredited any truth, or admitted any error, or credited any falsehood, he would have been changed in all the feelings of his heart and in all the conduct of his life. Had he not believed that sin is an evil, he would not have hated it with such hatred, would not have labored with such zeal to destroy it, would not have suffered to deliver us from it. Had he not believed there was a heaven of ineffable glory, he would not have spoken to us of salvation in such earnest words of love. Had he not believed there was a hell, he would not have warned us to flee from the wrath to come, even at the loss of all things, declaring it is better for us "to enter into life halt or maimed, rather than having two hands or two eyes to be cast into hell fire."

So true it is that Christ himself was moved in all his holy sympathies and enterprises by his belief in the truth. And so true it is that nothing but living convictions of eternal truth could have wrought such results. Even in God himself truth is the basis of his moral rectitude, as it is the law and measure of his beneficence. In God himself, notwithstanding the infinite virtue of his attributes, distrust of truth or the adoption of error, would transform the infinite rectitude of holiness and the infinite beauty of benevolence into infinite malevolence and deformity.

And if it would thus affect the moral features of the Godhead, can man indulge with innocence? Can that which would waste and annihilate the virtue of Deity be innoxious and harmless to man? Go to Eden and see. Behold the fruits of unbelief in the mother of our race. What led her to the fatal tree, when she ate and damned the world? It was unbelief. Search the history of mankind. Whence came the curses and blasphemies, the hypocrisies and treachery, the war and the bloodshed, of six thousand years? They have all sprung from the same fruitful source—unbelief. Men have cast away the truth and have believed lies. They have rejected the counsels of God, withdrawn their reliance upon truth, and have followed the devices of their own hearts. But if such are the effects of unbelief, let us inquire,

II. What is it to be damned? It is just the

reverse of what it is to be saved. "He that believeth and is baptized shall be saved, and he that believeth not shall be damned." Faith and salvation; unbelief and damnation—these are the opposites. The word literally denotes *the rendering of the sentence of the law;* the *giving judicial judgment against* any one; *condemning;* and if *salvation* is taking the believing sinner from under the sentence of the law and exalting him to a state of honor and felicity, *damnation* is the rendering and executing of that sentence, leaving the unbelieving sinner to all the miseries consequent upon the act. The causes leading to the two states differ, and in like manner do the states themselves. What is the difference between believing and disbelieving? The same that there is between light and darkness. What is the difference between being saved and being damned? The same that there is between light and darkness. Belief and unbelief are the causes; being saved and being damned are the effects, and the difference of these is at least equal to the difference of those. Keep this in mind and you will not dispute when we say:

1. To be damned, precious soul, is to be deprived of your probation. Probation means a state of trial for the purpose of forming a character fitted and suitable to some coming state. This life is our probation. We are warned, therefore, "Whatsoever thine hand findeth to do, do it with thy might." Damnation and probation are not concurrent states. The latter precedes the former, and its abuse or misuse is the very ground and measure of that ruin denounced in the text. When Adam and Eve were placed in

Paradise, their state was probationary. A law was given and sanctioned by the reward of life and the penalty of death. The law and liability were a test of character, and constituted their probation. They sinned, and the curse succeeded. But by the interposition of Jesus, they, and we, their children, were put again upon trial under an administration of grace. The terms of their first probation were, "In the day that thou eatest thereof thou shalt surely die," with the implied reward of life if obedient. The terms of our probation are, "He that believeth shall be saved, and he that believeth not shall be damned." For Adam, indeed, there was found a sacrifice for sin; but for us the Scriptures affirm of him that believeth not in Jesus, "There remaineth no more sacrifice for sin, but a certain fearful looking-for of judgment and fiery indignation, which shall devour the adversaries." God forbid, then, that we should look for another probation. "It is appointed unto men once to die, but after this the judgment." Our final hope is suspended upon the issues of the present life. God has placed our race upon two probations—one of law and the other of grace. We live under the latter. It is the last trial of humanity. Be mindful, therefore, of this affecting truth. When the terror and pains of this damnation come upon you, they will find no alleviation in the chance or possibility of escape. Seed-time will be gone forever, and all that remains will be a harvest of unmingled vengeance. But,

2. To be damned, is to be excluded from all the pleasures and comforts of the present life. This, if you will reckon it correctly, is no trifling evil. You

have seen no example of such wretchedness on earth, much as you have seen of sorrow and suffering. Who is there upon the broad earth that hath not some food, though scanty or coarse? some friend to speak a word of comfort? Who has not the privilege of sunshine and shade, and sightly scenes to rouse and refresh, and cheer? Who, at least, has not the air to breathe, and a drop of water in the midst of a raging thirst? But the subjects of this threatened cause are deprived of all. Your hearts would sink within you if God should take from you but a small part of your blessings. If your wealth were scattered, and you were reduced to abject poverty, how would that grieve you, and bow your heads to the earth! If your friends should turn from you in scorn, and hide their faces from you in trouble, yet the world would be before you a spacious field for action and for enterprise. Suppose that world should turn with demoniac zeal to haunt your life, setting upon you the mark of reprobation; yet yours is the privilege to fly from your persecutors, and yours is the comfort of hope at least. But what comfort can remain for him whose wealth, whose friends and strength, and hopes all die to be buried in one common grave! It is the purpose of God, in his long-suffering mercy, now for a time, and during probation, to leave the unbeliever, the atheist and blasphemer even, in the possession of varied measures of earthly good. If conscience suits, if the law condemns, if retrospections are bitter, and the future overhung with threatening clouds, yet the ungrateful wretch finds alleviation in the solace of earthly comforts, and may partially forget himself in sensuous engrossment with perishable things. But what will he do when deprived of all these, and left under the naked action of sin upon a moral nature created only for the enjoyment of God, and to which sin is like fire to the flesh! The doom of unbelief is banishment from all the blessings of this life, and like the gateway of Paradise, the flaming sword of wrath, turning every way, forever prohibits the return of the exile, or any participation of the forfeited pleasures.

3. To be damned is to be excluded from heaven; to be "banished from the presence of the Lord, and from the glory of his power." It is enough to know that it is the opposite of salvation, the opposite of heaven, the opposite of holiness, and of happiness; in short, the condition of the whole being exactly opposite to that for which we were created, and for which we were redeemed by Christ. It is that which both the law and the Gospel warn us against, and wherein both are arrayed against us. It is not a merely negative state. What is death but the opposite of life? Or sickness but the opposite of health? The absence of humility is pride; of obedience, transgression; of love, hatred, and all the kindred sisterhood of infernal furies. It is to be left of God, forsaken by his Spirit, separated from the means of grace, withdrawn from the society of the pure and the good, and left to the soul's own choice—unbelief—and to its idols forever. It is, as the word denotes, to be left under condemnation, when the last offer of remedial mercy is withdrawn. "He that believeth on the Son hath everlasting life: but he that believeth not the Son shall not see life; but the wrath of God abideth on him."

Whether the punishment of the wicked is by positive infliction, or by the operation of constitutional laws in a moral condition of the soul exactly opposite to that for which it was created, it may not be proper for us here to discuss, but a careful examination of Scripture, in connection with the providential government and the moral constitution of man, afford a strong presumption, if not a decided proof, that the latter is the case. The elements of punishment are within us. So are the capacities of angelic happiness. Fearful or glorious is the operation of this wondrous machinery of mind. In holiness and righteousness it is adjusted to the most exquisite delights. In a reversed condition it becomes the seat and instrument of the profoundest suffering. Through faith in Christ we attain the former; but unbelief reverses the action of all the moral and intellectual powers, and they are turned into ministers of death. Conscience becomes penal only in its action; memory, judgment, perception, imagination, and reason, all affect the sensibilities, through the conscience, like the touch of fire! Alas! what being can endure its own existence when, self-condemned, self-corrupted, self-destroyed, it beholds the law, the Gospel, the attributes of God, arrayed in just, and truthful, and holy, and everlasting condemnation of its character, and in the light of that law, that Gospel, those attributes, left to this self-abhorred character as its everlasting heritage!

. . . . . .

The remainder of the sermon wanting.—Ed.

VI.

FRIENDSHIP WITH CHRIST.

A SACRAMENTAL SERMON.

"*But I have called you friends.*" John xv, 15.

WERE not this the language of Jesus himself, we should pronounce the sentiment incredible, and the speech presumptuous. But as it proceeds from His own blessed lips, we are to receive it as one among the many examples of that condescension which leads us to exclaim, "Behold what manner of love the Father hath bestowed upon us." Let us, with deep humility, receive this saying, and compose our minds for a few minutes' meditation on a theme so full of delightful interest.

Man is so constituted that society is necessary to his happiness. Let him command every thing else; let the abundance of the world be his; let the sea and the dry land accumulate their treasures, and pour them at his feet; let him subsidize the riches of the universe, and hold them (if possible) by an immortal tenure, and still he must be inconceivably wretched, unless he can find one friend, at least, to whom he can speak of his prosperity, and communicate the intelligence of his happiness.

"The friendless master of a world is poor."

But friendship, however necessary to our happiness, exists only in a very defective form among the children of this world. Here it is incident to many irregularities, suspicions, and interruptions which mar its comforts, and sometimes transform its sweet into bitter, its bliss into the pain of severe disappointment. Sometimes it is only in word. It is commenced and carried on by deceitful professions which conceal the selfishness or malice of a heart as empty of love as is the sepulcher of life and beauty. Or, if it be sincere it is impotent as childhood, and short-lived as the vapor of the morn. If not destroyed by some trifling offense, it terminates in death. The ties which unite the ungodly in this life will be severed by the king of terrors, and there will be no friendship in hell.

But how pleasant it is to know that we can obtain a Friend whose love is sincere, efficacious, and everlasting; one from whom nothing can separate us; one from whom death can not remove us, but will only serve to transmit us to his immediate presence, and promote us to an intimacy unspeakably delightful, such as we can not, *even now*, conceive! Some of you, beloved, already know this Friend, and have had sweet communion with him. And you, like his disciples who surrounded him when he spoke these blessed words, find him not ashamed to own you as his friends. For to you he has said this day, while you gathered around the board to feast in his presence, "Henceforth I call you not servants; for the servant knoweth not what his Lord doeth; but I have called you friends."

We shall consider

I. How the friendship of Christ and his disciples is unlike the friendship of men.

II. The resemblance between them.

I. *Their differences.* They differ,

1. In their origin. This union between man and man commonly arises from some supposed congeniality of temper; or from the imprudent ardor of youthful passion; or from the interchange of kind offices, or from some community of interest. But the friendship of Jesus had no such origin. We were his enemies. We hated him with cruel hatred. We were as unlike him as hell is unlike heaven. We were rebels against his government. When, by incarnation, he came within our reach, we abhorred his person, as well as his authority, and persecuted him with cruel wrath, until our hands were wreaked in his blood. And yet, on his part, there was nothing but friendship and love. While we hung, with fiendish joy, around his cross, and feasted on his agonies, affection sprung, spontaneously, from the immeasurable goodness of his own pure and spotless soul. If we now love *him*, it is because he first, even while *we* were enemies, *loved us*.

2. The friendship of Jesus differs from that of man in the *degree of its affection.* In earthly loves that of Jesus can find no parallel. We may have felt the glow of fraternal, parental, and even conjugal love; but neither of these can afford us any just conception of that boundless, fathomless ocean of love which dwells in the bosom of Christ.

So far from comparing it with any thing earthly,

we should say, let history be silent. Let not the profane exhibit Damon and Pythias, nor the pious speak of David and Jonathan in connection with the sacred theme of Jesus' love for man. If angels desire to understand it, let us not suppose that from amidst a race polluted by sin, we can find any thing to shadow forth this everlasting and all-glorious mystery. "Greater love hath no man than this, that a man lay down his life for his friends." Look well to the meaning of these words. *No man* has any greater *love than this.*

The man who will die to save his friends, will die also to be revenged upon his enemy. Here is the grand distinction between the love of Christ and the love of sinful creatures. Christ commendeth his love toward us, in that while we were yet sinners, he died for us.

This is an example of love which stands isolated in the universe of God. Heaven itself has furnished but one solitary example of a love like this.

3. The friendship of Christ differs from that of man *in its efficiency.* However sincere and ardent the friendship of man, in a thousand cases it is impotent and useless. In our most pressing need, the one who loves us may be far away. Our cry for help will not reach him, and he will not come to support or save us. Even if near at hand, he can not always disperse our gloom, nor ease our pain, nor heal our wound. In our distressing cry for some anointing hand to touch the wounds of sin and heal them, that our conscience may find some peace, and our heart some crumb of comfort, what can *man* do for us,

though he were to die in our behalf. What could his friend do for him, who, in the paleness and agony of death, exclaimed, "*Remorse, remorse, remorse!*" Alas! he could only listen, and sigh, and suffer, and resign the suffering victim to the cheerless meditations of his dying hour.

Not so with our gracious heavenly Friend. He is ever present. Our softest whisper of grief reaches him in a moment. He listens and he flies to our relief. He can shed light upon the regions of death, and perfume the very grave. He can anoint the wounded soul with the oil of joy and gladness, and bring peace and assurance of hope to him who folds his hands in death. His rod and staff can comfort us, even in the gloomy vale, and his almighty arm can seat us on the hills of Zion forever. He is a very present help in time of need.

4. The friendship of Jesus *will endure forever.* That event which consigns other friendships to oblivion, serves only to the consummation of this. The Church is the espoused of Jesus Christ, waiting for the hour of death, to be decked in bridal robes, and introduced to her well-beloved. The Christian, in this world, is somewhat like one who waits knocking at the door of his friend, till he shall be heard and bid to enter. And, while he waits, darkness surrounds him, and the piercing winds chill his frame. Death, at last, opens the door, and behold the glory of the mansion revealed. A living splendor is all around him. The banquet is spread. Heavenly harmonies swell in ten thousand times ten thousand voices through all the courts of bliss, and welcome

him into the presence of his everlasting friend, with whom he is to dwell, loving and beloved forever.

II. Having seen the difference between the friendship of Christ and that of man, let us now consider *their resemblance.*

1. Friendship, in its perfect form, implies a *harmony of sentiment between the parties.* Although Jesus loved us when we were enemies, yet we can have no comfort of this love, and no benefit can accrue to us unless we love him in turn. Where there are opposite views, and warring opinions, and hostile sentiments, there can be no peaceful fellowship, nor true friendship. Christ has revealed to us his views and feelings, and these views and feelings must be ours, or we must be his eternal foes. This enables us to test the sincerity of our professions as disciples of Christ. Do we think and feel as he did on the subject of sin? Do we view it as an evil so dreadful as to deserve the punishment of hell? Do we view it as an evil so dreadful that to stamp it with merited reproach and reprobation, it was wisdom in Christ to die as its victim, and thus proclaim its exceeding malignity to all the creature universe? Do we feel as Christ does on the subject of holiness? Do we view it as the crowning attribute of Godhead, as the true honor and happiness of his creatures, without which "*no man* can see the Lord?" Do we view this world as Jesus viewed it? vain and transitory; unworthy to be made the portion of the soul, and the love of it fatal to our everlasting happiness?

Do we possess the Savior's views of death, judgment, heaven, and hell; both as to their certainty and their awful import, and the necessity, also, of being ready for that judgment and that heaven? Do these solemn truths influence our whole conduct and lives, making us men of one enterprise, namely, the pursuit of everlasting life? These sentiments do not possess the worldly mind. But if we are the friends of Jesus, they are our sentiments as they were his, and they exert an influence *upon our hearts* and lives.

2. A second principle in friendship is LOVE; or a sincere and mutual admiration. There may be forms of civility without any personal esteem. But all the customs of polite life are unproductive of the pleasures of friendship. They are as cold and cheerless as the grave, unless they be attended by the light and heat of love. Love imparts life and bliss to the union of Christ and his disciples. Jesus has manifested his love for his people in a manner which forms the joy of earth and the wonder of heaven.

Let us, my brethren, never forget that he expects us to reciprocate the sentiment. Our affection is to correspond with his. He loves us with an everlasting love. With all his infinite affections, he sets his heart upon us. We are, in return, to love him with supreme ardor. With all our finite affections we are to set our heart upon him.

3. A third particular, in this Divine friendship, is *an identity of interest.* There is a friendship which endures so long as prosperity lasts, but withers under the frosts of adversity. Thousands will smile upon us when Fortune smiles, who will frown also when she frowns. But, alas! who would value a friendship which ebbs and flows in all its sympathies, obsequi-

ous to the waxing and waning influence of changeful and treacherous fortune? Yet, such are often the friendships of the world. From such friends we may pray to be delivered. Where friendship is sincere and virtuous, adversity does not separate, but binds the faster. The parties will cleave more closely together while they drink the cup of sorrow. They will clasp each other with a more vigorous embrace, as they sail down some rushing current, and realize the danger of being dashed upon the rocks, or buried beneath the angry waters.

So it is with Christ and his true disciples. The interests of the Christian are identified with those of Christ. The Savior delights to have it so. As he and his Father are one, *so are* he and his people one. In all their joys he rejoices ; in all their afflictions he is afflicted. He feels a tender interest in all their movements, wants, and sufferings. Do they present petitions to God? He joins them in their intercessions, perfumes their prayers with his precious blood, and bears them to the presence of a propitiated God. Have we formidable adversaries, the world, sin, and the devil to oppose? He, as the Captain of our salvation, assumes the van of battle, spreads over us the banner of the Cross, inspires our hearts with heavenly courage, teaches our hands to war, and our fingers to fight, and leads us forth to glorious victory. Are we to bear a cross? He inspirits us with courage and strength, till the cross seems to rest lightly upon us. Must we drink the cup of bitter bereavement? He sustains us with precious promises, and consoles us with tokens of his gracious sympathy as he did the mourners at the grave of Lazarus. Are we cast into the fires of affliction and persecution? He comes to us as he did to Shadrach and his brethren, loosens our bands, and walks with us in the midst of the flames. Do we long after the glories of heaven? He has purchased for us the blessed inheritance, as our forerunner has for us taken possession, and is preparing its mansions for our reception, waiting with smiles to see us arrive. And while Jesus is concerned in our interests, we, too, are concerned for his.

The salvation of immortal souls lies near the Savior's heart. For this he wrought the wonders of redemption. For this he toiled, and wept, and died. For this he sustains this lower universe, and administers its high concerns. For this he has published His Word, appointed the holy Sabbath, and raised up the ministers of his truth. For this the Holy Spirit is come to convince the world, and sanctify believers. Some of his professed friends feel no interest in this enterprise, and care not for the salvation of the million who sigh in darkness and sink to despair. But the real friend of Christ, knowing how the soul of his gracious Benefactor "travails" for the salvation of man, is led by every principle of grateful love to travail also in the same behalf. The true friend of Jesus asks with Saul, "Lord, what wilt thou have me to do?" He longs, with ardent zeal, to see the lost gathered into the fold of Christ. His labors, prayers, substance, and influence are all placed at the command of Heaven. And, in all this world, he tastes no joy equal to that of seeing the pleasure of the Lord prosper in his hand.

4. Another requisite of true friendship is *mutual confidence between its parties.* To say that a man is talented, amiable, and interesting; that his morals are pure, his manners polished, and his conversation agreeable, is saying much of him as a candidate for friendship. But it is not enough. If he lacks firmness and decision of character, he lacks almost every thing. What avails it to *admire* if we can not *trust?*

One of the most delightful privileges of friendship is the communication of secrets. And this is one of the privileges of that divine friendship which subsists between Christ and his disciples. Mark the language of the context: "Henceforth I call you not servants, for the servant knoweth not what his Lord doeth; but I have called you *friends,* for all things that I have heard of my Father, I have made known unto you." Sweet are the expressions of confidence. Divinely precious are these tokens of the Savior's confidence in his disciples. It is not surprising that the Christian should repose confidence in his Savior, that he should retire from the world and even from his family to commune with Christ in a manner too intimate and familiar for the observation of his nearest earthly friend; exploring all the secrets of his own heart, and presenting them, both in his confessions and prayers, before the Holy One. It *would* be surprising if he did not seek to unburden his soul by spreading all his sins, and weakness, and wants, in undisguised simplicity before his compassionate, bleeding Savior.

But the friendship of Christ and his disciples implies more than this. There is a communication of secrets on the other side. Jesus opens his mind to his disciples. Even the things which he has heard from his Father, he makes known to his disciples. To those that fear him, he imparts the secret of the Lord. "The secret of the Lord is with them that fear him." Sometimes this is true in a very open and miraculous sense. When God resolved to overthrow Sodom, and the cities of the plain, he could not hide it from Abraham the faithful. He became the Patriarch's guest, and while conversing with his beloved child, he says, "Shall I hide from Abraham this thing which I do?" No, he could not withhold the secret, because Abraham was his friend. Look at Enoch and Moses; at Elijah and Elisha; at the three Hebrews in the midst of the fire; at Daniel, watched by the angels of God. Look at Paul and Silas in the dungeon, and at Stephen, as he kneels to die with all heaven open before him; and the throne of God, and the lovely Savior all revealed to his delighted gaze.

Every friend of Christ possesses secrets of greater worth than any of these—secrets which a thousand worlds could not purchase from him, even if the alienation were his privilege. The secret of the Lord is still with those who fear him—a deep knowledge of the things of God, of the import of his Holy Word, of the nature of sin, the blessing of pardon, the power of faith, and the bliss of love, such as the renewed in heart obtain from God through the blood of Jesus. "Eye hath not seen, nor ear heard, neither have entered into the heart of man the things which God hath prepared for them that love him; but God hath revealed them unto us by his Spirit." The Spirit which "searcheth the deep things of God" makes known to us the "hidden wisdom" of God, which "none of the princes of this world knew," which the natural man neither understands nor receives. To the real friends of Jesus only the Spirit reveals this "secret wisdom." To them also he gives "a new name, which no man knoweth, saving he that receiveth it." "They have the mind of Christ," not only in the sense of possessing his disposition and spirit, but of understanding his will, his purposes, his thoughts. The friend of Jesus exclaims, in reverent wonder, "How precious are thy thoughts unto me, O God!" To none others are these loving tokens given. Thus the friendship of Christ and his disciples is confidential.

Sinner, let me entreat you to cast around, and, convinced of your true condition, see your need, and secure Jesus for your eternal friend. You now exult in your youthful associations, but, alas! these will soon give place to others, and these to others still, until death shall bury, in everlasting oblivion, all the friendship of this vain life.

The changes which tend to such result are passing upon you in rapid succession. Already your early friends are gone, and their places are filled by others.

> "Where are the elves that your children caressed,
> And the friends that in boyhood attended your way?
> They are sunk like the bubble on ocean's rough breast,
> Like the mists of the morn they are vanished away!"

And other revolutions are just before you till there remains no room for another. And when you have selected your friends for the last time, and these shall also have gone, what then? Can you look forward from that point and not tremble? The gloomiest scenes of your existence will then lie before you. And must you encounter them in lonely and friendless solitude? in the hour of death, when deserted by the gay, and forgotten by the ambitious, and lamented by the pious, and abhorred by an abused, insulted Redeemer, what wouldst thou not give to have Jesus for thy friend? What wouldst thou not give, when heart and flesh fail thee, and thy farewell look upon all thou hast here loved is turned away downward to the valley of death, there to meet the Savior, there to lean thy fainting head upon his bosom, and smiling, say, "Lord Jesus, into thy hand I commit my spirit?" I now offer thee this Divine Friend, and stand up, in the name of Christ, to entreat your acceptance of his overture. We plead with you by all his tears and blood, and agony, cast away the weapons of your rebellion, and receive him who is all-merciful to pardon and all-powerful to deliver. Receive him and you shall not be friendless in time, nor shall you be friendless in eternity.

My brethren, we have this day made new covenants with Jesus. We have been in his heavenly society at the table of his love. We have eaten and drunk in his presence, and to seal our friendship forever, he gave us his flesh to eat, and his blood to drink. Shall we violate our engagements, and be guilty of a breach of this covenant? Let us beware how we dip our hand with Jesus in the dish, and then hurry forth to betray him. Let us go forth to the world exclaiming, "The vows of the Lord God are upon me."

That we may retain the friendship of Christ, let us repudiate the friendship of the world. We can not retain both, for the friendship of the world is enmity with God." And can we be willing to take the world and be severed from Jesus? Have we not been already sufficiently deceived and abused by the world? And who of us will be deceived again? How nobly did it promise us before? And which of its promises was finally fulfilled? It flattered us with the prospect of rest, and peace, and joy. Where are all its exquisite satisfactions, and when did we possess them? Alas! The world has been to us a deceiver, alluring us from scenes lovelier than Eden with all its charms. And when she promised us a couch of down, we found ourselves on a bed of scorpions. When we laid ourselves down to repose, stings and terrors assaulted us on every side. We felt the poison of the wounds, and waking from the delusion, exclaimed, "Avaunt sorceress," and fled her presence. And then followed the gloomy wanderings of our stricken souls, through dry places, seeking rest, and finding none, till One from heaven met us in the way, and poured upon our wounds the oil of gladness, took us into his banqueting house, called us his friend, his bride, his best beloved; watched us with the eye, soothed us by the voice, and breathed upon us with the breath of love. And now shall we turn from this Divine Friend and go back to the dungeon whence we came out? God forbid! No, thou most adored One, lovelier than the sons of men, "chiefest among ten thousand," we will still hear thy voice, and behold thy smiling countenance. We will still weep at thy cross, watch at thy sepulcher, and worship at thy gracious throne. And when death shall chill these hearts, and distill its dews upon these foreheads, let us, like Stephen, behold thy face, and yield our departing spirits into thine arms of everlasting love! Like Asaph, may we say, "My flesh and my heart faileth; but God is the strength of my heart and my portion forever."

VII.

GOD THE RIGHTEOUS JUDGE.

"*Shall not the Judge of all the earth do right?*" Genesis xviii, 25.

THESE words relate to one of the most memorable scenes in the history of man. That spot which is now covered by the odious waters of the Dead Sea, once revealed one of the most pleasant and fertile valleys in the world. Lovely hamlets and flourishing cities decked its sun-lit fields, and proudly looked down upon its waters which then sparkled like the eye of childhood in all the purity of curseless innocence. But sin prevailed, and the wrath of God followed in its train. The inhabitants of those regions became the most abandoned and guilty of the human race. Long did offended Heaven hush to sleep its disturbed vengeance, and repeat its missions of mercy to save them. At last their iniquities went up over their heads, their cup of transgressions was filled, and the uplifted thunder would no longer delay. In an hour the God of battles overwhelmed them in death, and commissioned his curse to dig their grave. The caves of the sea are their sepulcher, the waters are their winding-sheet and monument, and the bitter curse rests upon them, even to this day.

This retribution was as righteous as it was terrific and severe. It was preceded by an open inquisition of the abominations which provoked it. In verses twenty and twenty-one, God is represented as instituting an investigation of their conduct and crimes. And this is intended to show us that he acts in the character of a judge, whose business it is to know before he condemns.

In those days the Patriarch had pitched his tent upon the plain of Mamre, while before him lay the doomed cities of the plain. He was the friend of God. Jehovah came unto him as he sat in his tent, accompanied by two angels, and after receiving the hospitalities of Abraham, and having sent the angels forward toward Sodom, he communicated to his servant the purpose of his holy mind which had devoted to destruction the surrounding cities. Abraham interceded with his Almighty Friend for the salvation of his abandoned neighbors. "And Abraham drew near and said, Wilt thou also destroy the righteous with the wicked?" And thus continues the strain of his earnest intercession. And how strangely does the prayer of this righteous man prevail! While he pleads, Jehovah listens. While he presses his suit with persevering importunity, enlarging his request at every repetition of it, Jehovah yields, step by step, until the promise is given that ten righteous persons shall save the city. And here Abraham paused; or Sodom *might* have remained to this very day.

Observe the argument of the Patriarch's prayer. He pleads the righteousness of Jehovah, as the judge of the whole earth. "That be far from thee to slay the righteous with the wicked: and that the righteous should be as the wicked; that be far from thee! Shall not the judge of all the earth do right?"

We proceed to invite your attention to the rectoral character of the Supreme Being as the righteous Governor of the whole earth, in the following propositions:

I. SOME EVIDENCE THAT GOD GOVERNS THE WORLD.

II. A CONSIDERATION OF THE GROUND OF HIS AUTHORITY.

III. THE NATURE OF HIS ADMINISTRATION.

I. *What evidence, then, have we that God governs the world?*

1. We infer it from his nature. God is a Spirit, *incorporeal, intelligent, and active.* We conceive that a pure spirit, an unincumbered intelligence, must be unceasingly active. Such a spirit is God. We infer, therefore, that God is unceasingly active. Again, it will not be disputed that wherever God is, there *he acts.* But God is every-where. He lives in heaven, he lives on earth, *he lives* in hell. All creatures are filled with his presence. And as his presence fills all things, it follows that in all things and in all places he is *an active* spirit. Once more, wherever God acts his actions are regal and supreme, or they are loyal and subordinate.

One of these must be the case, because there are other agents in the universe besides God, and either he or they *must be in subjection.* But is God in subjection? Certainly not, as we infer from the fact that God is

2. *The Creator.* The Creator is incapable of

subordination to the creature. God, therefore, is not subordinate to his creatures, nor are his actions subordinate to theirs, but they are supreme, and constitute government.

But it is sometimes urged that this world is of too little account to engage the attention and secure the supervision of Jehovah. If this be true, why then did God create this world? Surely if it be beneath him to govern, it were equally beneath him to create such a world. But if its plan were of sufficient interest to employ his energies to create it, it may, when created, be of sufficient interest to secure his regal notice. Or, must it be presumed that he who made the world, lost all interest in it the moment it was formed? Must it be credited that God created life in a thousand forms and even endowed a portion of it with the noble attributes of intelligence merely to pass it by and yield it to any influences which chance or ambition might usurp over it? Would God bestow such powers and not be interested to watch their exercise and gather the fruits? Would he adjust such a system and disregard its operation? Would he people a world with intelligences, and teach them that he is their common Father, and then forsake them to the desolations of such a dreary solitude as this world must be if God is not present to cheer, and rule, and save it? No. If the creation of the world and its inhabitants were not beneath the dignity of God, neither is its control or government. If their creation was for his glory, so is the supervision. If, for his pleasure, he formed them, so also for his pleasure he still sways his scepter over them. If he brought them into being through the impulse of his benevolence, his benevolence is equally gratified in sustaining, guiding, guarding, and perfecting his creation. From the fact, then, that God created, we infer that he governs the world.

Again: It is generally allowed, either by open or by implicit concession, that the world is under government of some sort. Thousands, we know, profess to deny it, yet in a multitude of instances you find them ascribing to the world a subordinate station, and placing *chance* or *nature* as a sovereign upon the throne. In some such forms of speech does the sentiment declare itself that the world is under government. And we ascribe its government to God for this reason, namely: he alone has been proclaimed and confessed to be its governor. They who deny him this character and refuse to acknowledge his authority, ascribe subordination to the world, and then either invest *nature,* or *chance,* or *fate* with the attributes of supreme divinity, or, more properly, provide none to govern or control. We, therefore, ascribe to God that office of supremacy, and we do this with the greater confidence from the fact that there are in the order and the motion of things around us what appear to us certain tokens that there is an efficient system of government in operation over this world. Observe the good order which prevails, and the delightful harmony which obtains so far around as your eye can behold. How came these powers so nicely adjusted; these systems so skillfully balanced; these worlds revolving noiselessly through the fields of immeasurable space, without the least interference or pause, or disorder, amidst machinery so vast and so complex that no finite mind can admeasure or trace? Look upon it! Could such harmony prevail without some agency to secure it? Must not some power continue it as well as originate it? Does it require less power to preserve the worlds in safe and orderly motion than it did to start them in their sublime career? Does it require less power to reproduce Summer and Winter, and seed-time and harvest now than it did to produce them at first?

Much is said of the laws of nature; and much to proclaim the folly of those who say it. Let it be granted that Nature hath laws by which her operations are now conducted. Then it must be conceded that God upholds these laws, makes them efficient, and that their force or efficiency is naught but his power. If these laws be the instruments of Divine power in ruling the world, they only serve to remove the Divine hand a little farther off. And is God less the governor of the world because, instead of laying his naked hand upon it, he moves a spring which produces all other motions around us? Assume the extremest position consistent with the lowest type of Theism—the theory of development and order in nature from the operation of laws impressed upon primitive monads of matter—and still, if we reject atheism on the one hand and pantheism on the other, and adhere to the doctrine of a personal God, we are forced to acknowledge him as the Creator, and the wise Being who gave to matter these laws, and that his intelligence foresaw an *end*, and his benevolence determined that end to be *good*, and thus he projected the entire scheme of government for beneficent ends for which we plead. The distance of time, or the multiplication of subordinate agencies between the efficient cause and the final end of things, can make nothing against the wisdom, power, goodness, and glory, much less the reality of the government of all things by the one originating and supreme God. From the evident fact, therefore, that the world is under government, we infer that God is its governor.

We proceed to inquire

II. *By what right God governs the world?*

Men acquire authority over their fellows in several ways, as

1. By usurpation, when the crafty boldness of one man triumphs over the pusillanimity and simplicity of many.

2. By inheritanee, which is a covert usurpation; but yet is of a conciliatory character, and claims to be by a tacit consent of society.

3. By popular suffrage, which alone creates right, and confers an innocent and valid authority. But on neither of these grounds does God exercise authority over the world. To say he is an usurper were profane and blasphemous. Inheritance implies predecession, which God's eternity must of course exclude. The suffrage of his creatures is necessary for their holiness and comfort, but not for the purpose of conveying to him authority. He has an equal right to govern with or without their suffrage. God's authority is more sacred than even suffrage itself can bestow. It arises from his creative acts, by which all things are made that are in the heaven or upon the

earth. Creation confers upon God an absolute and indefeasible property in all things, so that he may possess them, use them, and derive from them the utmost satisfaction, praise, and glory. Usurpation and suffrage both imply the acquisition of authority and the investiture of office. There can be no such thing implied concerning God. God was always sovereign from necessity, and by necessity he must always be sovereign, not by assumption or suffrage; not by usurpation, or by hereditary right. His sovereignty is inherent in his nature. It is inalienable as his own essence. He can not divest himself of the attributes of sovereign any more than he can of the attributes of Creator.

Were he to vacate his throne, and cast away his crown, and resign the government of the universe, or any portion of the universe, it would be treason, and by that treason the universe must perish. So high and holy, and awful and glorious is the authority by which God governs the world! We shall now proceed to consider

III. *The nature of the Divine administration.* Generally, it may be said to abound in all that is considered excellent in government, namely: *Wisdom, energy, and beneficence.*

1. The Divine administration displays wisdom. It proceeds upon a perfect knowledge of every thing that transpires within his vast dominions. Human dominion is exercised in absolute ignorance of much that transpires within its limits. It often mistakes the innocent for the guilty, condemning the former and acquitting the latter; depressing the worthy and

exalting the vile. But no such errors are committed by the universal Judge. Under his administration, innocence has nothing to fear, guilty impenitence has nothing to hope. He leaves no secret places empty of his presence, or veiled from his eye, where crime may be concealed, unnoticed, and unpunished. He fills the universe, extending in all space, moving in all motion, enduring in all eternity, animating all that lives, thinking in all that thinks, imparting energy to all that acts; and can any thing be concealed from his omnipresent mind?

2. Another trait in the Divine government is energy. Omniscience and omnipotence are blended in Godhead. When Deity has laid his plans in infinite wisdom, nothing can defeat or retard their execution. There is no device against the Lord God Almighty. When he arises to battle it is vain to contend; when he pursues it is in vain to flee.

By a word he spoke the worlds into being, and raised up the dwellers upon the face thereof. By a word he can undo the mighty work, and resume the solitary station of his own primitive eternity. By his omnipotent energy the obedient of his subjects are sure of a reward, and the disobedient are sure of punishment. For these his treasures of wrath, and for those of his love are inexhaustible. A spacious heaven and a spacious hell are prepared and wait his purpose of retribution. Do you ask for some signs of his power? You have it in the diluvian tempests which drowned the world, and in the fiery deluge which whelmed the cities of the plain. You have it bursting up beneath your feet in all the vernal charms and glories which surround you. You have it in the lightning's flash, in the thunder's peal, in the volcanic blast, and in every shock of the terrific earthquake.

3. Beneficence is conspicuous in the Divine administration. God seeks the highest good of his creatures in all his acts of government. True, there are examples of punishment frequent and severe, under his administration. Such examples will remain forever to testify his veracity and answer the demands of justice. But, in judging and in punishing, God will be clear and irreproachable. In the destruction of the old world he sought to purify our race from corruptions so prevalent, and deep, and damning that no hope of reformation or salvation remained. In the destruction of Sodom and her sister cities he proceeded upon the same ground. In the former instance only a solitary family remained uncorrupted, and the whole world besides was filled with violence. In the latter instance ten righteous persons could not be found among the thousands who crowded and defiled the cities of the plain. Why, then, should they be spared? Were it better that they should live to prepare for a deeper hell, and to transmit their corruptions to succeeding generations as long as time should last? Doubtless benevolence dictated their destruction, and there was mercy in the wrath which consumed them. But it may be queried by some mind why God, in the exercise of omnipotent energy, did not reform rather than destroy them; and why he does not uniformly prefer reformation to punishment, correction to destruction? This query goes

upon the supposition that the Divine government operates mechanically or physically, and that matter and mind are subject to its influence. But this is error. God's government is adapted to mind, and cautiously counsels its attributes that it may commit no invasion upon its sacred prerogatives, but may rather preserve and confirm them. Whatever influence he can exert for the reformation of the depraved, without invading their prerogatives, that he will exert, but no more. He can not interpose his power for moral reformation in a way to derange or destroy the Godlike freedom of the human will. This would be to infract his own laws written in the constitution of his noblest creatures, and for the purest and noblest ends. He can not contradict himself. This would be to ruin the universe. Innocency itself could not be safe in the hands of a supreme ruler who could change or infract his fundamental laws at will to accommodate the guilty.

It is very pleasant to contemplate the Eternal God as the Father and friend of his creatures. It is very cheering to view him as a being of infinite benevolence; as a fountain of mercy; as guiding the steps, supplying the wants, and alleviating the sorrows of man; in a word, as clothed in all the attributes of gentleness, condescension, and love. But were we to view God only in these aspects and characters, we should betray a thoughtless mind or a vicious heart, and should be guilty of a dangerous and fatal error. We should behave like children who, pleased with the brilliancy of the flame and ignorant of every thing but its luster, rush into the midst of it, and find, too late, that its beauty hath power to torture and consume.

God is indeed our Father and Friend. But he is also our Governor and Judge. In each character the Scriptures reveal him with equal certainty. The history of the world, no less than Holy Scripture, proclaims the same truth. All the records of his providence, all its observed provisions and tendencies, all the monitions of conscience, pure and unseared, join with the uniform testimony of Scripture to prove that God is the Judge of the whole earth. That which proves the existence of a Divine government proves also its rectitude. "Shall not the judge do right?" How closely here and elsewhere do the sacred records blend the sovereignty and the righteousness of God! To affirm one is to affirm both. Like *depth* and *height,* they correlate. One can not exist, even in idea, without the other. But it is the justice of God as expressed in penalty to which men most object. They profess difficulty in reconciling punishment with love, especially sore punishment. But what is penalty? Is it the offspring of vindictive feeling? It may be so in the hands of a capricious tyrant. But in the righteous government of the universe, it is the offspring of benevolence. It is the office of penalty to guard the precept, first, by deterring from sin; or, secondly, by correcting and reforming, or finally by placing the offender beyond the power of injuring the innocent, and where his condition shall fitly express the evil of transgression and the Lord's hatred of offense. The punishment, in its essence, in a moral government, must consist in leaving the offender under the action of those principles which he has voluntarily chosen for himself, and in that condition to which those principles, by their tendencies and consequences, would consign him. And this, in any government, after suitable corrective discipline had failed, would not only be just to the offender, but the dictate of love to the obedient and loyal, and for the well-being of society in general.

Such only is the penalty of the Divine government. It assumes the accountability of men, and supposes all those actions to be free which commend men to the praise, or expose them to the censure of their judge. The world harmoniously reprobates that judicial iniquity which condemns for that which is inevitable. Those actions which are subject to judicial inquisition must have been free and avoidable. It were monstrous to suppose that God would preappoint the crimes of the Sodomites, and then visit them with overwhelming ruin for those very crimes. He avoids the imputation of such tyranny by representing himself as coming by his messengers into the midst of the city to examine the morals of the people and decide by holy inquest as to the course he should pursue. If God had determined all their moral conduct, surely this language would exhibit him in the unlovely aspect of affectation and hypocrisy.

In forming an estimate of the beneficial tendencies and results of the Divine administration, it is necessary to refer to its principles, and if these are pure, and reasonable, and excellent, it only remains to inquire whether God does strictly adhere to them in the details of his regal conduct. Now it is claimed in the Scriptures that God "governs the world in righteousness, and the people with his truth." It is claimed that "justice and judgment are the habitation of his throne." Will any dare to challenge the Almighty and charge him with a departure from righteousness? Can any, by searching the records of his administration, sustain so bold a charge?

But God has claimed, in his government of this world, to have done more for it than sheer justice demanded. He has not, according to his own showing, rendered unto sinful man his due. He has studied successfully to avert from our rebellious race that overflowing wrath which justice had directed. In his government of man, "mercy and truth are met together, righteousness and peace have embraced each other." He not only acquits innocence and sustains and blesses it, but by the Gospel of his grace, even the penitent guilty are made partakers of the same life and blessedness with the unoffending. God forbears with men. Forbearance is a suspension or delay of the penalty for the purposes of grace and reformation. "The long-suffering of the Lord is salvation." It is for this end. The principles of law and obligation laid down in Holy Scripture he departs not from in judgment and in rewards. Yea, he overpasses the strictly legal aspects of the case, and with the pitying heart of a Father, he condescends to entreaty and expostulation, and reformative methods, and long-suffering, in order to win back the revolted soul to obedience and love. Such is the beneficence of the Divine government. Infinite goodness proposes the end; infinite wisdom determines its model and methods, and infinite energy sustains it, while in awful array the moral attributes of Jehovah are drawn up as solemn guards and pledges of the eternal rectitude of its administration.

Conclusion.—My hearers, if these views of God and of his government be just, we entreat you to consider the affecting relation you sustain to him as his dependent subjects. Surely, if God be your judge, if he be present to you in your deeds, words, and thoughts; if his eye is never, for one moment, removed from your hearts; if such be his almighty energy that he is only to will it and all moving nature pauses in her course, chaos succeeds to the harmony of innumerable spheres around us; if he will by no means suffer the guilty to escape condemnation, but will pursue them by the ministers of justice until they are destroyed; surely if God be such an one, and you have served against him, it is no time for us to rest fearless of the awful curse, and unmoved by the lightning of his vengeance. To leave upon your minds a distinct and deep impression of your accountability to this judge, and of the measures which he proposes toward those who profane his holy name and trifle with his majesty, we invite you to look at Sodom in its glory and in its ruins, and be admonished.

Uniformity is an important characteristic of good government, and it belongs emphatically to the Godhead. So that by ascertaining the course of the Divine conduct in given examples, we learn its course in all similar circumstances. Let us examine then, the history of those cities here referred to.

1. Consider the partial history *of the Sodomites.* They were of a high and holy lineage. A few generations bring them back to their righteous progenitor, Noah, whose godly example was sanctioned by the forbearance and the judgments of Heaven.

Sinners in this assembly may boast an equal advantage, may claim an honorable and Christian birth and culture.

2. Those inhabitants were as highly favored in condition and fortune as they were nobly descended by birth. Their dwelling was almost a paradise. The spot which is now covered by the waters of the Dead Sea was doubtless among the most pleasant and fertile valleys of the whole world. Moses, whose eye for the beautiful was as correct as his heart was devout, says of it, that "the plain of Jordan was well watered every-where, before the Lord destroyed Sodom and Gomorrah, even as the garden of the Lord," or Eden. And this is but an emblem of your prosperity under the smiles and blessings of Heaven. But sin grew up and prevailed over all those scenes of loveliness which were designed by Providence to draw the heart toward God. So, sinner, it has been with you. Goodness has superabounded in order that thus you might be led to repentance.

3. But the inhabitants of those fair regions became thoughtless, and vicious, and profane. With them lavished mercies and delayed judgments became only new occasions of impiety and self-corruption. Still God repeats his messages of grace, but still they refuse to hear. So, sinner, it has been with you. At last their cup was full. "Their iniquities went over

their head." The wrath of God followed close in the train of their sins. God awoke to vengeance, and the impatient thunder-bolts could no longer be restrained. The elements were summoned as executioners, and a sulphurous sea of death became at once their winding sheet and sepulcher, even to this very day.

O sinner, darker clouds impend over thee this day, than ever lowered over those regions of death. And they are charged with lightnings fiercer than those which glared upon the doomed cities of the plain. Hear your sentence from the lips of the Judge. "It shall be more tolerable for Sodom and Gomorrah in the day of judgment than for thee" who hast trampled under foot the Son of God, and counted his blood unholy. God has spoken it. The word is gone out of his lips, and let it be according to his Word. Shall not the Judge of all the earth do right?

O sinner, flee speedily to some sheltering Zoar or the tempest must overtake thee. The wrath of God as a sea of fire rolls its angry floods just behind thee; make haste, or all its waves and billows will go over thee forever.

VIII.

THE WAGES OF SIN.

[Some years before his death, the lamented author attempted to prepare this sermon for the press, but was unable, from ill health, to accomplish it. The present form, excellent as it is, gives little idea of the wonderful effect of its oral delivery. An infidel who had heard it from the glowing lips of the author, remarked to a friend, in allusion to the closing words of the sermon, that "for days after nothing rang in his ears but *wages! wages! wages!*"—ED.]

"*For the wages of sin is death.*" Romans vi, 23.

EVERY portion of Holy Writ is worthy of the name of Gospel. Though it has curses for its foes as well as blessings for its friends, yet it is a system of pure benevolence. Like the colors of the rainbow, its variety of truth betokens and tenders peace to the world. But the covenant which stipulates the terms, consults not only our wants but our faculties, approaching us as parties, and persuading us as rational. Even in the last resort, refusing to invade the grand prerogative of mind, it proceeds no further than to enjoin us as agents, God himself conceding that our liberty is sacred.

The Gospel proffers happiness. It is the sealed instrument to convey "joy unspeakable," and is waiting for delivery—waiting, not because the Holder is slow to alienate, but because the alienee does not approach and take it. Why then the difference in men's moral states? Not from God's partiality. His

Gospel offers its benefits to all—to all on equal terms. But some will not accept its benefits; and such, like the sluggard who will not sow and reap, remain in that condition of destitution and distress which that same Gospel is commissioned to relieve. And refusing that "gift of God" which "is eternal life," they inherit the "wages of sin," which is the second "death." The text leads us to consider,

I. SIN IN SOME OF ITS PECULIAR ASPECTS;

II. THE PUNISHMENT OR PENALTY OF SIN;

III. THE RIGHTEOUSNESS OF GOD IN ITS INFLICTION.

I. Let us consider sin under the aspect which the text intimates by the term "wages," which suggests,

1. That sin is a *service*. And why? Because it enlists the energies—the physical, mental, and moral powers of the agent. What single sin can you think of, which, in its conception, growth, and development does not oblige us to effort and action? Not one. And it is servile action, in the employment of Satan, who "works in the children of disobedience," led captive by him at his will. Surely this is a service. If holiness is serving God, sin is serving the enemy of God. If the former involves labor and effort to obey God and persuade others to obey him, having for its precept, "strive to enter in at the strait gate," the latter involves more painful struggles to oppose and dishonor God. It employs the whole unregenerate man, the hand, the head, the heart. In other words, it engages the members of the body, the powers of the mind, and the ardor of the affections. The whole being is enlisted for its inception and enactment.

Religion is called a service, because it calls its votaries to a noble and blessed employment; but sin requires at least an equal degree of energy from those who seek its pleasures and pursue its ways. Was not the life of Cain as full of toil as that of Abel? Were the men of Sodom less laborious in their war against God and his servants, and his truth, than was Lot, the friend of God, in his righteous calling? Was not the service of Saul, the fickle and faithless king of Israel, more exhaustive of the powers of soul and body, than that of David, the "man after God's own heart?" Did not the course of Balaam, the apostate, in serving Mammon, cost him labor more severe than would have fallen to an honest prophet of God? Were not the priests of Baal, in their contest with Elijah, when bowing before their god from morning till noon, with loud, unheeded cries, cutting themselves with knives to propitiate an answer, in greater distress and labor than the calm and truthful prophet of God?

But leave the sacred history, and look out upon the world. Observation will convince us that sin is a most painful service. Inspect the different classes of the worldly and the vicious, and see if their pursuits require no toil. Can pleasure pursue its course of lawless gratification and not reduce the noble, the mighty, and the wise to the mere wreck of that which was magnificent in manliness? Can avarice reach its aim without a painful struggle? Can ambition win its honors without fiery contest? Can intemperance allow indulgence without a fearful sacrifice of health, comforts, and constitutional strength? Worldly and wicked men are the greatest drudges in the world. The excesses of worldly and selfish appetites, of carnal and unsanctified desires, are simply martyrdom in sin. Those sins which a wicked world agrees to pardon or applaud are never venial, as is seen by consequences. To say nothing of a future but certain retribution, they exhaust the powers of life, and reduce the strong and gifted to the mere wreck of all that is noble in humanity.

Thus you perceive that sin deserves the name of service. The sinner and the saint has each a work to do. Both devote themselves to laborious occupations. The Christian's work is in the sanctuary; the sinner's at the assembly room, the theater, or gambling house. The former seeks the closet, the latter his debauch. Pass down the stream of life and watch them in their course, and you will behold them encountering rough and smooth, always actively employed as the friends or foes of God. Nor could we easily determine whether it be more difficult to sustain the Christian's toils or endure the sinner's drudgery, were it not for the blessed fact that the Christian's course is aided by heavenly succor, and that his toil is relieved and sweetened by heavenly consolation.

2. Sin is a *voluntary* service. By this I do not mean that the human will begets man's wicked dispositions as they appear in the infant mind. To affirm this would be neither philosophical nor Scriptural. If the will of infancy beget its unlovely dispositions, what originates that uniform bias of the will by which it produces only sinful or corrupt states? The ques-

tion is unanswerable. But we avoid the difficulty by holding that Scripture truth, "Behold I was shapen in inquity"—a truth which we believe inculcates moral doctrine and not a mere physical fact.

We hold that moral depravity is man's natural inheritance—that he enters the world subject unto sin, whose early dominion over him is without his let or hinderance. We hold that its first working in the members confers no guilt, and that all its concupiscence of whatever sort, requires no condemnation till the eye of conscience is opened, and its monitory voice warns him of a right and a wrong in human actions. But while we hold these sacred truths, we neither deny nor doubt that sin is a voluntary regard and pursuit of things forbidden by God's commandment.

But this voluntariness of freedom of the will in things pertaining to God we hold again to depend on the aid of God's Spirit, which, by well-invented and prescribed means, such as the study of the Scriptures, prayer, and the ordinances of the Church, "helps our infirmities," and imparts a gracious power to choose eternal life, to adopt a course of seeking by which we surely may attain it. With the diligent and persevering use of means, God has connected eternal life; in the habitual and persevering neglect of means prescribed, we are sure of final ruin. The former we attain only through Divine grace helping us; the latter we reach by the proclivities of our own nature, when grace is spurned.

Now it is plain that the use or disuse of these means of grace is voluntary with man, as would be the adoption or the rejection of a remedy for sickness, from which it differs only in the certainty of its results. Adopt the *means* of grace and their *end,* salvation, is sure; reject them and it is impossible. We voluntarily choose or reject the means; and by the same suffrage we voluntarily choose or reject the end. Thus sin is a *voluntary service.*

3. Sin is a *fruitful service.* It requires a reward. So says the text. The Scriptures reiterate the same alarming truth. They teach us that man's probation is prolific—that in it he prosecutes a sort of moral husbandry, which will bring a following harvest. "Whatsoever a man soweth, that shall he also reap; he that soweth to the flesh shall of the flesh reap corruption." Not only they who have done good, but they also who have done evil, shall come forth to a resurrection of just retribution.

"Sin, when it is finished, bringeth forth death"—produces that which is well suited to its devices and its deeds. Yes, brethren, sin hath wages. It merits and will meet its due reward.

The word rendered "wages" was used to designate the pay of a Roman soldier for services performed. We are called to be soldiers. The soul of man may be considered the seat of war. The contending armies which occupy the field are recruited from heaven and hell. Satan and his legions preoccupy the ground. The Captain of man's salvation invades this cursed encampment. War rages. The soul in this position is forced from her neutrality. The issue of the conflict depends on her behavior. At first her powers divide. The passions, earthly, sensual, and devilish, declare for the prince of darkness and arm against the Spirit. Reason and conscience with earnest protestations condemn the unworthy deed, and commence to plead the cause of Truth and Righteousness. Celestial and infernal powers stake all upon the issue. Yet both abet the onset. Satanic charms inspire the passions and fire them for the conflict. A heavenly influence imparting light, and pressing truth upon the conscience, rouses the nobler powers to maintain the cause of God. The Savior's strength and promise assure victory to conscience, unless, transformed to traitor, she betray her sacred trust. Does she betray her trust, go over to the passions, and join the standard of God's enemy? *'Tis treason,* and under the authority of the King of Kings, the traitor in the camp of Israel, as well as under the Roman eagle, is sure of his award; for "*the wages of sin is death.*"

II. The punishment of sin—"*death.*"

Let us consider *the nature of this death.* The word death has various meanings. Its most natural and of course its common signification is the separation of soul and body. Is this its meaning in the text? By no means. Because the death here mentioned is something from which the Gospel proffers us deliverance. But the Gospel proffers no deliverance from dissolution and the grave. The separation of soul and body is the common lot of all. It is an event which comes on the righteous and on the wicked. Would Justice prescribe that as a punishment for treason which comes also on the most faithful and patriotic soldier? Surely not. That death, then, which is the common lot of all the sons of men, can not be a penal dispensation toward the wicked; for such a dispensation must bear peculiarly and exclusively on the wicked, and not involve the righteous also. The death threatened in the text is not, therefore, the separation of soul and body merely.

Death sometimes denotes the separation of the soul from God—its destitution of the graces and comforts of the Holy Ghost. This is sometimes called *spiritual death.* Is this what it means in the text? Certainly not. For this spiritual death is the very offense for which punishment is threatened; and it can not, therefore, be the punishment itself. Let us attempt an illustration. A traitor is arrested, tried, found guilty, and waits his sentence. The Judge proceeds to pass that sentence, and in the progress of his remarks uses some such words as these: "The commission of this high offense proves that you are *dead* to all sentiments of patriotism for your country and of attachment to your king; that you are *dead* to all those generous emotions which can render you a worthy and useful citizen, fit to enjoy the sacred privileges which the laws and constitution secure to the loyal and patriotic. Thus, *dead* to every ennobling virtue of humanity, it is not fit that you should live to annoy and curse the land which you will no longer adorn and bless. Most justly, therefore, does the law which you have violated award the penalty of *death* which I shall now pronounce upon you." He then proceeds to sentence him. Here you perceive the word death, in its grammatical variations, is applied: first, to describe the guilty and depraved state of the vile malefactor; and, second, to designate the penalty of his crime. And would the officer of public executions be in any danger of confounding the two, or mistaking them for one and the same thing? Could he so misinterpret the sentence as to infer that the criminal's death to honor and to virtue is the only death he is to suffer under the sentence of the court? Now apply this illustration.

The Bible teaches that the sinner is spiritually dead—that is, dead to every sentiment of love and loyalty to God. This, it teaches us, is his *crime*, alleges it as a matter of accusation against him. And *for* this it pronounces sentence of *death* upon him. And will any but profane lips affirm that the death threatened as a punishment is no more than the very same death which constitutes the crime? Surely not. It is most evident, then, that the death mentioned in the text is not spiritual death. What, then, is meant by death in the text? Undoubtedly it is eternal death, or the retribution which overtakes the impenitent in another world. *Eternal* death is not a Scriptural phrase, but it is a Scriptural doctrine. Death, like the word corruption, is evidently considered, by inspired writers, as implying, of itself, perpetuity. This is evident from the fact that they often place it in antithetical relation to the phrase "everlasting life;" and also use the words "everlasting punishment" in the same connection. For example, "The wages of sin is *death*, but the gift of God is eternal life," etc. Here the opposition is of *eternal life* to *death*. But again, "These shall go away into everlasting punishment, but the righteous into life eternal." Here the opposition is of "*life eternal*" to "*everlasting punishment.*" Now, as "death" and "everlasting punishment" are both used in this construction, or are indifferently connected antithetically with the phrase *eternal life*, the principles of fair criticism clothe them with the same signification and force as to duration. In other words, they are, in this respect, synonymous, or exactly parallel. But it may be asked, what is the import of "*everlasting punishment?*" I answer, the exact opposite of "*everlasting life.*" And further than this I need not reply. Why should I argue that it signifies endless misery? Could I prove it, the phrase *endless misery* is just as liable to cavil as the other phrase. I could not come to any conclusion as the result of my argument, which is not just as equivocal as the phrase "*everlasting punishment,*" with which I set out. Should a man argue that white means white, or that black means black, how could he conclude his argument with a statement more plain than that which he defends? No word in Greek literature could more definitely set forth duration without end than that rendered everlasting and eternal in the passages we have quoted. I leave you, therefore, with the declaration of Jesus, "these shall go away into everlasting punishment," as my exposition of the nature of this "death."

III. But is this view of the subject consistent with the revealed character of God? Is God herein righteous? Can we reconcile it with his attributes of wisdom, power, and goodness, that he should award to the sinner everlasting punishment? In reply to this question we must be mindful of these things: 1. He has procured for us a most unmerited probation. 2. God wants us to spend it in his service, and stipulates its reward in the spirit of infinite benevolence and love. 3. In view of our disrelish of divine things, he supplies us with the Holy Spirit to help our infirmities, and renew in us a holy admiration and relish of his service. 4. He warns us that unless we serve him we oppose him, and ally ourselves to his enemies. 5. He admonishes us that by this course we increase our opposition to him, and render it impossible for him to make us happy by his society and friendship, because, in this state, these can not, in the eternal nature of things, be pleasant to us. 6. He teaches us that all our privileges are bought by the death of Christ, and that their neglect or abuse involves the heinous crime of scorning that rich grace thus dearly purchased, and the madness of rejecting the only method for our salvation.

Now, in all these things it will doubtless be confessed that God displays his goodness. When we turn to the analogy of his earthly administration, we acknowledge God's goodness to be properly displayed in those arrangements which place security and happiness within our reach, and then permit us freely to apply the kind provision. For instance, we call it goodness in him to cause the sun and rain to fructify the soil; and we never presume to charge upon him the misery of man who suffers nakedness and hunger as the fruit of indolence in seed-time or harvest. We acknowledge his goodness in setting his bow in heaven, as a token of his covenant that he will no more drown the earth. But we never charge it to malice that he does not interpose and force the wretch to live who resolves to drown himself.

We acknowledge his goodness in supplying plants and minerals whose virtues, prudently exhibited, restore the sick to health; but we do not say he is malevolent, because these salutary remedies are often made the instruments of suicide and murder. In such cases as these we acquit the Almighty of wrong, and credit him as good and wise, because he has placed security and comfort within our reach, and instructed us to apply the benevolent provision.

Why can we not judge with righteous judgment on other subjects also, in which the same principles are involved, and where the course of the Divine administration proceeds upon the same rule? God has placed us upon trial for eternity, and in circumstances, too, most friendly to the acquisition of a holy and happy mind. He reveals the bow of mercy. Jesus and the Spirit shed rain and sunshine on the soul. He charges all his truth with a healing virtue, and every believing application approves its efficacious power. Does not this display his goodness and his wisdom? And after all, shall we charge it to his malice that he does not force the wretch to live, who madly drowns himself in destruction and perdition? or who has resolved to make the medicine of the Gospel the perverted instrument of the soul's eternal ruin? Little will it avail us in the day of retribution to have passed the time of probation, given for repentance, in censuring our Judge. We shall wonder why we did not lay it to heart that we were made subjects of so holy an administration, that our whole probation was a display of love on his part, and of enmity on ours.

In these circumstances, supposing, as we do, God to be good and wise, and mighty, we still ask how is he to display these attributes toward us? We have been active, moral beings, under his dispensations of law and grace, and our whole probation has been crowded with displays of love ungratefully applied by us. In the close of this scene God must change his measures with us, or resign his dignity as governor of all worlds. He can not treat us as obedient, worthy subjects without disregard to truth, for we have not been obedient or worthy. He can not treat us as sinful, but pardoned subjects, because we treated the Gospel and its Savior with neglect and contumely, as well as the law and its Author with scorn. In addition to this, we have not moral taste or capacity for one single pleasure which blooms in all the regions of the celestial world.

What disposition, then, will he make of those who have reduced themselves to a condition so forlorn that nothing can bring them joy, because they have ruined every faculty for the fruition of it? Were God to introduce them into the heavenly world, and recall to every sense its choicest good, the eye, and ear, and taste, and all would be in anguish worse than hell. His courts on earth were disagreeable, though the tokens of God's presence were but feebly discerned. How, then, could heaven be borne, where God displays his glory in intense, eternal splendor to all its gathered hosts?

Do you say that Omnipotence can still create the

soul anew, and form it for the pleasures of that holy world? I answer, he *will not* do it. God could do many things as an Omnipotent Being that he never will do as a wise and holy Being, even though it might seem that in doing them he would afford striking evidence of goodness. The wretch who drinks his poison may say with perfect truth that God can counteract it and save his periled life. The monster who kills his neighbor may affirm with equal truth that God can, by his act, resuscitate the dead. But God will do none of these things. It would be poor encouragement to virtue, and poor discouragement to vice, if God were to busy himself, not in arresting the spread of sin, but in averting its fatal consequences from the guilty. His wisdom and his goodness assure the universe that it needs to apprehend no misfortune of such a magnitude. What the law of moral fitness requires is as essential to Deity as his perfection or his existence.

Do you still say that God can, in eternity, renew the ruined soul and fashion it for pure and heavenly entertainments? I answer, yes, and in the same instant he can, if it be a mere question of power and independence, transform the sainted spirits who, through tears, and pains, and blood, have entered into heaven, and fashion them for all the woes and agonies of hell. *But he will not do either.* One event is just as probable as the other with the self-assumed obligations of his eternal truth. He *can not* do it. Once he sought the privilege at your hand of effecting your renewal. He sent his Word, and sent his ministers, and his providence, and his Son, and his Spirit to perform this blessed work. These waited all the time that probation lasted. He bounded that probation, and warned you of the fact. You mocked his gracious offers till you had passed its limits, and as he proved to you his goodness and mercy while you lived, he will now prove to you his decision and his justice. How? He will suit your wages to your work, and your reward to your capacity. The universe shall see and approve it, and shall adore. The lost shall see it, and feel to all eternity that hell is the wages paid by justice to the reprobated soul. A sense of this will kindle fiercer all its lurid fires; and if, amid its flames, the soul should cry out, "What meaneth this great wrath?" a hand, scarred with wounds of cruel crucifixion, shall come forth and write, "THE WAGES OF SIN IS DEATH!" and every sheet of fire shall reveal the startling truth, "*the wages of sin is death.*" And the smoke of their torment shall ascend forever and ever, and on each convolving cloud, as it curls upward from the pit, that hand shall write in blood, WAGES! WAGES! WAGES!

IX.

THE GIFT OF GOD.

[This, as well as the preceding, of which it forms the counterpart and completion, is found only in the rough sketch from among the Author's MSS. Yet, like that, though the less complete of the two, its rich suggestiveness stamps it with value.—ED.]

"*The gift of God is eternal life, through Jesus Christ our Lord.*" Romans vi, 23.

IN our last discourse we attempted to explain and enforce the first clause of this text. We then remarked that every portion of Holy Writ is worthy the name of Gospel. For though it has curses for its foes as well as blessings for its friends, it is a system of pure benevolence. We then directed your attention to some of its darker shades. We now propose to your meditation more cheerful, if not more salutary views. Then our text introduced us to scenes of death, of wrathful retribution. Now we may speak of Christian life and Christian joy, of Jesus and heaven. The Gospel is a system of pure benevolence. Infinite love speaks by its voice, infinite light shines through its doctrines, infinite munificence adopts it as an instrument to convey eternal riches to the sons of men.

Merciful God, assist us by thy Spirit to listen to this voice; to rejoice in this light; to take through this sacred instrument an inheritance incorruptible, undefiled, and that fadeth not away!

Let us consider the tenor of this instrument by noticing,

I. ITS DONATION.

II. THE METHOD OF ITS SEIZIN AND ENJOYMENT.

I. *Its donation—eternal life.* By this we are not to understand perpetual being merely. If so, it might imply an evil, not a good; a curse, not a blessing. To perceive the excellence of this life we must advert to the nature of that death which constitutes the wages of sin. The wages of sin is not annihilation. Man was made to be immortal. He was made to be the image of God's eternity. This purpose of his creation will be fulfilled. Man must live forever. Sin, if it could annihilate, would be comparatively a trifling evil. Annihilation would be an effectual, though a mournful remedy for the wounds it gives the soul. But though sin can not annihilate, it can kill. It can convert all the light of our existence into darkness; all its sweet into bitter; all its joy into agony; all its immortality into an eternal dying. It can fill the living soul with anguish more intense than all the pains of dissolution in its severest forms. This is Scriptural doctrine, but it is taught by Providence as well as Scripture; by experience as well as Providence; by observation as well as experience; by history as well as observation.

Inspect the scenes which history has rescued from oblivion, and in them you will perceive such sufferings as illustrate this truth, that "*sin has power to kill.*" Look at the scenes of life as they spread around and pass before you, and in their crime and misery you may read the fearful truth, that "*sin has power to kill.*" Look into your own heart, and in its corrupt and painful passions you have affecting proof that "*sin has power to kill.*"

The Scriptures in this instance serve to confirm, and not reveal, a doctrine which history, and consciousness, and God's instructive providence do, by fair interpretation, suggest to every mind, and impress on every heart. While the Scriptures assure us of the malignant power of sin to destroy our peace and murder all our joys, we can perceive, if we examine, that it has already commenced this dreadful work. Can you not perceive it? Are you not witnesses to yourselves that it has disturbed your hours of rest; transformed your pleasures into pain, armed conscience with a scorpion's sting, and inflicted worse than serpent wounds upon your bleeding, poisoned hearts? And while these scenes, composed of sin and suffering, of crime and anguish, are within and all around you, will you dispute or doubt that Scriptural statement which confirms the vision of your eye and the consciousness of your souls? Surely not; and if not, you will believe that sin is working death within; that it can and will, if permitted to take its course, convert your endless being into immortal pain and agony. It is inveterately hostile to the happiness of man. It assails his pleasures in their bud; blasts them in their blossom. It sows the seeds of care and pain in the Spring-time of his being, matures them in its Summer, and stores the poisoned fruit as the bitter treasures of the soul's eternal Autumn.

This is death: that death of which the Scriptures warn us; and which they do assure us is in its milder form the condition of our souls, uninfluenced by the reviving virtue of the Gospel.

Miserable condition! Dreary, terrifying prospect! How does it sicken all the soul, and make it cry with earnestness, and struggle with utmost energy for the devouring gulf of dark annihilation! And still it finds, as it struggles, that its energies are immortal, and its very struggles after death proclaim its painful doom to live forever, and live the victim of an immortal dying.

> "O, wretched state of deep despair!
>
> What! to be banished from my Lord,
> And yet forbid to die!
> To linger in eternal pain,
> Yet death forever fly!"

Yes; the wages of sin is death.

> "But, lo! a voice of sovereign grace
> Sounds from the sacred Word."

For though the wages of sin is death, and we have all begun to taste the bitterness of its remuneration, yet the Gospel interposes and proclaims a joyful rescue. The same communication which reveals our true condition displays to us the method and means of blessed deliverance. The ultimate aim of this Gospel, in all its representations of man's sinfulness and wretchedness, is to save him from so forlorn a state.

The information it communicates is painfully affecting, but the object which it seeks is divinely benevolent. Like those medicines which are bitter but salutary, the Gospel bears, under the cover of severity, the elements of heavenly life to ruined, dying souls. True, it teaches man his ignorance, but it is to make him wise. It proclaims to him his misery, but it is to make him blessed. It indicates his sickness, but it is to bring him health. It displays to him his poverty, but it is to make him rich in the possession of the gift of God through Jesus Christ our Lord. It paints in striking colors the doom of the transgressor, but it is to warn us of his ways and turn us from his paths. Last of all, it exhibits in impressive figures the rewards of Christ's religion, to attract us to its altars and enlist us in its service. Here, that reward is called "eternal life." Eternal life! How sweet it sounds to the soul that has enjoyed the least experience of it!

That soul was dead, but is revived. Its present life is found to be the very opposite of that dying state which was its birthright and its curse until, by new creation, it partook of the enjoyment of this most blessed life. This, then, is a general description of eternal life, namely: It is the very opposite of that death which we have just described as constituting the wages or the punishment of sin.

For, if sin kills the soul, the gift of God revives it. The gift of God imparts a consciousness of energy for holy action, and this is life eternal. It imparts fortitude for patient suffering, and this is life eternal. It inspires the soul with holy raptures, and this is life eternal. Does sin convert the light of man's existence into darkness, religion transforms its darkness into light. Does that convert his sweet into bitter, this converts his bitter into sweet. Does that convert his comfort into pain, this transforms his pains into pleasure. Does that fill the living soul with worse than dying horrors, this inspires the dying with raptures all immortal. And religion, like sin, begins its work on earth. Experience is the Christian's demonstration of those Scripture statements which announce this life eternal as the gift of God to man. The Christian has blessed admonitions, from what he feels in his own heart, that the book of God is true. He finds that life, eternal life, has commenced its blessed reign, and in its swelling raptures he is then satisfied. Now he can exult in the prospect of immortality. The gift of God is boldly counteracting the power and work of sin. It restores that rest which sin disturbed, disarms the conscience of its sting, heals all the wounds of his aching, bleeding heart; while peace and purity, joy and holiness, spread all abroad within him, confirm the blessed doctrine of man's eternal life.

Well may he triumph in the thought that man must live forever. For religion converts his endless being into immortal joy and rapture. It nips his *sorrows* in their bud and blasts them in their blossom. It sows the seeds of peace and bliss in the Spring-time of his being; matures them, and treasures them as the riches and the glory of the soul's eternity.

Such, my brethren, is the precious gift of God. So excellent and lovely is that eternal life into which your souls have entered by the second heavenly birth. You are now, in the peace and comfort of your faith, enjoying the infancy of an eternal life. You have yet attained but little of that which is in store for you, yet this little is more than this vain world can give. Your life, though just commencing, is sweeter far than all the joys of sense. And if the bud of this new life affords such strange delights, O, what may we expect from its blossoms and its fruits!

II. We shall proceed to inquire by what method we may possess this eternal life.

1. This inquiry is very necessary, as we learn, not only from the tenor of God's Holy Word, but from the fact that thousands of the human family exist without this life, and even pass from this world without any signs of its enjoyment. And why? Surely not because it is limited by the Donor's partiality to a few of this great family? No! The instrument which proffers it urges its acceptance upon all the sons of men. The Gospel, in strains as sweet as those of Heaven, invokes a suffering world to seize these everlasting riches. In many varying tones it appeals by turns to every passion which sways the human heart, to every principle which prompts to human action. With a voice of wisdom it speaks to the understanding, with words of promise it rouses expectation. Its fearful threatenings are addressed to our fears, and its tender invitations to our hopes. Conscience is assailed by its bold accusations, while our gratitude is moved by a thousand indications of its kind and tender purpose.

But, alas! to thousands its voice of wisdom and of promise, of warning and entreaty, is like the idler's tale, unheeded and despised. And this is the reason that men have not this life eternal. Gospel manna is rained down to them from heaven, but they refuse to eat it. The water of life flows in floods all around, but they refuse to drink it.

Sinners, are any of you now otherwise disposed? Do you look upon this divine life as a gift not unworthy to be sought and cherished, and preferred to all that the world can promise or present you? If there be one such present, let him diligently consider that this eternal life is an absolute gratuity. In the language of the text, it is a "gift." It is a gift in the simplest, least qualified sense. There never was a benefit conferred in which the beneficiary was so undeserving. Undeserving, did I say? Call it ill-deserving. Nay, that is insufficient. Call it hell-deserving. This donation is not like that of A, who owed B nothing, but capriciously presented him with one hundred dollars. Nor is it like C, (though this is nearer to it,) who forgave D a debt of one hundred dollars, and added another one hundred dollars as a largess.

The Gospel benefice has not a parallel in earth or heaven, and why do we present one? The degradation of the beast and the malice of the devil combine in the wretch whom Jesus died to save. I say the wretch, that it may rouse, not your pride, but your humility. I say the wretch, and this may prove the fitness of the name. He had not only fallen, but he was averse to rise again. He had not only sinned, but he refused to cease from sinning. He had not only warred with God, but the zeal of his hostility waxed warm, and bold, and devilish, while God was seen descending with him, intent to pacify him. Yes, the zeal of his hostility waxed hot against Immanuel, till its cursed, cruel wrath wrought the sanguinary horrors of the cross; and weep, O Heaven! blush, O Hell! the God who came to save was made the victim of a tragedy! Jesus died, and rising from the tomb, all pale in the visage and attire of the sepulcher, he presents to his murderers the gift of life eternal. He presents to you, and all the world, the same gracious offering. You, and all the world, are fallen, depraved, and enemies to God, just like those who arrested Jesus in the Garden, and cried, with one accord, "Crucify him! crucify him!" A thousand times our hearts have felt the same, and thousands of our deeds have been as sacrilegious as the taunt and the blasphemy which mocked his dying pains. Yet he bears to us the offer of everlasting life. And well is it denominated the "*gift* of God."

2. But you may say, what are we to understand by the *conditions* of salvation? I answer, by the conditions of salvation you are not to understand any performances whose merit moves the Gracious Donor to kindness toward his creatures. These conditions are scarcely conditions, either in the legal or popular sense. They are rather the method, or the mode, of possessing the gift of God. In every thing there is a method. There is a method of allaying thirst, namely, by swallowing fluids. There is a method of allaying hunger, namely, by eating food. There is a method of nourishing the body, namely, by digestion. There is a method of making the atmosphere

contribute to the immediate support of life, namely, by inhaling it into the lungs. But God does not bestow water on condition that we drink, nor food on condition that we eat, nor air on condition that we breathe. Fruits grow, whether we eat or not; fountains abound, whether we drink or not; the globe is girt with atmosphere, whether we breathe or not.

The gift of food, and drink, and atmosphere is absolute, and independent of all conditions. And so it is with the provisions of grace. The bread of Heaven, the water of life, the atmosphere of truth fall, and flow, and circle all around us, whether we eat, drink, breathe, or not. And do you, then, conclude that all is safe, and that you have nothing to do but sleep your way to heaven? Pause and consider! Will the fruits of the earth nourish you unless you eat them? Will the gushing fountains revive you unless you drink of them? Will the pure air invigorate you unless you breathe it? No! And so, although the bread of heaven and water of life are spread and poured around in profusion as rich as the mercy which bestows them, yet you must eat and drink or perish in the midst of the abundance.

3. To meet this view of the subject, then, we propose to speak of the *method*, not the *condition*, of enjoying the gift of eternal life.

This method is described by the Instrument which offers to us the gift. And what does it affirm? "He that believeth on the Son of God hath everlasting life." "Now the just shall live by faith." Faith is the method of enjoying life eternal. By faith, the soul eats the bread and drinks the water of life. By faith, it breathes the atmosphere of heaven. Faith fills the soul with heavenly light and love, and communicates unto it the joys of fellowship with God.

But this faith is in Jesus. "*He that* believeth on the Son of God hath," etc. The text affirms that "the gift of God is eternal life, through Jesus Christ." Faith in him, whose nature is like our own by the everlasting mystery of Deity incarnate, unites the soul so closely to God, manifest in flesh, as to diffuse his life divine throughout our being. "Jesus lives," "in him is life," and whoever is vitally joined to him lives also by the quickening energy of his Spirit. Faith constitutes the soul a branch of Jesus Christ, who is the living vine, and communicates to every branch a living vigor, a divine and heavenly beauty.

But how may this faith be exercised? How may its blessed operations be commenced in the unbelieving soul? If you will keep in mind that by faith the soul feeds its inward life, our answer to this question may seem more readable. Birth must precede the full development of life. It must precede the voluntary use of food, and drink, and atmosphere. So the soul must be regenerated, must be born of the Spirit, before it can, by faith, partake of the elements which nourish this new life.

By birth the child is introduced into this world and all its scenes of sorrow or of joy. By birth, a second birth, the soul is introduced to the rapturous experience of the new and heavenly life.

Except a man be born he can not see the light nor enter into the scenes of this checkered mortal life. So, except a man be born again, he can not see the kingdom of heaven. Would you, then, have this blessed life? I say to you, in the words of Christ to Nicodemus, "ye must be born again." Do you ask "how shall a man be born when he is old?" I answer, "seek, and ye shall find; ask, and ye shall receive; knock, and it shall be opened unto you." Adopt the method and God will secure the result.

And now let us close this discussion by entreating your attention to this gift of life eternal. We earnestly persuade you not to reject a donation so incalculably precious, purchased by such suffering, and offered in such pity, to souls so needy, so fallen and distressed. What objection can you have to be partakers of this life, to seek that regeneration which will introduce you to it, and that faith in Christ which will nourish and consummate it? Array before us your most formidable difficulties, and let them be examined by the light of truth divine.

Do you say that the doctrine of spiritual birth is a dark, forbidding mystery? And does your judgment slight it because your reason can not trace it? I answer, this mystery is not more difficult than the origin and development of that vital animation which is displayed by man in the commencement of his being. Do you say that the work of faith is a mystery, and that you can not perceive how its influence does serve to nourish this holy, heavenly life? I answer, the office of food, and drink, and atmosphere is a mystery to me, and I do not perceive how they operate to nourish the vigor of my frame. If you will, by any demonstration, solve my difficulty,

I will, by fair analysis, solve yours. Do you say that you are witnesses of the fact that meat, and drink, and air, administer life to your bodies, but you know nothing, by experience, of the nourishing powers of faith upon the souls? I answer, on this principle, we might array against you the lily and the oak, as witnesses that yours is but a vegetative life, and that the idea of your possessing vital animation is dispersed by the condition of the whole vegetable world. Do you insist that all the living are conscious of a life superior to that of the lily and the oak? I answer, all the pious are conscious of a life superior to that which they lived in the flesh. Yes, you know by experience, (though you can not explain it,) that food, and drink, and air, are grateful to your appetites, and nourish your frail bodies. And we know, by experience, that faith in Jesus Christ nourishes us in this eternal life; a life grateful as happiness and glorious as heaven. Do you still doubt, take not our word, but test our proposition by one fair experiment, and if false, then cast it from you. Seek this birth, and faith, and life with half the diligence with which ambition toils, and you shall know whether this doctrine be of God, or whether it be of man.

If you neglect this life under the impression that it is an idle fancy, and it should prove at last to be a blessed reality which thousands *have* enjoyed, and *will* enjoy forever, but which you in folly have despised, and in madness have rejected, what then, I pray, awaits you? Death—death, never past, but always present—a death which implies the corruption of an immortal spirit—a corruption of all that was designed to be holy, and lovely, and godlike in the soul—a corruption which will render our nature base, according to its dignity; which will render what was purest the most loathsome; what was freest, the most servile; what was loveliest, the most hateful; what was healthful and attractive and altogether blissful, the most sickly, and disgusting, and distressing—like those forms of life which, the more delicate and lovely they seem amid the charms of health, the more unsightly are they in their lifeless putrefaction. O sinner! will you devote yourself to a destiny so horrible?

To the sincere and humble Christian we would say, Child of God! life is yours. You have not now to win this excellent possession. It is yours simply to cherish and retain it. The joy of this life is now thrilling in your soul. And yet this is only life in embryo. What, then, shall we expect from its blessed consummation? Look beyond you and above you, and rejoice with joy unspeakable. Here you have life in the midst of death, whose gloomy scenes spread in terror all around you. Soon you will have life in the midst of life, whose unwithering beauty will pervade the heavenly regions, and crown with everlasting glory the immortal heirs of God. Here you are confined to the inferior manifestations of this Divine life. A moment of endurance will bring a mighty change. Another step and you may launch upon the blissful ocean. Another gasp and your impatient spirit may spread the pinions of immortality. Be thou, therefore, faithful unto death. "For we are not of them who draw back unto perdition, but of them that believe to the saving of the soul."

X.

THE SUFFERINGS OF CHRIST.

A SERMON PREACHED AT A COMMUNION SEASON.

"*For Christ also hath once suffered for sins, the just for the unjust, that he might bring us to God.*" 1 Peter iii, 18.

IT is believed by serious minds that God is righteous, and that the perfect development of his righteousness is reserved for a future state. It is also confessed that its development involves man's immortal interests, and that man whose interests are thus involved is depraved and guilty.

The belief of doctrines, sustained as these are by ample and conclusive evidence, is not surprising. But it is surprising that such doctrines, believed, produce no more effect upon the heart and life. What! can we believe that we have sinned, and that God is just, and yet remain indifferent to our present condition and future prospects? Yes, and in doing it we claim the rank of Christians! But would not any other name suit us better than that of Christ?

Atheism is the child of folly; but not an only child. To waive all solicitude with regard to our future state, and do it in the confession of God's righteousness and man's sinfulness, is the twin sister of atheism. Their names should designate them as of common parentage and birth. Yet in some respects they are unequal. Atheism is confined by narrow limits, and operates mostly upon the vulgar and profane. Speculative levity prevails every-where, and its victims are the noble, the modest, and the worthy. To such we address ourselves this day, beseeching Almighty Goodness to sharpen the arrows of his truth, and direct their unerring flight.

Reason and conscience, with revelation, pronounce that the *wages of sin is death.* But neither reason, nor conscience, nor the works, nor the providence of God can discover the means or warrant the hope of escape. Do you doubt? make the experiment. Retreat into thine own bosom, and ask, "Can God justify the ungodly?" Reason, abashed, declines to answer, and conscience replies, in the language of accusation, and points to the *wrath to come.* Turn from reason and conscience, dark and guilty as they are, and explore the works of God, they reveal to you a thousand examples of order, magnificence, and utility, but not a trace of pardon. Search the abodes of rebel-spirits who lost their first estate, and you shall behold chains of darkness and vials of wrath, but not a glimpse of mercy. Search the fields of light which angels occupy before the throne of God. Ask them if the Holy One can save a sinner without prejudice to his glory. Silence seals up their lips of love, and ye are driven back within yourself, in solitude and despair to waste the span of life in the agonizing dread of its eventful issues.

But while you sit, chilled with the ague or scorched by the fever of despair, God sheds upon your path the light of his blessed Gospel. It dispels those forms of horror which stalk around us in Nature's gloom. It reveals to us the "Word made flesh," as an angel of peace, and a minister of life to immortal minds. The *Word* made flesh presents us overtures of peace, and invites us to be the purchase of his blood.

The language of the text exhibits Christ as suffering in just that character which meets and sustains the views of orthodox Christians. It exhibits his sufferings,

I. As PENAL—He suffered for sins.

II. As VICARIOUS—the just for the unjust.

III. As PROPITIATORY—that he might bring us to God.

I. The text asserts the *penal* sufferings of Christ: "*hath suffered for sins.*"

If there be a God such as the Bible reveals, sin can not go unpunished. Its impunity is inconsistent with God's nature and government.

It is inconsistent with his nature. He is intensely holy. He loves holiness in his creatures, and is eternally opposed to every thing which is contrary to holiness. Sin is an abominable thing which he hates. It shall not dwell in his sight. He abhors transgressors as well as transgression. He sets his face against them. Wherever sin is found, there the curse of God is seen, proclaiming his unchangeable opposition to sin, and his inflexible purpose to punish it. He sets his name, his glory, his attributes, yea, his very being, against it, and pledges all these to secure its punishment.

But the government of God secures the punishment of sin. God is a sovereign, ruling the whole universe and governing all worlds. His *will* is law supreme, and his omnipotence secures its fulfillment. Sin is rebellion against the will, the law of God. It is an expression of hostility toward him and toward his creatures. If it pass with impunity it can not harm God, but it can harm and does vitally injure him who is guilty, and those who are affected by its example. Sin is an effort on the part of the creature to throw off his dependence upon God; and could he sin with impunity he would effect his object and become independent. But independence in a creature is an absurdity. The punishment of sin, therefore, results, necessarily, from the Divine supremacy of the universe.

God is a righteous sovereign, as well as supreme. He sitteth upon the throne judging right. But a righteous governor must punish crime or he is no longer righteous. To punish vice is as essential to rectitude as it is to reward virtue. Righteousness consists in rendering to every one his due. And to be exact in this rendering is the perfection of righteousness. If God punish no sin he is destitute of every principle of righteousness. If he punish for some sin, but not all, his righteousness is imperfect, and entirely defective as to the ends of supreme and universal government. Sin must be punished, because its punishment is intrinsically righteous, and can not, therefore, be remitted by a righteous God. Its punishment is not a question of political expediency, but of moral rectitude, and it must be inflicted, or the administration of moral government must be dishonored and denounced.

Again, one of the principal ends of right government is the protection of the innocent. Justice owes this protection to the obedient subjects. This protection requires the punishment of transgressors. To indulge a spirit of rebellion against the lawgiver, inflict upon the rebel no tokens of displeasure, would most certainly provoke universal defiance of God's authority, and the invasion of his rights. It would encourage the desolating march of sin; would give efficacy to the contagion of its example; would facilitate its conquests and multiply its triumphs, till its influence, uncontrolled and unchastised, would blot out from the minds of creatures the impression of its wrong, and annihilate the distinction between sin and holiness in the moral world. And would *that* be the protection of innocence which legalizes sin, places it on an equality with holiness, affords to its agents all the good, and comfort, and benefit which are generally supposed to constitute the peculiar rewards of devotion and obedience? It is impossible for God to afford protection to the innocent, and, at the same time, screen the guilty from reprobation.

These views of the opposition of God's nature and government to sin are sustained by the system of administration adopted toward man. The law of morals prescribed to our race is armed with a vigorous penalty, which nature itself is commissioned faintly to indicate, and which God has expressly announced by his Word. The Divine administration is in this world singular and without a parallel. In other worlds, whether obedient or rebellious, there has either been no preparatory state, or otherwise it has been allotted to holy beings, whose first transgression converted their probation into a state of retribution and punishment.

Man, on the other hand, has a *sinful* probation, and God has undertaken to provide and apply a system morally restorative in its effects. But in prosecuting the glorious experiment he evidently resolves upon no sacrifice of the vital principles of his government. He still exhibits to the sinner the prospect of punishment, unless the plan of mercy be carried into execution in a manner so peculiar that the interests of his throne shall suffer no detriment, and his glory no disparagement. This plan merely embraces in itself an exhibition of deeper hostility to sin than the universe had ever witnessed. It proclaims more impressively than the pains of hell could do it, the uncompromising integrity of the Godhead and the inflexibility of his restored justice.

But by what expedient does God make manifest the rigor of his justice in the pardon of sinners? It is announced in the text, "For Christ also suffered for sins." His sufferings were endured that the penalty might be remitted to the penitent guilty. He made satisfaction to that law and justice which threatened the offender. Atonement is not an abandonment of law, nor of the purpose to sustain its honor, but it is a support of the law on the ground of a satisfaction, instead of penalty.

II. The penal nature of his sufferings being established, the question is whether these sufferings are vicarious, or endured in man's behalf? This is also affirmed in the text: "He suffered, the just for the unjust."

He did not suffer on his own account. He *could* not, because he is here called "*just*." He is every-where represented as holy; as having done no evil, practiced no guile; as being the likeness of God's glory and the express image of his person. Surely, then, we are forbidden to suppose that he was wounded for his *own* transgressions, and was bruised for his *own* iniquities. No; he was wounded for our transgressions, and was bruised for our iniquities; he bore our griefs and carried our sorrows; he was made a *curse* for us; the Lord laid *our* iniquities upon him.

But to this procedure we often hear objections. It is said to be inconsistent with the Divine righteousness to inflict the punishment of sin upon an innocent substitute. Of this God is probably the best judge. The fact is susceptible of the clearest proof from the unequivocal declarations of Scripture. We might simply say, "Nay, but, O man! who art thou that repliest against God?" He has declared it, that "Jesus has borne our sins in his own body on the tree;" that "he has made him to be sin for us who knew no sin, that we might be made the righteousness of God in him."

But we may venture to scan this proceeding of Divine Wisdom, and inquire if it be so utterly at war with the nature of justice and the providence of God, as some suppose. Justice, as we have argued, demands the punishment of sin. But justice has no further demand than that every transgression receive a just recompense. Ordinarily the offender is her victim. And why? Simply because in no other way can she express her abhorrence of the offense, and be secure from the repetition of it. Her quarrel is with sin, and not with the sinner, except it be on *account* of sin. If, by any means, the sinner can be separated from his guilt, Justice has no more to do with him, for she can not war with the guiltless. The sin which provoked her indignation may remain and demand a retribution, but not upon the person of one who is innocent in the estimate of the law.

Now, in every pardoning act of God toward sinners, there is a separating of the sin from the sinner. Pardon remits the guilt for which the sinner is threatened, and pursued, and arrested, and condemned by the justice of God. Such pardons are believed to be extended to many souls by those who object to the doctrine of vicarious atonement. But pardon without atonement appears to us an express violation of the principles of justice, because, in such case, sin passes with impunity; guilt escapes rebuke; no homage is paid to the stern principles of justice; and the law takes no vengeance of the offense. Now let it be granted that Christ died for the pardoned sinner, and you at once waive every such difficulty. In the sufferings of Christ atonement is made, because guilt is rebuked, condemned, and an equivalent to its literal punishment offered to God. Justice takes a full satisfaction, government is sustained, the law is honored and magnified, God exhibits testimony against sin, and all this in a more striking manner than if a world had sinned and sunk beneath the curse of an offended God.

The principle involved in this doctrine of vicarious atonement is often introduced into the operations of society, and is never regarded as unjust. The business transactions of life proceed by it in a thousand forms, and no man challenges its propriety or utility. The merchant reaps the gain or loss resulting from the wisdom or folly of his agent, and never objects to that principle by which his fortunes are thus controlled. A nation is blessed with prosperity or involved in disaster by the policy of its government at home or of its representatives abroad, and never reprobates the principle upon which her liabilities depend. This is the very principle involved in the interesting facts that, by the transgression of the first Adam we were made liable to sin and death, and that by the suffering of the second Adam we become partakers of holiness and heaven.

The providence of God allows, perhaps *establishes*, this liability to good and evil on the principle of representation. It will not be disputed by the pupil of the Bible, at least, that the world fell in Adam; that its generations became subject to sin and misery by his transgression. God announces to Israel that his curse or his blessing awaits their children, according as they, their fathers, obey or disobey his word. The murderers of Jesus said, "Let his blood be on us, and on our children." And to this very day his blood is on the descendants of Israel, and is a curse more fearful than that which lighted upon Cain, or blasted the fields of Sodom. The patriarchal malediction which fell upon Canaan for the offense of Ham, his father, has descended upon every succeeding generation, and cleaves unto them to this very day.

In all these examples the very principles which are objected to the vicarious sufferings of Christ are evident and indisputable. Providence approves and adopts them. And if we die in Adam, why may we not live in Christ? If the former ruined us by transgression, why may not the latter save us by his obedience to death? If, without any let or hinderance, we be partakers of Adam's curse, why may we not, by faith, be partakers of Christ's blessing? If ruined by one representative, may we not be restored by another? The sin of our first parents was vicarious to procure our offense, and the sufferings of Christ are vicarious to procure our expiation. We conclude, then, that the sufferings of Christ are vicarious.

III. The text teaches that the sufferings of Christ are *propitiatory*. That is, they turn away the wrath of God from the sinner and invite toward him the pity and, if he repent, the complacency of the Godhead. Several Scriptures, besides the text, ascribe this attribute to the atonement. "And he is the propitiation for our sins." "Herein is love, not that we loved God, but that he loved us, and sent his Son to be the propitiation for our sins." "Whom God hath set forth to be a propitiation through faith in his blood." It is objected to the doctrine of propitiation that it assumes facts derogatory to the dignity and glory of God. It assumes that God is angry with the sinner. No, brethren, it does not assume, if assumption signify unsupported assertion. The Scriptures tell us that God is "angry with the wicked;" that "the wrath of God is revealed from heaven against all ungodliness;" that the "wrath of God abideth upon unbelievers." The day of judgment is called "a day of wrath."

We do not suppose that the wrath of God is like the rage of man. We do believe that God is just; that his justice is punitive as well as distributive; that his holy mind is displeased with sin, and that such displeasure is essential to his perfection. Though we do not believe that God is ever moved by any wrathful or revengeful passions, we believe he is disposed to vindicate his law and maintain the rights of his throne and the principles of his government, and when these are violated, the protection of his honor and the support of his government lie in the enforcement of the penalty. If he loves the precept for its perfect symbolization of his own eternal purity, and the only condition of moral happiness and perfection in his creatures, he must hate, with inverse intensity, all violation of that precept. If his holiness, benevolence, and truth forbid him to abrogate or relinquish the precept, so do these same attributes, and all the moral attributes of his nature, bind him to uphold the penalty as the awful guard of the precept, and to express the evil of sin and his eternal hatred of it, by the certain punishment of all iniquity. He excludes the offender from his fellowship, and withdraws from him the tokens of his love. And his fellowship and love are not regained but by the mediation of Christ; nor without his mediation as an atoning high-priest, whose blood is an offering acceptable to God.

And now, brethren, is there not a wonder in this doctrine, a wonder full of beauty, and comfort, and glory? Consider the history of all society where this doctrine is not revealed, and see in what gloom and misery its absence involves the soul. Such is the effect of heathenism, Islamism, and Judaism, whose wretched sons, goaded by conscience, wounded by guilt, deceived by false tradition, and abused by base imposture, attempt a thousand vain expedients to propitiate their gods. The Pagan and the Papist would attract the smiles of Heaven by an ablution, or a pilgrimage, or the penance of a strange and blind asceticism. Others lavish wealth in costly sacrifices, and inflict pain upon the body for the good and safety of the soul. But, O, how vain! "Will the Lord be pleased with thousands of rams, or ten thousands of rivers of oil?" "Shall I give my first-born for my transgression, the fruit of my body for the sin of my soul?" Alas! the evil lies deep, and these remedies can not approach it. Neither men nor angels can offer a sacrifice that will be to God of a sweet-smelling savor. The offering is for man, and he can not be the priest to make that offering. The offering *is* man, whose nature must be sacrificed according to the curse, and angels have no such nature to present as an offering to God.

Who, then, shall be the victim, who the priest, and what shall be the manner of the sacrifice? The priest must be holy, the victim spotless, and each must possess such a merit and a dignity as becomes the honor of God's government to accept in behalf of the sinner; such as will offer a safe ground of pardon. The principles of God's government admit of our release on no other ground. O for some friend able to supply it—able to lay his hands on both parties and make them to be at one again! But behold! Who is this that cometh from Edom, with dyed garments from Bozrah? It is one who "speaks in righteousness mighty to save." He is the son of God, in dignity; in humiliation, the son of man. He is full of grace and truth. He comes with ample offerings for atonement, and commissioned for the work of our salvation.

The offering is made. The Lord is well pleased for his righteousness' sake. "He hath set him forth to be a propitiation through faith in his blood, that he might be just and the justifier of him that believeth in Jesus." Forgiveness is now proffered to the sinner, and peace shall be the fruit of its acceptance; for God is in Christ reconciling the world unto himself, not imputing unto them their trespasses.

Here is an atonement which well assorts with the majesty of the violated law and the glory of its insulted Author. Here is a victim pure and spotless as the law whose demands it honors—pure as the throne whose rectitude it sustains. Here is an exhibition of mercy, but not at the expense of truth, of justice, of righteousness. Here, "mercy and truth meet together; righteousness and peace embrace each other." The creature can not guess

> "Which of the glories brighter shines,
> The justice or the grace."

Each is displayed in brilliant colors, as an object of delightful admiration to eternity.

My brethren, forget not the aim and the possible result of Christ's sufferings, as announced in the text. They are designed "to bring us to God." We have known the unhappiness of being alienated from God; for this is the uniform condition of the soul unregenerate by the Holy Ghost. We have all been separated from the Divine life; we have all been excluded from the Divine presence.

O most gloomy and miserable state! to live in a universe filled with God, and yet neither know, nor behold, nor enjoy him; to feel that he is our enemy and not our friend; to dread his frown and not hope for his favor. What state so much to be deprecated? What blessing can compare with our escape from this condition? And then to take its opposite; to possess the life and feel the presence of God within; to find ourselves resting beneath his shadow and his smile; to realize his presence everywhere, converting all our seasons and abodes into resemblances of heaven; and to know that we travel in a path which will soon conduct us to his immediate presence, and establish us in possession of "joy unspeakable and full of glory."

All this is proposed in the propitiatory offering of Christ.

But be not deceived. This atonement can not take effect for our salvation unless it be applied by faith. It does not place us in a condition of safety without any care or action on our part. If we have no anxiety for the pardon of our sins or the sanctification of our hearts, we are not proper subjects either for the one or the other. Christ distributes pardons to those who anxiously apply for them, and sanctifies the heart which diligently seeks him. He feeds the hungry and refreshes the thirsty soul. "Blessed are they that hunger and thirst after righteousness."

This is the language of his lips, and the rule by which his holy charities are dispensed. Do *we* hunger and thirst after righteousness? Do we wait this day at our Savior's feet, with earnest longings to be baptized by the Holy Ghost? Are we now opening our hearts to Christ and imploring his triumphant entrance there?

Be comforted. He for whom you wait is not afar off. The Lord whom you seek shall come to his temple. Be comforted. He will reveal his presence to your waiting soul. He has suffered that he might save you. He has commenced the blessed work. He has already convinced you of sin. He has forgiven your iniquities. He is even now working in your hearts to subdue all sin, and impress upon you the beauties of his holiness. And this is but a preparatory work. When his mercy has accomplished it, there remains for you a lot unspeakably desirable. Prepared as a bride adorned for the bridegroom you shall be conducted to "a house not made with hands," and introduced to the presence of the Father, and the Son, and the Holy Ghost.

We are about to celebrate the sufferings of this Jesus. He has taught us to be familiar with certain symbols, expressive of the mournful scenes of the

17

cross. These symbols are soon to be exhibited that we may behold them and weep; that we may handle them and taste them, as a token that we hope to be healed by the virtues and sustained by the strength of our crucified Lord.

Would you have this feast graced by the presence of the blessed Jesus? Make haste, then, and prepare a place in your hearts. Draw near to this communion with contrition and faith, and you shall depart with holy exultation, and exclaim, in the fullness of your soul:

> "Blest Jesus, what delicious fare!
> How sweet thine entertainments are!
> Never did angels taste above
> Redeeming grace and dying love."

XI.

DELIGHT IN THE HOUSE OF GOD.

A DEDICATORY SERMON.

"*For a day in thy courts is better than a thousand. I had rather be a door-keeper in the house of my God than to dwell in the tents of wickedness.*" Psalms lxxxiv, 10.

SUCH are the feelings of the devout soul, long exiled from the house of the Lord, and now panting with enlivened hope once more to tread the "holy courts." The whole Psalm is a lively description of the feelings of those pilgrims to Zion, who went up to the house of the Lord to worship in his holy hill. Of them it might be said, "the high-ways are in their hearts," (verse 5,) so that, although their way be rough and desert-like, as through the "valley of weeping," yet their cheerful songs, and buoyant hopes, and devout aspirations transform it as into a land of "wells" and "pools" of water and fertilizing showers. (Verse 16.)

And having arrived at Zion, the joyful soul drinks in the holy delights which God has prepared for them that love him, and sitting at the gate of the holy place, exclaims, "I would rather sit at the threshold of the house of my God than to dwell in the tents of wickedness." (Verse 10.) To him all is holy. With

Jacob he exclaims, "Truly, God is in this place." And the summing up of all his blissful experiences in the worship of God is thus given: "O Lord of Hosts, blessed is the man that trusteth in thee." These are but tastes of the pleasures which are enjoyed in their fullness in the heavenly sanctuary. We will speak,

I. Of God's house.

II. Of the Godly man's delight in it.

I. Of the *house* or *courts* of the Lord. Certain things, common of themselves, are made sacred by Divine appointment. The Holy Sabbath is an example. Originally all days were equal, but God pronounced the seventh day holy, commanded us to consecrate it to religion. And that authority which made time sacred, can impart to places and other objects an equal grace or dignity. He who sanctified and gave to man a Sabbath—who sanctified Israel and made them a *holy* people—who sanctifies bread and wine for sacramental uses, has also been pleased to sanctify altars and temples. And by God's approbation, some of these sanctified edifices have been called "*the house or courts of the Lord.*"

For example: First. God revealed himself to Jacob in night visions, who, when he had received the Divine communications, roused from his slumbers, exclaiming, "How dreadful is this place! This is none other than the *house of God!*"

Second. God commanded the preparation of the tabernacle in all its details of construction, furniture, and religious ritual, and it was called *his* tabernacle.

Third. The building of the temple was by his ordering. He selected Solomon as the chief agent, inspired him with a purpose for the enterprise, gave to him wisdom, and to his servants cunning, for so great a work, and finally received the edifice at the hand of Solomon, baptized as his own house, and proved his seizin of it by the kindling lights and glories of his presence. But it may be asked, *Where is God's temple now?* I answer, its site is profaned, and unholy structures rear their turrets upon the sacred mount. Yet God has not forsaken Zion. The Church is built upon a rock which hell shall never move. She therefore still lives and battles with her foes. She is unconquered and unconquerable. In her the God of Israel "still has his abode"—still "he loves the gates of Zion."

But can the Church still claim her sacred edifices, and are the tokens of God's presence in them as of old? It might seem discreet to raise no such question; but circumstances call for it. We are here to dedicate this house, and the services of this hour associate this humble edifice with the temple which Solomon consecrated to Jehovah. True it is that circumstances differ. Solomon was explicitly enjoined from heaven to build. We plead no direct behest. His edifice, with its splendors, seemed worthy of God's notice; while ours can pretend to nothing like such rare magnificence. His was the chosen spot for national sacrifice and worship. Ours will secure the partial regards of but one or two city wards. His was openly possessed by the great God of heaven, who kindled fires on its altar and shone forth between the cherubim. Ours will display no proof to sense that "Jehovah hath desired it to set his name there."

We might pass these differences by, in the hope that our hearers would lose sight of them. But silence would almost savor of a fraud, which we would choose not to mix with sacred things. We say, then, though this house is built by no specific Divine mandate, is very modest in its show, will accommodate but few, and will be graced by no visible Shekinah, yet will it be God's house, the container of his presence, graced with his own lights, while oracles of power, such as Israel never knew, will sound forth from its most holy place. To justify this faith, we will now offer a brief hint, and then adjourn the argument to the close of this discourse.

God sometimes moves his servants to particular deeds and duties by direct outward mandates. At other times he guides them by general principles and inward monition. In the earlier dispensations, calls to duty were more commonly external and specific; but as the canon of Scripture enlarged into the Christian Dispensation, these calls became more general, by "the *sure word of prophecy*," and in word *by the Holy Ghost.* In the Biblical notices of the patriarchs and prophets, and early kings of Israel, we have examples of the former, while past and current Christian times afford instances of the latter. Under the former, if God would have a temple reared to his name, he gave a special order and commission for the work; but under the Christian regimen we are left to infer our life warrant from his Word, in its plain principles or examples, or other forms of teaching. Now, in building Christian churches we profess no special order like that imposed on Solomon, but we claim a *Scripture warrant:* "Forsake not the assembling of yourselves together."

Omitting further explanation, we shall proceed to inquire,

II. *Why the devout man delights in God's house.*

1. He delights in it because it *is* God's house. Such it is called, and, he believes, with God's approval, who, in a glorious sense, takes it for his own, and sets his holy name there. It is *God's* house; and because it is *his*, the devout man delights in it. For this word "*his*," in such an application, refers not to those ideas of *meum and tuum* which prevail among men. For in this last sense—the common sense—all space and all worlds belong to God. Hights and depths, clouds and caverns, the limitable and the illimitable, bear his all-pervading presence; which led Solomon, amazed, to cry, "The heavens—even the heaven of heavens, can not contain thee."

What, then, is the higher significancy of these possessives, as ascribing property to God? What does Solomon mean with these possessives on his lips, in his prayer of dedication just read? What does David mean in the reiterations of this Psalm, pleading all along God's ownership of the Tabernacle, as earnestly as though it were all the estate that God can claim on earth? Is it fiction, or is it an unmocking claim set up for God, and well-pleasing in his sight? It is not fiction. It is not fancy. This special claim of God to an altar—to a temple—and we will add to the ten thousand Christian churches which grace our land and other lands, is a sweet and savory principle, "exceeding full of comfort." Let us briefly trace that principle.

God owns the soil as truly as he owns the altar. All the tents of Israel are his as truly as the tabernacle. All the dwellings of Zion are his as truly as its temple. Our private habitations are his as truly as the churches which we so devoutly consecrate. So also the universe is his. Nay, we may go farther. Hell is his, and its thrones are his—if it be a question of ownership—as truly as heaven and its glories are his. But what then? Does the word "*his*," as applied to heaven, mean no more than when applied to hell? The question unlocks the gate to meditation. The universe is God's—space is his—hell is his. But O how differently—how gloriously true it is, "*heaven is his!*" Let us apply the principle.

The world is his, for he made it—the pirate's haunt is his—yonder vile drunkery is his. But how different the meaning when we say, Yonder house of prayer and praise and holy sacramental services are his! And having explained, we now simply repeat that the godly man delights in the house of the Lord *because it is the house of the Lord—his Father's house.* It is his by an act of special, approving acceptance, for his worship and his holy habitation.

2. He delights in God's house *for the instruction it affords.*

There, like the children of a parent who administers prompt and wholesome admonition, he is "taught of the Lord." Instruction is made a special order of God's house. In the ancient worship both the tabernacle and the temple were graced with the ark of the *covenant*, in which was carefully preserved the "*law of the Lord*," and the testimonies of Israel, out of which priests and prophets were to feed the people with knowledge. From the times of Ezră, instructed scribes became the teachers of the law. In modern times the house of God is well provided with the offices of instruction. True the *ark* of the covenant is removed, but the *covenant* remains; for the Bible now being in every man's hand, needs not so close a custody, lest it should be blotted from being and from memory. Yet the chief ornament of the pulpit, in every well-ordered chapel, is the HOLY BIBLE, resting in simple majesty where every eye can see it, as it seems to announce, "*Lo, God is here!*"

This book is the source whence the minister of Christ is to borrow all the saving truths which he proclaims to the worshipers. He is commanded to "preach the Gospel to every creature." The apostles began to do it in streets and prisons, and, when permitted, in the synagogues. And their successors in spirit and vocation—not after the law of a carnal commandment—follow their example and proclaim this Gospel. They who are called of God and faithful, set forth the following doctrines as of Divine authority, and as vital to salvation:

(1.) *Original sin, or human depravity*, which lies at the foundation of the Christian system. The view taken of this doctrine generally infers a sound or a lax theology through all depending departments. Probably no statement of the doctrine is more precise than that which constitutes the seventh Article of Religion in our Discipline: "Original sin standeth not in the following of Adam, (as the Pelagians do vainly talk,) but it is the corruption of the nature of every man, that naturally is engendered of the offspring of Adam, whereby man is very far gone from original righteousness, and of his own nature inclined to evil, and that continually."

This doctrine is opposed to Pelagianism. The former teaches that man is inherently and totally defiled: the latter assumes that he is radically pure. One looks for a new creation to start man on a career of piety; the other claims that mere cultivation in the sense of development can fit him for heaven. On this point the seventh Article, above recited, states the thesis which will be maintained in this pulpit, as the basis of all the peculiar doctrines of Christianity—the religion of fallen man.

(2.) The doctrine of *the Trinity*, which involves also the Godhead of Christ, (as well as his incarnation and atonement,) is cardinal in this system of salvation, their shadows being partly found in the tabernacle and temple services, but their glorious realities being ministered to us. All these, as before suggested, stand or fall with the doctrine of original or birth sin. Diverging from the Bible on this last point, none will fall back upon the Bible in the view which he shall take of Christ and his death. Lost man and a restoring Christ infer both incarnation and atonement. He who agrees to the former will permit the untortured Scriptures to hold their own language in regard to the latter. On this point our Church confession is: "The Son, who is the Word of the Father, the very and eternal God, of one substance with the Father, took man's nature in the womb of the blessed virgin; so that two whole and perfect natures, that is to say, the Godhead and manhood, were joined together in one person, never to be divided, whereof is one Christ, very God and very man, who truly suffered, was crucified, dead, and buried, to reconcile his Father to us, and to be a sacrifice, not only for original guilt, but also for the actual sins of men."

(3.) In close alliance with this doctrine of atonement is that of *justification and sanctification by faith alone.* We say in close alliance, because they are not often separated in Church creeds. It is difficult to sunder them; for if Christ died for our sins it constitutes a violent presumption that we can not merit pardon, and by unequivocal declarations of the Bible that presumption is made a certainty. On the other hand, if Christ has not thus died, why should we not propose to be saved by works, seeing there is no foundation for faith? But Christ declares "he *that believeth* shall be saved." In regard to *justification* our Church confession runs thus: "We are accounted righteous before God only for the merit of our Lord and Savior Jesus Christ by faith, and not for our own works or deservings. Wherefore, that we are justified by faith only, is a most wholesome doctrine, and very full of comfort."

(4.) The doctrine of *divine influence by the Holy Spirit to regenerate and sanctify* is vital in this gracious system. Man is morally defiled as well as legally guilty. He must be inwardly purified as well as relatively vindicated. Justification removes a legal hinderance to his salvation, but it *does not save him.* The fires in his own bosom must be quenched, and on its altars, instead thereof, holy flames must be kindled by the indwelling Spirit, or he *is not saved.* The first stage of this inward work is called regeneration—which is the birth of holy affections into a soul, where, until then, *all* was unholy. "The carnal mind is enmity against God." But as this new birth—like the breaking of day, when light and darkness intermingle—is not the *destruction of all unholy desires,* a further work of the Spirit is necessary to fit the soul for heaven. This is called sanctification, which is mostly gradual for a time, but is instantly accomplished in those who come fully to believe. The faithful minister always looks for the Holy Spirit to regenerate and sanctify the heart. It is a work for *Omnipotence.*

(5.) The doctrine of final, eternal retribution belongs to this Biblical system. It unfolds a hell for Dives as well as a heaven for Lazarus. Christianity abhors "*partialism,*" and therefore maintains that there is a "*reward for the righteous,*" that "there is a God who judgeth in the earth." In the same line of doctrine with *depravity, atonement,* and *salvation by faith alone,* we find the doctrine of future, endless punishment.

(6.) Finally, that these Christian doctrines may be taught and urged on man's attention, a ministry is provided and a class of men are divinely called and authorized to state and vindicate them, and persuade the children of men to receive them into good and honest hearts as the seed of life, and their only preparation for, and their only hope of, heaven.

In these and kindred doctrines God has thus provided that his children should be taught, and should be grounded in the truth. As a son over his own house, Christ has ordained the preaching of the Word as the ordinary method of impressing these doctrines on docile and believing hearts. For this, devout souls love the house of God, and under such ministrations they can often exclaim—" How sweet is thy Word unto my taste, yea, sweeter than honey to my mouth!"

3. The devout have great delight *in the sacraments of God's house*, namely, *baptism and the Lord's Supper.* These are not only *signs*, but also channels of grace; for when properly received God is pleased by them so to work in us as to quicken and confirm our faith in him.

Baptism is a sacrament of regeneration, shadowing forth birth by the Spirit. It is also a sacrament of admission into the Church of Christ. It is the right of parents and of children, and should be ministered to both. As our birth is one this sacrament should be but once and finally administered to all the subjects of it.

The Lord's Supper is a sacrament of *refreshment*, or nourishment; and as life depends on frequent refections, this sacrament should be often repeated. These are the only sacraments of Christianity. Some fond superstitions have been profanely styled sacraments, for since Satan contrived to appear among the sons of God in Job's day, we shall not marvel if he multiplies sacraments until himself is honored with a "*host.*"

How "exceeding full of comfort" are these authorized sacraments they know who rightly enjoy them. What reliefs they have been to thousands on thousands of God's misgiving saints! How often has Jesus met the weary at his table and they have felt their loins fresh-girded! While we refuse to add *unauthorized* sacraments, let us beware that we neither despise nor neglect the *instituted.*

4. The devout delight *in the fellowship of God's* house. It is their *Father's house,* and is *the home of their Father's children,* with whom they love to commune. Home, with its fraternal fellowships, is sweet. The meeting of separated brethren at the parental board is a scene for a monarch. David had an eye to it when he sang "I was glad when *they* said unto me, Let *us* go into the house of the Lord." He loved a plurality in the tabernacle. "*Our* feet," he says, (not mine only,) "shall stand within thy gates." Ps. cxxii. God's courts seemed doubly attractive when he saw "the tribes go up, even the tribes of the Lord, to give thanks unto the name of the Lord." How amiable the scene when this comely temple shall invoke to God's worship many scores of whom it can be said "this and that man was born there!" Hasten the time, blessed Jesus! Move by thy Word and Spirit on many hearts, and bring in hither the poor, the maimed, and the blind, yea, and the rich and the honorable, if they will yield to come, that a great family may surround thy table, and as a holy broth-

erhood, take sweet counsel together, and walk to the house of God in company.

5. The devout love God's house *because God himself is there.* The Father here dwells among his children. (Ps. lxxxiv, 2.) David "*thirsted for God,*" and, therefore, for his *tabernacles,* where he expected to find God. All about the tabernacle were seen the token of God's presence. Over the door was the cloud of glory—a sensible mark of God's inhabitation there. Other symbols gave to the tabernacle, and afterward more especially to the temple, a very glorious appearance. "Yes," says one, "and if such lights would now kindle up before us, and those mysterious oracles could be heard in these courts, we would confess this edifice to be the house of God. But where are the furniture and graces of God's ancient courts?"

This question throws us back on our deferred argument, namely, that the present Church of God has truly sacred edifices inhabited by the Most High, though they be without the symbols and shows of the tabernacle. Yes, it is true that God's presence is now revealed in his earthly sanctuaries, if not openly yet more effectually than it was in ancient times. We confess that both the altar and the ark are gone; but a sacrifice remains without the altar, and the covenant without the ark is doubly sure. The sacrifice remains, and is of perpetual force and virtue, without daily or yearly repetitions. The covenant remains, is enlarged, and is established on "new and better promises." It includes a second testament, and, sealed in blood, is delivered over with solemn forms, into the hands of us all, the Testator having died to give it everlasting effect. The instrument is not confined in the ark of testimony. Here it is, openly adorning the courts of God's house, and is being published to the nations that they may be our fellow-heirs.

The ritual sacrifices, to be sure, are ended, but were they not mere symbols? Some have taught that the altar was significant of the cross, and its sacrifice a picture of Christ crucified; that the consuming fires from heaven report Christ to be accepted as a true offering for sin. Be it so. Then shadows yield to substance. Then, too, atoning blood, which can never lose its power, always pleads for your pardon and mine. Then you and I may enter daily (unlike the high-priest, who entered once a year) into the holiest of all. The mercy-seat and cherubim no longer meet the eye. The Shekinah shines not outwardly. But these mere shadows are supplanted by realities. We have now a surer light. The "Day Star" himself has risen on our hearts. The wings of the cherubim overspread our *souls*, and the Shekinah *burns within us.*

In the absence of "Urim and Thummim" do you demand of us the responses of an oracle? You shall have them. But what would you inquire? Do you ask for man's state by nature? The oracle announces, "Dead in trespasses and sin." Do you inquire if he can live? It answers, "I am the resurrection and the life." Do you ask *how?* It answers, "He that believeth in me, though he were dead, yet shall he live." Full of grief, and heavy laden, would you inquire for rest?" The oracle replies, "Come unto me, and I will give you rest." Do you ask for happiness? It declares, "Blessed are the pure in heart." Or for hope beyond the grave? It answers, "Blessed are the dead that die in the Lord." Encouraged to press the inquiry for the particular state of the soul, what are its utmost bliss and dignity in that beatific state? The oracle upbraids not, but pointing upward with a glow of holy charity, exclaims, "To him that overcometh will I give to sit down with me in my throne."

This is the true oracle. That voice proceeds from a "more excellent glory" than dwelt within the veil. It is a voice from heaven. "In these last days God has spoken unto us by his Son." The faithful Gospel minister, standing in God's courts, catches the very syllables from his heavenly Master's lips, and reverently announces them to the listening multitude.

And now shall we be challenged when we may claim that this very edifice is become the house of God? Surely not by Christian lips. The antiquated ritual, with its altar and its victim, with its duller lights and scanty oracles, is gone. But these fading "shadows of good things to come" yield to brighter glories than Mount Zion ever saw.

In God's house are three degrees of growing light and privilege, until all are supplanted by an approaching perfect day.

The first is the *degree of shadows* already pointed out, which, with its yoke of labored rituals, neither the children nor the fathers were well able to bear. And yet it was so good, as David thought, that he was all in raptures over it; for the gleanings of the tabernacle seemed to him a joyful harvest.

The second was the degree of *outward substances,* when Shiloh came—when Christ, in person, took possession of the temple, and made it "to excel the former house in glory." For then was seen (affecting vision) God *in flesh!*—in *servile meanness!*—in *sorrow* and in DEATH!

The third degree is the Spirit's; that is, the degree of power—of new creations, which the Spirit only could dispense. For Jesus, in his earthly lifetime, laid up his power to rest. Or his deeds, like characters in sympathetic ink, were to be warmed into fruitfulness by the Comforter which he sent, who should "take the things of Christ and (as flames the pen-marks) should show them unto" *us.* This third degree is ours. It is the ripest stage of mercy. Our temples entertain, and our anthems echo it. It should cause every springing heart to leap for joy. Surely we may say that the halleluiah part of all the songs, the creeping notes of David's day, belongs, of right, to us. They sang, we swell the chorus. For on us fall the Gospel culminations of that glory whose overrunning measures not only fill God's house, but turn each believer into a living sanctuary, and make us all to be "*the temples of the Holy Ghost.*"

Moses longed for the cleft, where God should veil and hide him as he caught a glimpse of the insupportable glory. We, strengthened for greater things, behold not merely God's retiring train, but the front of all his graciousness in the face of Jesus Christ, and gaze thereon day and night. We, "with open face beholding," "are changed into the same image from glory to glory, even as by the Spirit of the Lord."

Prophets longed to see this day. Kings sighed after it. David knew that it should come, and as the sun the stars, quench the glory which went before it, though that glory seemed to him so great. For even then the tabernacle had a show and beauty which made his royal eye to stare, and his furrowed cheek to swell with holy smiles and gushing praise. And if he half forgot himself at sights like these, what would he do in our day? If he fell to dancing then at the movements of the ark, what would he contrive to do if he could be here among us, and could look upon the Bible, hear a thousand tongues proclaim its good news, and could fall in with a baptism like that of Pentecost? Would he begin to question whether this is the house of the Lord? Would he fall heart-sick at the absence of brazen altars, and long for the flares of Zion's temple to make his soul content? No, my brethren. David would feel that he had lost a rill, but gained a river—"the river of God, which is full of water;" that he had exchanged one of his pools for an unbounded ocean; that a lamp had gone out in the sanctuary, but a sea of light had drowned it.

In David's time the revelations of God's glory seem to have been gathered into the corners of one small tent, and then into the temple, not half filling it. This was not because Heaven begrudged the diffused and brighter glory, but because the world was not prepared to entertain it. But now the veils are lifted. Glory after glory opens on mankind, which tabernacles and temples by no means contain. It bursts these narrow bounds. It flashes over seas and continents, and is about to flood the world. How glorious its effects in these broad and full diffusions! It makes every vale a pool, and every hill a Zion. It stamps the very soil as holy. Nor need we any more search after sacred places, as though this *were*, and that were *not* "*the hill of the Lord.*" Neither in such a "mountain, nor in Jerusalem" need we worship. Wherever we may choose a spot and rear an edifice, thither comes "the man of sorrows," and brings the Father with him, to take a full possession, saying, "They that worship the Father must worship him in spirit and in truth. For the Father seeketh such to worship him."

Thus is this house erected, to the honor of his name, and to edify his worshipers. We are met to dedicate it to his service.

In the name of Jesus Christ we hereby consecrate it to the ever-blessed Trinity, *Father*, *Son*, and *Holy Ghost!* In all its materials, and parts, and forms, from apex to foundation, we yield it up to thee, O Lord, JEHOVAH! "Arise, O God, into thy rest, thou and the ark of thy strength." "The Lord is in his holy temple, let all the earth keep silence before him!"

XII.

DEPRAVITY OF THE HEART.

FIRST DISCOURSE.

"*The heart is deceitful above all things, and desperately wicked.*" Jeremiah xvii, 9.

THE moral character of man has been a subject of deep and exciting interest to the wise and studious of every age. It has provoked discussion and dispute in almost every school, and has produced sectarianism among philosophers of old as well as among polemics of modern times. But until a heavenly Teacher appeared, and gave us infallible decisions on this subject, the exclamation of the poet was just, which assumed that "man was a miracle to man."

As to the philosophers, it is not strange that they studied and disputed in vain. They had lost the only light which could illuminate the secret chambers of the soul, and display the sources of its ever-flowing griefs and joys. Or if, in solitary instances, they did press through every obstacle, arrive at some discoveries, and detect some of the soul's disorders, they could only gaze and wonder at the moral ruin, without the least conception of a remedy for wounds so deep, and dangerous, and painful.

But whatever may have been the condition of the ancients, our ignorance can not be winked at. God has supplied to us the means of self-knowledge in the rich revelations of his Word. From that Word we can infer the faculties with which he originally endowed us, the duties and prerogatives to which they designated us, and the woe which came upon us through their sad perversion. That holy book advises us of a safe and happy course, of the obstacles we must encounter in its pursuit, and of the means by which those obstacles may be surmounted or removed. It exhibits our moral state in fair analysis, and proposes regeneration as the method of exchanging that unhappy state for one of ultimate holiness and blessedness.

In order to avail ourselves of the sanctifying virtue of the Gospel, we must study it for instruction and conviction. We must labor to detect the base elements of our fallen nature. We must receive the testimony of Him whose guileless tongue proclaims, as the result of omniscient inspection, that the "carnal mind is enmity against God."

We propose in this discourse AN EXPLANATION OF THE DOCTRINE. In our effort to explain we will commence by protestation. That is, we will, if possible, separate this doctrine from certain principles which have too often been considered as its theological adjuncts, or rather as constituting the doctrine itself. Many objections to this doctrine are founded upon an entire misconception of it. They are, in fact, not so much objections to the doctrine itself, as they are to certain fancies which men have substituted in its place.

1. Let it be remembered, in the first place, that *moral depravity is not physical disability.* It refers not to the state of the body, but to the condition of the soul. Man, as a sinner, has become the victim of a withering curse, whose influence extends to the tabernacle without, as well as to the immortal tenant within. But by moral depravity we mean not to designate the *effects* of the curse, but the provocation by which it was procured. Whatever the body suffers, is consequential upon sin; but is, in no wise, sin itself. Such sufferings have come upon the innocent. The blameless, unspotted Lamb of God was made a curse, drank the bitter waters of dissolution, and tenanted the cheerless grave. Yet in him was no moral defilement. Corporeal states, therefore, are not designated by the phrase, moral depravity. It follows, of course, that our animal appetites are not directly implicated in the charge of moral depravity. They may be made the ministers of this depravity, but in themselves they are neither virtuous nor vicious. They become the one or the other, only as they are the means of expressing, and the instruments of executing, the holy or impure purposes of the heart.

2. Moral depravity *is not seated in the intellect.* It is true that the mind is a sufferer in the wide-spread ruin wrought by sin. Its suffering, however, is, as in the case of the body, a consequence of sin, not sin itself. It is in the character of retribution, rather than of moral offense, that mental weakness and disorder come upon us, and make us blind to the charms and insensible of the salutary power of truth. This is indeed a partial, not a perfect retribution. It is

such as is permitted by the all-wise God toward offending *probationary* beings, whose recovery to holiness is sought by an administration of forbearing mercy.

This one fact distinguishes moral depravity from all mental states. The most depraved in morals are not the most imbecile in intellect. The vile in heart are often the greatly gifted in genius. The moral and mental graces do not flourish and decay together. The former often deteriorate, while the latter rapidly improve. Thousands of our race pursue the wrong, with their eyes steadily fixed upon the right. The profligate generally become what they are by the gradual formation of corrupt and vicious habits while the youthful mind is in process of development. Moral depravity, therefore, does not consist of peculiar mental states or attributes. From this the inference is authorized, that in asserting the moral depravity of man, we assert nothing inconsistent with the manifest excellences of the human mind.

3. Moral depravity is not in *action* or *deed.* Its development in action is very common, but not universal. Among the unholy passions of men there is one, and that the unholiest of them all, which dictates the concealment of this depravity, and the show of moral purity in the place of it. That passion is pride. When pride becomes dominant, and rules the sister vices of the heart, it compels them to retire from observation. Like a prince ashamed of his subjects, or a parent of his offspring, pride blushes for its associates, and strives to hide them from the world. It ingeniously contrives to convert the

outward life into a deceitful token of inward rectitude and purity.

It is an interesting fact that a depraved heart is occupied by antagonistic passions. Were it otherwise, its vile passions would combine uninterruptedly to war against God and against his creatures. But the contest of the passions with one another, in some degree, prevents it; and instead of uniform, naked wickedness, produces many of the apparent virtues of mankind. Pride has done more for the world than all the world's virtues have done, setting aside the religion of the Cross. Yet pride is sin. It is one of the most odious vices of our fallen nature. Its utility is not from its own tendency to good, but from its hostile relations to other vices, which it aims to suppress; and, by so doing, without any good-will to the world, rescues it from that utter ruin which must follow the uncurbed indulgence of sinful lusts.

Pride not only conceals *other* base passions, but itself loves to be concealed. It seeks to fashion each evil of the heart, itself included, into an imitation of that which is good. This would be difficult under the scrutiny of a clear and cautious vision. But in the presence of erring man, whose prejudices unfit him to observe and to judge, it is an easy task. Besides the world does not test the actions of men by Scripture rules of moral purity. It claims that some vices are necessary to our comfort and our dignity. Pride is one of those "*necessary vices.*" How often is it said, "we must have some pride, or what will become of us?" Starting thus, no wonder that a "necessary vice," should soon come to be ranked among the virtues and "darkness be put for light, and light for darkness." When right and wrong are thus confounded, actions the most unworthy, and flowing from the worst passions of the heart, will pass without censure, and even with praise. Let the world be convinced that I am honest in my business, generous in my charities, honorable and amiable in my intercourse with men, and though I be proud as Lucifer of these shining attributes, my pride shall be no drawback on my virtues. I shall be called a good man, and he will gain but little credit for his labor, who shall strive to convince the world that my heart is depraved. But I seem to wander.

Although moral depravity is often displayed in action, yet pride sometimes restrains it. And this pride is not always apparent. When it has cast a veil over all the heart, so that none of its vices are exposed, itself last of all withdraws behind the curtain, and leaves every thing without fair and beautiful as a "whited sepulcher." It is true that wicked actions, like waters from the fountain, flow from a wicked heart. They are, as the Scriptures teach us, the evidence of its corruption. But they are not the only evidence.

4. Moral depravity lies not *in principle.* By principle here I do not mean a constitutional tendency, but a speculative or factitious law of human action—a conventional rather than a constitutional law of action—a rule of conduct which custom and the common sentiments of society may approve, without regard to constitutional tendencies.

Thousands, mindful of public sentiment, and regarding their evident utility, adopt worthy rules of life, and observe them with great caution and diligence. And they finally form such habits as render the observance of these rules tolerable, or perhaps agreeable. Indeed, these habits are finally so confirmed, and so fully sanctioned by reason, that to violate them would be painful. This we call principle. Moral depravity may pervade the heart, when these principles are, as it respects man, unexceptionable and commendable.

These principles may owe their origin and primary influence to the mere result of that contest which is carried on between corrupt, antagonistic passions. A man may be charitable in the sense of almsgiving, because the love of fame is with him a more violent passion than the love of money. Another may withhold alms because his avarice conquers his ambition. In the estimation of the world the former is a man of pure principles; but wherein consists his essential excellence? It seems that his apparent benevolence results from the peculiar strength of *one* base passion, or the peculiar *imbecility* of another. The example might be varied in several forms; but this is sufficient for illustration.

The most depraved of our species may, by this warring of the passions, adopt rules of life, which, were their motive pure, would do honor to the saint; and this may create habits, which confirmed, constitute worthy principles of action. But these principles *owe their origin to some of the impurest passions of the heart.* It may be said of such a man, that a storm of passion drove him upon the ground he occupies.

By accident, rather than by moral preference, he embraced righteous principles. Could his dominant passions find gratification in other modes by the adoption of different principles, he might not hesitate to abjure the right and adjure the wrong. Without religion, the grand moral features of the heart are the same. Whether our principles be liberal or restrictive; whether they license or restrain the passions, the difference is superficial, not radical. It is like the different shades of complexion among men, not like the specific animal distinctions. It leaves all within the man, of which moral action can be predicated, impure, and unsightly in the eye of God. The murderer reveals his depravity to the world; the *angry man reveals his to God.* The former permits the evils of his heart to grow early into a state of maturity; the latter checks his in their growth. But he does not eradicate them. Without the renovating power of religion, they can not be extirpated. They may be, for a time, artfully concealed, and even coerced into partial submission to reason or to principle. But like serpents in a den, they will live; and when factitious restraints are taken off, they will come forth from their concealment and do the work of death.

5. Moral depravity is not *the imputation of Adam's transgression* to the sinner. As depraved beings we are intimately connected with the fallen progenitor of our race; and severely suffer by his fall. He involved himself and his descendants in one common ruin. But his sufferings were *personal* and present as well as relative and prospective. They consisted

in the defilement of his heart, as well as in a condemned estate. So we, when born, are tainted with sin, as well as subjected (without a Savior) to the penalty of the Divine law. It is this personal defilement by sin that constitutes our moral depravity. And this is evidently communicated—not imputed. When communicated, it is *ours*, not Adam's. It is a disease, coursing with violence through all the moral system, and working death *within;* and not a name or relation appendant, merely subjecting us to danger or ruin from without.

When we assert the moral depravity of human nature, therefore, we do not assert the imputation of Adam's transgression to his posterity.

6. By moral depravity we do not intend *the guilt of sin.* Guilt is the just liability to punishment, and always implies moral accountability. Depravity is in the human *nature,* whether of infant or adult age; guilt is in the human *condition,* and is contracted by the violation of God's law. There may be depravity when there is no knowledge of God's law and no conscience to accuse the offender. But when there is guilt, there is knowledge of God's law and consciousness of wrong. That there is a difference between guilt and depravity is evident from the fact that their removal is not by one act or in one form. The removal of guilt is by justification; the removal of depravity is by sanctification. The former is the work of the paternal Godhead, the latter is by the Holy Ghost. By moral depravity, then, we do not mean the guilt of sin.

7. This depravity is not *in the conscience.* We

have before stated that it is not in the *mind* or *intellect*, and this would lead to the presumption that it is not in the conscience. For conscience is the exercise of the intellectual powers in relation to moral truths and actions, with the result self-applied; that is, it is an intellectual operation accompanied with moral emotion or feeling—the feeling of *approval*, or *disapproval;* of *complaisance*, or *remorse*. So far, therefore, as conscience is an intellectual faculty, it partakes of the nature of all intellectual powers, so that whatever does not primarily affect the mind or intellect, would not primarily affect the conscience. But the office of conscience is also judicial and retributive, to enforce upon the mind practical conformity to its best perceptions of right and duty, and herein it is allied to, yea, the source of the moral sensibilities. But as this function of conscience was not designed to *supply* a rule of action, but only to secure obedience to the best knowledge of duty the mind possessed, and as its action is never bribed, though often overruled by passion, it can not be the seat of man's depravity, however it may suffer by it.

Moral depravity does not imply an incapacity to discover duty and to discern or feel the consequences of its neglect or violation, but it does rather consist in a *violent disinclination to discharge duty*, and in an incorrigible attachment to the pleasures that it prohibits. It is plain, then, that moral depravity is not seated in the *conscience*.

8. This depravity is not *in the social sentiment*. By the social sentiment, we mean the affectional dispositions of mankind, considered as an endowment

of our nature. These are a bond of union and a law of social order and relation. Such tempers abound, and are both useful and praiseworthy in society. They impart almost the only charm to irreligious life, and without them the unregenerate world would be diabolical and wretched. But amiable as these dispositions are, they have no moral excellence whatever. They are common to man and brute, but, though enjoyed by man in a more refined degree, are yet of too low a character, allied too intimately with the involuntary and instinctive qualities of our nature to be accounted morally virtuous.

The mild and affectionate carriage of the brute is never considered as forming any thing like moral excellence. And why? Evidently because the brute does not act under any moral responsibility, and does not meditate the discharge of moral duties. But at the same time, the brute is not morally depraved, because he has not the capacities of a moral agent, and therefore violates no moral obligations. Now, to apply these remarks in illustration. The affectionate tempers and amiable manners of the natural heart are not *morally* virtuous. And why? Because they do not blend with attachment to God, and to his Son, and to his law, and are not associated with a holy and joyful obedience to the Divine precepts. But in this state man is *morally* depraved, because, unlike the brute, he acts under moral responsibility, with the capacities of a moral agent and with the privilege of a moral subject, and violates his most sacred obligations, which are commensurate with the total powers of his being.

This view of the subject is justified in the Scripture history of a young man, who came to inquire of Christ for salvation. He was so amiable in character and manners that "Jesus, beholding him, loved him." It was only necessary to prove that his excellencies were the fruit of attachment to God and his law. The Savior tested him and discovered at once that his heart concealed all the elements of fierce rebellion against his Maker. All this leads us to conclude that the affectionate dispositions of human nature are only praiseworthy when men are viewed as mere animals, and not when they are regarded as moral agents.

In asserting the moral depravity of man, therefore, we assert nothing inconsistent with all the enchanting exhibitions of natural and social loveliness which so often appear in the history of unregenerate humanity.

Having endeavored to show in what the moral depravity of man does *not consist,* we shall now proceed to show in what it *does* consist, by affirming,

9. That moral depravity is *in the heart.* The affirmation of our text is, that the "heart is desperately wicked." Here a question arises as to the significancy of the word "*heart*" in the holy Scriptures. The word literally signifies the seat of life in the human body. Upon the action and office of the physical heart depend the circulation of the vital fluids, and the growth, vitality, and active functions of all the members of the system.

Now, what is there in the soul of man that sustains such an important office, and operates such an essential influence as this? What is that which may justly be called, morally, the *heart?* We incline to the opinion that the *affections* sustain this office. We know it is a common opinion that the term heart is used for the whole soul, and embraces the understanding, conscience, will, affections, and even the memory; in short, the total power of the intellect and moral being. And it may often be so understood without any doctrinal error, or detriment to truth. But in discoursing on a theme like the present, it does seem necessary to explain with more critical caution, and qualify the term with more exact precision. And in attempting this we know not how to define the word better than to confine it to the affections. For certainly the affections, taken in the larger sense as comprehending the desires, passions, and the whole emotional nature, are the exciting cause of action, the seat of sensibility, and the fashioning power of character. If reason discovers the rule, the affections alone supply the stimulus, we might almost say the propelling power, of action.

This signification of the word heart, in its figurative and theological use, is confirmed by the fact that the sum of the moral law is comprehended in the right state and exercise of the affections, making all moral virtues to consist of a twofold manifestation of love, namely, first, loving God with all our heart; and, second, loving our neighbor as ourselves.

Our Savior declares that all the law hangs on these two commandments. They do undoubtedly divulge in spirit all the moral duty of man, and embrace the sum of all his obligations. "The end of the commandment is charity." This is a fundamental principle of ethics. Injury may result from an erring judgment and a consequent misdirected action; but crime—transgression in the moral sense—can never attach to actions flowing from pure love to God and man. It is in this purely moral sense that love fulfills, and the want of it violates the whole law. "Love is the fulfilling of the law." All the law is fulfilled in one word, even in "love." "He that loveth not knoweth not God, for God is love." Whosoever does not love God, then, and his neighbor, according to this great commandment, is morally depraved. For he is in a state of mind which the law of God does absolutely abhor; and in a state, too, which disqualifies him for any acceptable actions as a moral agent.

Let it be considered here, that although we place this depravity primarily in the affections, yet it can not be confined there, but quickly diffuses itself throughout the soul. Corrupt affections will rule the will into a corrupt choice, because the will is easily swayed by the affections, and in the natural heart exerts an agency accordant with their unholy dictation. He, therefore, who is not actuated by the love of God, will generally exhibit a careless inattention to religious duty, and an obstinate devotion to the pursuits and vanities of the world.

If this is moral depravity, we must see that the several negative propositions advanced for the purpose of explaining the doctrine of moral depravity are not opposed by the view we have *here* taken of that doctrine. If this depravity is in the affections, it is not primarily in the body or in the intellect. It is not primarily in action or in principle. It is not imputed sin, nor is it guilt. It is not in conscience or in the social sentiment, considered as a law of relation and action of our social nature, but lies farther back and deeper down in our nature, at the fountain-head of all activity and character, in the moral agent, in our affectional being, and consists in want of supreme love to God—or, as expressed in positive terms, "enmity to God," and the want of expansive, pure, universal love to man. This wrong state of the moral affections is sufficient to account for the darkness of the understanding, the obliquity of the will, natural selfishness and perversion, and the deadness to God of our whole nature. Like the fatal worm at the root of the vine, it withers every green leaf.

Pause, then, vain boaster, and from thy pride of reason and the lofty conceit of thy natural goodness, humble thyself to consider thy true condition. Behold thyself in the light of the inspired Word, corroborated by philosophy and conscious experience. In this doctrine of our common depravity is grounded the necessity of our regeneration by the Holy Ghost. "Marvel not that I say unto you, ye must be born again." This is the only way of salvation. "If we say that we have not sinned, we make him a liar, and his word is not in us. If we confess our sins, he is faithful and just to forgive us our sins, and to cleanse us from all unrighteousness."

XIII.

DEPRAVITY OF THE HEART.

SECOND DISCOURSE.

"*The heart is deceitful above all things and desperately wicked.*" Jeremiah xvii, 9.

IN this discourse we shall proceed to offer some proof of the doctrine of the moral depravity of our race. This proof we shall attempt,

I. FROM THE HISTORY OF THE HUMAN FAMILY.

We do not mean the history of human manners in detail; but we refer to the *general* history of man as a being—1. *Originally holy;* 2. *Afterward fallen; and* 3. *Finally restored.* By examining him in these three estates we shall be inevitably conducted to the conclusion that the middle or fallen estate is one of desperate moral depravity. Let us proceed to examine them.

1. As to the primitive state of man, we observe, it was the state of Adam before the fall. He is represented as having been made in the image of God.

"Let us make man," said the Divine Creator, "in our image, after our likeness. So God created man in his own image, in the image of God created he him." What image *was* this which adorned the person of our progenitor and crowned Eden with glory? It may have consisted of these seven particulars:

(1.) The spirituality of the soul.

(2.) The intellectual and moral capacities of the soul, including the freedom of the will.

(3.) The affections or dispositions of the soul.

(4.) The perfect holiness of those faculties and affections.

(5.) The dominion of the soul over the world.

(6.) The spiritual happiness of the soul.

(7.) The immortality of the soul.

Adam, possessed of these magnificent endowments, might justly claim to be in the image or likeness of God. And no argument is necessary to convince those who read the Bible with common attention, that he *did* possess these features of the Divine image.

2. The second state of human nature, to which we invite your notice, is its lapsed or fallen state.

The fall of man is, with one exception, the boldest and most affecting feature of his general history, as presented in Holy Writ. The history teaches us

(1.) That a law was prescribed by his Creator for his government—"And the Lord God commanded the man saying," etc.

(2.) That law is sanctioned by a most fearful penalty—"In the day that thou eatest thereof thou shalt surely die."

(3.) The history records the violation of that law—"And when the woman saw that the tree was good for food, and that it was pleasant to the eyes, she took of the fruit thereof and did eat, and gave also unto her husband with her, and he did eat."

(4.) The consequences of the fall are announced

in the Divine curse; are developed in man's woeful experience; are exhibited in the didactic Scriptures; and sound forth in the prophetic denunciations of both Testaments of God.

(5.) The Scriptures assume and proclaim an intimate connection between Adam and his posterity in the loss sustained by this act of transgression. Instance such expressions as the following: "As by one man sin entered into the world, and death by sin;" "For if by one man's offense death reigned by one;" "By the offense of one, judgment came upon all men to condemnation;" "By one man's disobedience many were made sinners;" "Through the offense of one many be dead;" "As in Adam all die." In these texts the fall of man, of his species, is plainly exhibited, and evidently attributed to the act of one man as the representative of the race. This fall, we presume, must have defaced that Divine image which at first adorned the human nature, for we can conceive of no degradation or fall but by the loss of that image.

We proceed to inquire, then, in what respect has man lost the image of God?

1. He has not lost the spirituality of the soul. The soul is now, as ever, immaterial. It is a spiritual substance, like the Divine essence, and retains, in this respect, the Creator's image.

2. He has not lost the intellectual or moral faculties of the soul. He retains the powers of perception, of memory, of reasoning, of imagination, and of conscience. He retains, also, the power of will, or choice. His constitutional faculties, as a moral agent, remain. They are impaired, indeed, and corrupted,

and depend for their right action upon grace, but as faculties they are still retained.

3. He retains the affections. He loves and hates with a surprising vigor of attachment or aversion, and might as well cease to be as to cease from these ardent emotions of the soul.

4. The soul retains its immortality, and looks forward with prospects as boundless in duration as does the Creator upon his everlasting throne.

If man retains the Divine image in these four particulars, his loss must be in one or more of the three remaining, namely,

1. In the holiness of the soul's affections.
2. In its dominion over the world, or,
3. In its spiritual happiness.

The Scriptures represent that in all these respects the fall has ruined us. From the time of the transgression and of the expulsion from Eden, all the direct descriptions and indirect allusions of Scripture advisory of man's condition, do indicate this threefold loss. From this moment the history of man becomes little else than record of crime, and degradation and woe. Instead of looking down upon a world filled with holy and happy beings, such as he had delegated to a joyful and immortal reign on earth, God looked upon the earth, and behold! it was corrupt, (Genesis vi, 12) "for all flesh had corrupted his way upon the earth." "And God saw (Genesis vi, 5) that the wickedness of man was great upon the earth." The heart, whose affections were formed in purity like God's, had become deceitful above all things, and desperately wicked. Moses, and David, and Isaiah, with Jesus Christ and his apostles, all harmonize in their descriptions of human nature, and the preceding quotations from some of them fairly exhibit their views on this subject.

We can not doubt, then, that Adam, and in him, his whole posterity, lost, by the fall, the holiness of the soul's affections. Inspired history settles the doctrine as a fact, whatever may be the theories or speculations of men.

As to the loss of the soul's dominion over the world, it is plainly signified by the same sacred authority, and abundantly corroborated by observation. The malediction pronounced upon the sinning pair immediately after the fall, must, of itself, have enforced the abdication of that dominion on the part of Adam. That curse dissolved the throne and scepter of the rebel, and placed the earth forever beyond his traitorous control. From sitting as a prince on nature's throne, to receive homage from all that moved in height above, or in breadth around, or in depth beneath, he is doomed, by a fierce warring with nature, to subdue the vices of the soil, the ferocity of beasts, the venom and hostility of lesser creatures, and forcibly possess himself of the stinted bounties of the harvest, and the diminished revenue of the earth. At the same time, one of the meanest of the reptile race, made to submit with the nobler orders to his dominion, now heads the rebellion of the brute creation against their fallen lord. Thus, the lord of nature becomes her servant—the monarch of ten thousand tribes sat down a slave upon the dung-hill. And the forfeiture which reduced the traitorous parent to poverty and shame has entailed upon us, his children, beggary and woe.

That the soul has, by the fall, suffered the loss of her spiritual enjoyments is also rendered certain by Scripture and by fact.

How evident is it that the transgression in the garden immediately introduced disquiet into the bosoms of guilt! The Almighty had, till then, met his unoffending children in all the peace and glory of their innocence. But now, when they listen to the approach of God, they hide themselves among the trees of the garden. The voice of God called them from their covert, and in answer to the question, "Where art thou?" they answer, "I heard thy voice in the garden, and was afraid." See, I pray you, how early this symptom of mental agony succeeds the tragic deed which blasted and condemned a world! Till that moment, think ye that this now trembling creature had ever quaked in any presence? Think ye that till then paleness had ever blanched his visage? Never. Till that moment there was music without and peace within. All was harmony on earth as in heaven. The hills were girt with beauty and were crowned with light and joy. The vales were filled with song, and ran down in floods of libation, which were nature's offerings to God.

Eden was dressed in richest robes and was filled and crowned with the presence and glory of God. Heaven looked down as upon some goodly scene, attractive to the eye and enchanting to the soul. And angels sung on high and the echo went up from earth. At this moment the serpent prevails. The hand is put forth. They pluck—they eat. Earth trembles. The songs of angels are hushed. Light and beauty fade from the hills, and there is neither song nor incense in the vale. Eden is in mourning robes, and there is woe and wailing in her bowers. God's presence and wrath are there, and the curse of his mouth rests upon all.

Such is the Scripture representation of man in his fallen estate. It is no myth, or allegory. It is God's record of a great event, lying far back beyond the origin of nations or of secular history, yet preserved by human methods in primeval simplicity, for the instruction of mankind and the settlement of a primary doctrine of revelation.

3. The third state is one of renewal or restoration. And a glance at this estate will confirm the view we have taken on this subject. Man is raised to this estate only by a radical change. This is indicated by the figurative descriptions of the sacred writings. It is called "a crucifying of the old man," and a "putting on of the new man," a "dying unto sin and a living unto holiness," a "resurrection with Christ," a "being born again," a "renewal in the image of God." And if any doubt remains respecting the signification of this last text, it may be determined by referring to Ephesians iv, 24: "And that ye put on the new man which after God [after the image or pattern of God] is created in righteousness and true holiness." This Scripture must convince us that in man's original state he possessed righteousness and true holiness; that he lost these by the fall, and that they are restored to him when he puts on the new man in

regeneration. Now, by receiving man in this threefold estate, we certainly must be convinced that the middle, or fallen estate is one of complete sinfulness and depravity. The account of his fall and of its consequences, of his recovery and its happy effects, is unintelligible, and even deceptive and farcical, unless it be conjoined with the doctrine of moral depravity in the unregenerate. Thus, from the general history of man, we argue the moral depravity of human nature.

II. THIS DOCTRINE IS SUPPORTED BY OBSERVATION AND EXPERIENCE. By comparing the actions and avowed sentiments of the unregenerate with the law of God, we can plainly discern the constant workings of this depravity.

We have seen that the Divine law requires us to "love the Lord our God with all our hearts; and our neighbors as ourselves."

1. Now, from our Savior's exposition of this law, it seems that the love we all bear to our friends and associates does not, in itself, carry us one step toward its fulfillment. He makes our enemy, as well as our friend, our neighbor—and if we withhold our love from the former, we need not account our love to the latter as worthy of the least reward. "Love your enemies; bless them that curse you; do good to them that persecute you."

"If ye love them that love you, what reward have ye? Do not even the publicans the same?" "If ye salute your brethren only, what do ye more than others? Do not even the publicans so?" Now, let us examine the unregenerate of our race by this rule of the Divine law, explained as it here is by our Savior, and we shall immediately perceive that all the warm and amiable affections of our animal nature do combine with the most abominable depravity of heart. For the sentiments and actions of the natural heart, so far as we can observe them, indicate the love of friends, and the hatred of enemies. Yes, corrupted nature blesses those who love and curses those who hate us. It returns kindness for charity and revenge for injury. And what then? Why, the love and benediction which we give our friends show us to be, in animal nature, equal to the forest tribes; while the hatred and malediction with which we follow our enemies proclaim us to be, in our superior character, as moral subjects, morally and radically depraved—or, in other words, we are proved to be wholly destitute of the spirit, and obstinately averse to the demeanor which this part of God's law requires of us.

2. But, again, the conduct of the unregenerate toward God is equally reprehensible when compared with the superior precept of the Divine law. That precept, as already stated, requires us to love God with all the heart. Now, the unregenerate never do love God. On the contrary, observation and experience here also corroborate the Scriptures, which represent them as even cursed with a heart of aversion to the great Creator. This aversion is manifested by the following facts:

(1.) Such men have *no curiosity to be acquainted with God,* or his truth.

Curiosity, or the desire of knowledge, is an ardent

passion of the human mind. It is as natural as the appetite for food, and belongs to all intelligent beings as such. In a healthful state of the soul it craves and relishes only that knowledge which tends to the purity and elevation of our being. It is wakeful and enterprising in the pursuits of science and of true philosophy. It rouses the soul to adventurous efforts, and enlists all its energies in the search for knowledge. But propose religion as the subject of study, or the theme of meditation, and how stupid and unaspiring is the irreligious soul! How impatient is it of the labor; how easily discouraged by the difficulty of obtaining heavenly wisdom! The most trifling objects in nature will engage the attention, and excite the mind to action; but nature's God exhibits nothing in the estimation of the sinner worthy the attention of his stupid, diseased soul. The structure and habits of the minutest insect; the class and order of the humblest weed of the dung-hill; nay, the analysis of an ounce of water from the fountain, or dirt from the hillock, is a matter of more interest to the wisdom of this world than are the discovery and adoration of all that wisdom, and goodness, and omnipotence which sustain and adorn the worlds of this wide-spread universe. This want of curiosity to know God, and become acquainted with the glory of his nature, especially the wisdom, justice, holiness, and goodness of his moral government, and above all, of redemption, indicates an entire absence of that supreme affection demanded by the holy commandment. The moral history of the heathen world is contained in the single statement, "And even as they did not like to retain God in their knowledge, God gave them over to a reprobate mind."

(2.) Our aversion to God is indicated by *a manifest disrelish of religious truth,* when made acquainted with it. Truth has a thousand charms, and exhibits them, in rich variety, to the children of science. The philosopher, the poet, and the statesman, live and feast with ever-flowing delight in her halls and bowers. But the poet, the statesman, and the philosopher will starve and die, rather than seek refection from the truths of our holy religion. For they are not willing to suffer the exposure of all the real poverty and misery of their souls, to cast away the dear-bought monuments of their intellectual glory, and come, like little children, to the feet of Jesus to be taught true wisdom there. That truth which will operate an effect like this, is not welcome to the spirit of pride, and when it is the subject of the mind's speculation, it awakens no harmony in the soul, unless the sanctifying Spirit has formed the man in newness of heart and life. The natural man "discerneth not the things of the Spirit of God, for they are foolishness unto him." This disrelish of religious truth when brought before the eye of the mind, distinctly indicates aversion to God.

(3.) The unregenerate evidence their want of love to God by their *neglect of his communications.* Every friend is a favorite author in the circle of those who love him, especially if his productions are affectionate epistles. If there be no harmony in his periods to others, yet doubtless there is to them. If all the world besides would trample his letters in the dust, yet *they* will not do it. Now, do the unregenerate claim to be the friends of God? Then for the proof of this friendship. God has sent to them epistles of mercy, which display the richest charms of language, and exhibit a thousand expressions of regard, and ten thousand offerings of love. Who among the irreligious open these epistles with haste, peruse them with holy pleasure, and treasure them up in affectionate remembrance?

Is not the Bible, which embodies these letters of friendship, generally exhibited as the mere ornament of the library? Is it not permitted to repose in dusty quiet in its alcoves, while novels and other frothy effusions of shallow and vain minds are sought, and devoured, and relished? Can any higher evidence be adduced of the vicious appetites of sickly souls? Be assured such neglect of God's Holy Word and such preference of the faulty, vain tattlings of fiction do furnish but a poor and disheartening evidence that we "*love God with all the heart.*"

(4.) That the unregenerate do not love God, is shown by their *disinclination to commune with him.* God has offered to all men this privilege, in the most direct and satisfactory form. He has erected the palace of his love within our reach, and there he has located the courts of his grace; adorning them with sweeter imagery than wings of cherubim, or mercy-seat. Love invites, mercy urges us to this sanctuary. It is entered by prayer. Corrupted nature refuses to approach, refuses to *enter* it; refuses all intercourse with the God who reared, and opened, and sanctified it, for holy conference between the creature and the Creator! How is this? If human nature be not hostile to God, if it cherish any affection for that spirit which so earnestly pleads for this communion, how is it, that with inclination for society, and with fervent devotion to the friends we love, we never seek, never *accept* the privilege of communion with this condescending and waiting God? The only reason that can possibly be assigned—the only reason that the *Scriptures themselves assign,* is a want of attachment to God.

III. Many questions have been raised in the theological world concerning the degree of human depravity. It has been strenuously maintained that human nature is totally depraved. Now the question arises, what is human nature, and what does the word *totally* mean? Human nature, taken without qualification, signifies the whole man; and the word totally signifies *wholly.* Now this is affirmed of human nature only in its relation to the claims of the holy and perfect law of God. It falls wholly short of meeting these claims. It can not renovate itself, nor raise itself out of its own ruined and sinful state. It can not of itself do works pleasing to God. Its total power of recuperation and holy obedience is in the assisting and renewing grace of God, not in itself. Yet it may perform many acts consistent with the higher animal, the social and intellectual laws of our being, without renewing grace. On the other hand, some have maintained that the corruptions of human nature are very slight, are contracted by education, and are easily removed by the unaided exertions of the moral delinquent. This mistake is radical, dangerous, and fatal error. Without borrowing any qualifying terms from the theological vocabularies, we are willing to submit to Scripture, and believe what it teaches. Let us resort to the Bible, then, and see if it will not aid us in settling this question of strife and war. It pronounces the heart (meaning, undoubtedly, the human heart in its natural state) *wicked*, in qualified terms; but in terms so qualified as to render every shade of the picture gloomy in the extreme. It is pronounced *desperately* wicked. This qualifying word is very significant. It means rashly; so as to set reason and prudence at defiance, and rouse the soul into the most presumptuous opposition to God's authority and omnipotence. It means furiously; so that the soul is in a moral rage, is wrought into absolute madness. It means hopelessly and irrecoverably; so that we may yield up all expectations of its being changed or improved if left to itself, as nothing can restore it except foreign influence. Such is the meaning of the significant word selected by the inspired philologist, to paint the moral state of the unregenerate. And it will be seen that this is no slander of human nature, if we consider:

1. How forward we are to sin. Unless God's grace prevent, we yield to the earliest and slightest solicitations. The least temptation will provoke our appetite. It needs no deep plot to betray, no captivating charm to allure us. Temptation is to our corruption like sparks to tinder. If it touch, it spreads without resistance, and in combustibles all prepared to facilitate its progress.

2. Our natural, inveterate opposition to holiness.

We are wise to do evil, but to do good we have no understanding. We exhibit an aversion to God that is absolutely invincible to every thing but his own omnipotence. As citizens of the world, motives of happiness will direct us into various courses of action, and will induce changes of sentiment and pursuit. But among all changes of sentiment and action, heart and hand will always cautiously turn away from the love and service of God. Though the motives to such service and love actually burden three worlds; though they are revealed to the suffering spirit from heaven, and earth, and hell, yet they can not tempt human nature to be holy. No condition of life, no apprehension of evil, no promise or prospect of bliss, can bring the natural heart to consent to an amicable alliance with God. Reason may declare for it, conscience may urge it, fear and hope may demand it, all else that belongs to man may offer zealous suffrage in its favor, and yet the heart will not yield. In such a heart, any thing can maintain successful rivalry with God. All that man hates shall become lovely to him, when it approaches him in company with God. When Pilate and Herod consumed their enmity upon the altar where the Lamb of God was slain, they sketched, with more than Raphael's skill, the abiding traits of human nature. We say abiding traits, because they can not be separated from the native character. They live or die with it. The heart of man can never be cursed, can never be blessed into any change essentially for the better, while the native moral elements remain. Curse may follow curse, till the suffering spirit refuses all alliances with the world, and still it will reject all overtures of friendship with God. Blessing may follow blessing, till Providence can give, or the subject can receive no more; and while the soul is buoyant upon floods of mercy, she will proudly set her sails, and hold her repulsive course away from the generous fountain which supplies the ample and overflowing stream. Why all this inveterate opposition to society and communion with God, if the heart be not wicked; desperately, rashly, furiously wicked?

3. It may be objected that this doctrine is inconsistent with a state of conviction and the desire of salvation. What is conviction? Is it not a feeling of discovery of this very depravity? Conviction implies self-knowledge. Is the conviction of the sinner the knowledge of his own purity? None will assert it. It must be, we conceive, the knowledge of sin existent and dominant within. So the apostle hints in that language, "When the commandment came, sin revived."

Now, if this is the conviction of the sinner, it is so far from being inconsistent with moral depravity that it is inconsistent with every state of heart except moral depravity. Conviction of sin is, in fact, very inconsistent with a state of moral purity. How could holy angels or holy men be convicted of sin? Moral depravity, then, is *not inconsistent with conviction.* Conviction of sin is no virtue, but a painful knowledge of the want of virtue.

Is it inconsistent with a desire of salvation? Salvation is the delivery of a sinner from the guilt, the pollution, and the punishment of sin. The very desire of salvation, then, on the part of the sinner implies that he now lies under the guilt, and suffers the dominion and is exposed to the punishment of sin. The desire of salvation, like that conviction which creates the desire, is so far from being inconsistent with depravity of heart, that it is inconsistent with every other state of heart but depravity. Desire of salvation in the unregenerate heart is not the possession of salvation. It arises from an intellectual perception of the excellency of holiness on the one hand, and a painful consciousness of sin on the other, and is the harbinger of reform, but not in itself holiness. The doctrine of moral depravity, then, is not inconsistent with a desire of salvation.

But the question may be urged, "Are not conviction and a desire of salvation *right?*" We answer, in a certain sense they are. If you judge them in comparison with a former and worse state of heart, they are right, as offering promise of reformation. It is right that the stupid sinner should awake and be convicted; and it is right that the worldly sinner should turn from the world and desire salvation. In this sense conviction and the desire of salvation are right.

But in another sense they are wrong. If you refer them to the law of God, which demands supreme love and perfect holiness *now*, it is certain that no state of mind can be *absolutely* right which implies the present *want* of love to God, and of holy tempers in the soul.

It is, in one sense, right for the assassin, who lies in wait to murder, to deliberate, to consider that the law of God and the laws of the land abhor the crime he meditates; but if at this moment his victim approaches, and dies beneath his thrust, who gives him credit for his moralizing? He did, for a moment, cast a wishful eye toward the temple of virtue, but the temple he did not reach, and the goddess he did not worship, and the oracle he did not obey. The law and his peers will say that his deliberations aggravated his offense, and consigns him to a surer and severer punishment. Now, as this deliberation is to the murderer, so, in a manner, is the desire of salvation to a sinner. The deliberations of the one, and desire of the other, are both, in a sense, right. But in each case, unless the deliberation and desire be connected with the purpose and the act of virtue and religion, they are abhorred by God and by man; and are so far from savoring of moral goodness that they only seem to betray the violent opposition of the heart to virtue and to piety.

We proceed, lastly, to improve this subject by observing,

1. That it casts *light,* as we have already suggested, *on the doctrine of regeneration.*

The remedy should be adapted to the disease. The disease is sin in the heart. What can cure it? The Scriptures prescribe a new birth, or regeneration. But what is this? One tells you it is acquiring a knowledge of the Scriptures, or improving the mind in theological science. This is a mistake, or else the wisdom of the Divine Physician has erred in the prescription, for the disease is not in the mind, but in the heart.

Another tells you regeneration is immersion in water, into the Name of the Father, and the Son, and the Holy Ghost; while others, still, would propose sacramental and ceremonial observances. But here is a mistake again; for the disease is not physical, and applications to the body afford but a discouraging promise of efficacy. Away with such moral quackery! You might as well poultice the head to cure a wound on the foot as to exhibit such mediums for the sicknesses of the soul. You might as well apply color to the palate, for refection, as to apply water to the body, or instruction to the mind, with the expectation of thus removing sin from the heart. That regeneration which the Scriptures propose, is a being "born of the Spirit" of God. The heart of man is the seat of this moral disease, and spiritual influence alone can reach and heal the spiritual disease.

2. This subject *should warn the mere moralist of his danger.* His hopes are vain. The *heart* must be changed or the soul must perish. Outward conformity to the Divine law will avail us nothing unless the inner man be adorned with the spirit of obedience. The stream can not be pure while the fountain is corrupt.

Vainly do we hope to impart to the grapes of Sodom the sweetness of Eshcol's fruit. The vine is bitter and its root corrupt, and the fruit must be deadly. Believe not that the whiteness of the sepulcher without betokens any thing better than foulness and loathsomeness within. You, sirs, possessed of generous minds, and rich in the display of all that can adorn and exalt the irreligious soul in the circles of the worldly, even you, unless changed in heart, are like the sepulcher, which, appearing outwardly adorned in beauty to the eye, conceals the most sickening abominations within. For how can the flatteries of a world, which is at enmity with God, commend your virtue before that law by which we all must be judged, and which prescribes love to God as your first duty?

No refinement of sentiment or of conduct can be of any moral worth in the sight of God while it sets aside, or makes no reliance upon, his law, his judgment and counsel, his will and doctrine. How can that be religious which makes no necessary recognition of God and his will? How can that be truly moral which is not approved by the Holy Law of God? How can that be amiable and refined, in any truthful sense, which grieves and offends the Spirit of Grace? We may be every thing admirable in human esteem and every thing abominable in the sight of God—"The friendship of the world is enmity with God;" "What is highly esteemed among man is abomination in the sight of God."

Alas! while the world acts upon us with its flatteries and witcheries, to persuade us that we are happy, and *shall be happy*, all things demonstrate our hostility to God, and all *hell* waits to reward us for that hostility. Were we, who are in an unchristian state, to see ourselves as we are; were we fully to discover that our carnal minds are "enmity against God," according to his Word; were we to catch the reflection of our moral image from that Word, as from a mirror which neither flatters nor deforms, do you believe we could endure it? No, we could never endure it! Let us, I beseech you, hold this glass before the irreligious of this assembly, and see what images the light will paint upon its bosom! Lamb of God, what have we here? I see a beaten path, smooth and slippery as the fused glass, surrounding the pit of despair. And here, on the very verge of hell, Pride tosses her head with scorn, and Vanity trips in airy giddiness, and Pleasure wantons in poisoned relishes, and Avarice grins and grasps its gold, and Rage pursues its abhorred victim, and Drunkenness, and Perjury, and Blasphemy, descend half-way down the precipice, look up from amidst the smoke of the pit, and cry "come on!" See here, sirs; do you know these features? O pass not these images by because of their unsightliness! Study the piece awhile with your best diligence, and, after all, if you doubt "what this meaneth," each one of you may read for label in front of the piece, "*gnothi seauton*," *know thyself*. And now, to gain some quiet to thyself, wilt thou close thine eyes, or put aside the mirror, or complain of its injustice and say, like faded beauty, that the image owes its deformity to the vices of the reflector, and not to the gracelessness of the original? Alas! do not so wickedly, we beseech you! Seek no false quiet this day by closing thine eye, or turning it askance, or accusing the Word of thy God and Redeemer of injustice. There is a region of better prospects beyond you, if you will but step into the path which conducts the wanderer thither. And, blessed be God, it is the happy office of the pulpit to direct, to persuade, to beseech you to fly to those regions of peace. We are commanded not only to spread before you the canvas on which God has sketched the gloomy features of your corruption and woe, but also to point you to that blood whose application will transform the darkest shades into beauty and loveliness. Yes,

> "There is a fountain filled with blood,
>   Drawn from Immanuel's veins,
> And sinners plunged beneath that flood,
>   Lose all their guilty stains."

Ruined and dying souls, we point you to those arms of mercy where the lost are saved. We urge you to that bleeding bosom where the weary sweetly repose. O, to be embraced in those arms, to lie down upon that bosom is sweeter than all that Paradise contained, when our parents rested in its bowers and ate its choicest fruits! May you soon enter this region of life and love, and learn what is the exceeding greatness of His power to usward who believe, and what are the riches of the glory of His inheritance in the saints!

XIV.

THE WISDOM OF GOD.

"*O the depth of the riches, both of the wisdom and knowledge of God!*" Romans xi, 33.

WISDOM and knowledge are kindred attributes. They may be blended, therefore, in discussion, without impairing that simplicity and unity which are demanded by the canons of pulpit discourse. At all events, they are associated in the text, from which may we be enabled not only to derive instruction, but to catch the very spirit which breathes forth in the apostolic exclamation. Let us introduce this text to your notice by some general observations.

Knowledge is the apprehension of truth. Truth is reality. The shining of the sun is reality. The vision of its light is a reality. The emotion which attends its perception is a reality. And all these, namely, the light, the vision, and the emotion, are for truth; reality is truth. The perception of these realities, or the mental apprehension of these truths, is knowledge. We have said that wisdom and knowledge are kindred attributes. Yet they are not the same. Knowledge is an essential element of wisdom, and benevolence is its sister element. Knowledge and benevolence, then, combined, constitute true wisdom. God tells us in his Word, that the knowledge of *the holy* is understanding, that is, wisdom. But how different simple elements appear in different combinations! Blend knowledge with holiness, and it is wisdom; combine it with sin, and it is the most extravagant and fatal folly. Of the holy it may be said, the more knowledge the more wisdom; but of the wicked it may be said, the more knowledge the more folly—like stagnant pools of putrid flesh, whose loathsomeness is always increased by the accumulation of the fluids or solids which constitute the source of the offense.

Wisdom belongs to all holy minds; to angels in heaven, and in a lower degree, to the pious on earth. But there is only one example of perfect wisdom in the universe. That example is referred to in our text. Infinite knowledge and benevolence constitute God perfect in wisdom. The apostle, as he dwells upon this theme, and contemplates the knowledge and wisdom of God in the gracious providence which is over mankind, bursts forth in this exclamation, "O the depth of the riches, both of the wisdom and knowledge of God!" Let us mark this language; and, as we have, in a former discourse, spoken of God's goodness, let us now inquire, What are the riches of his knowledge?

I. First, then, the knowledge of God is rich *in extent.* We can not say how extensive it is; for we can not admeasure the interminable field within which it expatiates. True, we can talk of the universe; but we talk about that of which we know almost nothing. Could the snail speak, it might discourse of the world; but the theme would scarcely suit its habits of confinement to one square foot of earth, without an eye even to survey the dusty bed whereon it rests. Man, as a sublunary dweller in this vast universe, has a vision so confined and imperfect, that the things unseen are as the world to a reptile; while the field of his survey is, in comparison, like that reptile's foot of earth.

The universe must be supposed to have an inconceivable extent. From what we behold with the naked eye, from what we discern by magnifying instruments, and, more than all, from what we perceive of the active tendency of the infinite mind, we have an ample warrant for the opinion that the universe, though not absolutely infinite, is so in relation to creature minds. Bold speculations there have been on this interesting subject. But the most daring curiosity is best suited to the theme. Here fancy needs no reins. The fervid imaginations of Milton and Chalmers are tame and stupid in such a field, though they carry us far beyond our customary walks. Taking from one of them a simple hint, let us not so much suppose as believe that the solar system is only one among millions of systems, formed into one superior, with its own remote invisible center; and then, again, that this superior system is but the fragment of another still superior, composed of millions like itself; and then, again, that a thousand other systems rise in succession, one above another, each succeeding one embracing its antecedents, and bearing to them the same relation as a genus to its species, till at last the thousandth, embracing all circles around God's everlasting throne, whose omnipotence binds together its solid forms, preserves its everlasting harmonies, and moves it in its everlasting course through the infinite space of the universe. In the midst of such a universe, where is man? In the midst of such a universe, *what* is man? Of such a universe can he see or can he know any thing that deserves the name of knowledge? Alas! it is more than he can do to meditate even the *existence* of these worlds, and set them forth with some orderly reckoning.

But what then? Is this universe an unsurveyed and solitary waste? Do you fancy that there is no presence to cheer it, nor eye to look upon it forever? Ah, brethren! there is an eye whose vision is spread all over this amazing scene. There is a mind present unto it in all its illimitable extent. A majestic and awful presence is familiarized to every portion of it. The eternal One, at the same moment, converses with its immeasurably remote extremes. Yes, sirs; there is a mind to whose intelligence all this amazing vast of worlds on worlds, and suns on suns, and systems on systems, is more distinctly apparent and familiar than are to you the features of the landscape, as its shadings are thrown from your pencil on the canvas. Is such the unlimited vision of the Godhead? Well, then, may we exclaim, in the language of the apostle, "O the depth of the riches of this knowledge!"

II. The knowledge of God is rich *in comprehension*. Although it is as extensive as the universe, and reaches to both actual and possible existence, yet it comes not from hasty glances; it does not consist of confused visions and superficial discoveries. It is not a knowledge of open forms and prominent principles, to the neglect of secret qualities and concealed attributes.

It is difficult not to judge our Maker by ourselves. We lose in confused vision what we sought to gain by amplifying its range. The more we multiply the subjects of our study, the less we know of any one of them, for we can not carry our attention to several without diverting it, by turns, from all. But the mind of God is just as familiar with each minutest portion of the universe as though he were employed in its exclusive and everlasting survey. His eye is always on *each portion* of the boundless whole. His attention is at once and forever fixed on every point of its distant verge, and on every point of each circling line which Omnipotence might describe, between its remote circumference and its glory-beaming center. This is not all. To his eye all things are transparent. Before him all depths are uncovered. His vision penetrates through them and beyond them. To him darkness itself is light. Egyptian and infernal glooms yield to his omniscient glance, the forms, and motions, and properties of all which they vainly sought to immask or disguise. Every atom in this magnificent immensity, whether sinking in its depths, or aspiring in its heights; whether resting at its axis, or whirling on its verge, is watched by the intense and eternal scrutiny of the omnipresent and omniscient God. "O the depth of the riches of this knowledge!"

III. The knowledge of God is rich *in variety*. This

might be inferred as a corollary from the preceding heads. If Divine knowledge is so rich in extent and comprehension, it must consist of an opulent variety. And this variety regards things material and spiritual with all that rank under their respective heads. As to things material, God perceives all natural truth; such as inheres in the millions of systems—rather, in the millions of generations of systems—with the millions of worlds appendant to each. In all these, what swarming varieties must rise to that mind whose subtile vision detects all that belongs to their physical aggregation, constitution, arrangement! God surveys them all. All the grand and minute, in the posture, relations, impulses, and movements of things created; in systems superior and subordinate; in worlds and their satellites, and in their separate and composed elements—all, from their maximum to the minimum, are presented in naked exposure before the eye of God.

And the universe of *mind* is equally familiar to Him. Of mind, how little does man know; of its substance, nothing; of its attributes, enough to give them names and rouse this world to a ceaseless war of words; of its connection with matter, the interesting fact unexplained, and full of mortifying mystery. But here every thing is familiar unto God. He knows the very substance of mind, the nature and purpose of its society with matter, and the secret of its active and passive sympathies in virtue of its mysterious union. God looks upon the soul as a thing of form, of countenance, of expression. By his sagacious mind its secret energies are traced to their source, as well as followed out in streams of creature action.

God is equally familiar with the endlessly varied schemes of *moral life.* He not only discerns that sin and holiness are at everlasting variance, and produce variant effects upon mind, in the pains of the one and the peace of the other, but he perceives what constitutes their difference, and from what principles flow their contrary effects. He clearly apprehends how and why a consciousness of guilt associates with sin, and a consciousness of innocence with purity and righteousness. He perceives, too, why a consciousness of guilt stings with remorse, and why a consciousness of innocence solaces with rapture. Now, consider what a multitude of forms, and elements, and principles, give variety incalculable to a small portion of matter in its senseless and unorganized states; consider what a variety of mental action is presented to a solitary mind in the space of one solitary hour; consider what changeful successions of passion, in the form of love and hatred, of desire and aversion, of fear and hope, of regret and gratulation, of ambition, jealousy, and rage, or of penitence, meekness, and charity, by turns possess one heart and yield it up again, like current waters which leave the shore behind; and consider, again, that though the subjects in which these unstable passions and principles inhere are countless as the earthly atoms, yet God beholds them all in their infinite and minutest shades of variation. Consider, that not an attribute of mind or of matter, in its ever-changing operations and tendencies, has ever, for a moment, escaped the all-pervading vision of the Godhead, that in the universe of mind not a thought or passion has ever occurred, but he has noticed it in its generate, rising, and waning stages, with every circumstance tending to aggravate or palliate the vice, and to heighten or deteriorate the virtue. Consider that by a permanent and boundless vision he discerns all states of all that is, of all that breathe, of all that think, of all that feel, of all below, above, around; of all that dwell on earth, or sigh in hell, or sing in heaven; of all that occupy the unreckoned worlds which trespass upon the boundless void and journey around the Eternal Throne. Consider this, and you may join in the exclamation of the apostle, "O the depth of the riches of the knowledge of God!"

IV. Divine knowledge is rich *in accuracy*. In our childhood we were taught that "to err is human;" but reason teaches us that to err is also superhuman. The liability to false impressions is doubtless not confined to human beings, but is common to all creature minds as such. This seems to be implied in the very capacity to increase knowledge. The acquisition of knowledge implies its pursuit; its pursuit supposes inquiry; inquiry is a confession of ignorance, and proclaims a liability to misconception, or false conjecture. The purest creature intelligences doubtless err by innocent misconceptions. But as no error would be harmless in God, the universal and supreme Governor, so God is not liable to err. He can not err. He acquires no knowledge, pursues none, inquires for none. He conjectures nothing and, therefore, can not conjecture wrong. He conceives nothing in relation to things that are, as to what or how they are; but he perceives all things. His knowledge consists of simple perception, and is, therefore, unmixed with error. It is light without darkness. It is pure, intense, perpetual light, without an obscuring cloud or shadow.

V. Divine knowledge is rich *in permanency*. Man acquires knowledge with toil, retains a portion of it with difficulty, but loses far more than he retains. Three things, like banded enemies, commit successive invasions upon his mind, and divide between them the spoils of their success. These are sleep, forgetfulness, and old age. Either of these can reduce man to partial or absolute idiocy. When the wise man is wrapped in slumber, search for the glances of the eye of fire; listen for the notes of spirit-stirring eloquence. You see no token of his wisdom, nor hear any thing but incoherent folly. The slumbers of Solomon stultified his mind and reduced a third of his life to idiocy.

Old age ravages the intellect, and sometimes renders it a frightful desolation. The palsy-smitten patriarch will tell you that he has forgotten more than he now knows; that time, whose hand has plucked off his locks, and bleached the scanty remnant with a snowy whiteness, has wrought beneath them a sadder desolation, because it fell upon that which is immortal.

Memory is man's only store-house of truth. Attention is the guard or sentinel which keeps it; and, while the sentinel is drowsy, or the guard is seeking rest, time steals in upon the treasures, and, by repeated larcenies, robs him of his jewels, and leaves him to poverty, perhaps insolvency of mind. Knowledge among men is like health or riches; it ebbs and flows, and sometimes takes to itself wings and flies away.

We conceive of Divine knowledge very differently. Let us speak with modesty, however, when we differ from one most eminent and worthy, whose opinion our remarks here call in question. Blessed be the memory of Adam Clarke, whose very errors are almost hallowed by the purity of his motives, and the sanctity of his life. But it is not necessary to hallow his errors. His virtues alone are sure to win as much of human admiration as a mortal should receive, and his errors are all needed to temper it. He suggests that God's omniscience consists not in actually knowing all things, but in the ability to know them; just as his omnipotence consists, not in actually doing all things, but in an ability to do them. As God can do many things which he does not choose to do, so he supposes that God can know many things which he does not choose to know. We reply to this suggestion:

1. The Scriptures never assert that God *does* all things; but they do assert that God *knows* all things.

2. The Scriptures proclaim the suspension of God's *acts;* but they nowhere hint at a suspension of God's *knowledge.*

3. The word omniscience, in its etymology, does not signify *ability* to know, but actual knowledge; whereas the word omnipotence, on the contrary, does not signify actually *doing*, but mere *ability to do.*

4. Omniscience and omnipotence are, therefore, improperly compared, for the purpose of illustrating the former by the latter.

5. Omniscience and Omnipresence should be compared, as they are resembling attributes. None will for a moment suppose that God can withdraw his essential presence from any portion of the universe, by choosing to be no longer Omnipresent. But the science and presence of God are coëxtensive. He can no more limit the one than the other. His science depends on his presence; and so long as he is Omnipresent, he must be Omniscient also. These attributes can not be severed. It follows, therefore, that God's knowledge is as permanent as it is extensive. It is not only infinite, but it is immutable. All states are present to his mind. Past and future, temporal and eternal, are known by a vision as clear and certain as that which scans the passing present. With God the past is not remembered. With God the future is not anticipated. To God all things are near—nothing is remote. He is every-where, and of course all things are equally proximate to him in place. He fills all eternity, and of course all events are equally proximate to him in period. His knowledge, then, unlike the creature's, hath no change by loss or recovery. It ebbs not while he sleeps by night, to flow again when he wakes by day. It is subject to no waning or waxing influences. This ocean is tideless and eternal. It embraces and retains forever and ever the infinite of space and the infinite of duration. "O the depth of the riches of this knowledge!"

VI. The *method* of the Divine knowledge constitutes it rich. On such a theme it behooves us to entertain no thoughts unless they are devout and reverent. Yet it is not profane to infer from the Bible and from God's omnipresence, that God knows all things by direct perception. His knowledge is not by effort of mind. It is spontaneous, like his own existence. It is acquired by no reasoning process. To reason is to seek for unknown truth; and as no truth was ever hidden from God, he can have no occasion to reason. The glance of his eye demonstrates and analyzes every thing.

How different is it with man! Our knowledge is sought with painful diligence, and is acquired by gradual discoveries. We creep like the sloth, through fields of truth, scarcely perceiving the diamond treasures which sparkle around like lights from eternity. If we gather them up, it is so unskillfully that their gems are obscure in the multitude of rubbish; and the acquisition is so scanty and impure, that we almost doubt the utility of our toil. We climb the steeps of Science by the toilsome paths of demonstration and induction. And often, as we are entering the vestibule of her temple, a careless step precipitates us from the height, into a depth proportioned to our giddy elevation. Or that temple scenery is the creation of a dream, and, just as we hoped to see the beauty of its courts, the vapory show vanishes away, scornful alike of our hopes and our toils. When the artisan would erect a splendid mansion, he proceeds to the wood or the quarry, selects his materials, and fashions them for use. Then he lays his broad foundation, and upon it erects the superstructure. So do we, in building up the soul. We go for materials to the fields of nature; draw out, by intuition and analysis, the facts and postulates which constitute our firm foundation. Demonstration, induction, or slow-progressing argument, rears the superstructure, ornate, perhaps, with decorations of a chastened eloquence.

Did God proceed thus in the creation? He said, "Let there be light, and there was light." All his creative acts were as simple as this. For six successive periods, mandate followed mandate; and the firmament above—the earth with its gathered waters and fruitful soils—its animated surface, atmosphere, and oceans—crowned at last with its new-born heir and lord, arose by the enchantment of a Divine invocation, such as called to its birth the bright morning of the universe. And be assured that the vision of the Godhead is as simple as his action. As he made he saw and pronounced all very good; not from any experiment of their merit, but by the mere analysis of vision. He saw all things. Seeing, he knows. His omnipresence explains, as far as possible, the fact of his universal intuition. He is present to all things—present in all things, and must, therefore, know all things by a direct and most intimate apprehension of them. "O the depth of the riches of this knowledge!"

VII. The knowledge of God is rich *in utility*. Divine knowledge is not a fruitless field—a barren waste. It affords ample and infinite productions. But its fruits are neither poisonous nor bitter. They are sweet and wholesome, like the pure and balmy air, which bears upon its wings both health and fragrance. The boundless treasures of Divine knowledge are all subsidized by infinite benevolence, in the glorious work of diffusing happiness. God's benevolence is the source of all the happiness which the universe contains; and his knowledge is the channel for its dispersion over the fields of the universe.

We call that man merciful whose charities relieve the sufferings of the distressed. This relief God could accomplish by blotting the miserable from the fair creation, and terminating their pain and their existence together. But Divine charity seeks to do more than relieve distress. It would impart unutterable joy, and render the states of creatures not merely tolerable, but unspeakably and eternally blissful. This is what the apostle means by the wisdom of God. Knowledge and benevolence commingled, flowing forth in confluent streams, prolific of life, intelligence, and rapture, in constant and boundless diffusion, constitute the wisdom of the infinite mind.

And now, who can contemplate such a mind?—rich in the knowledge of all that can be known, conversant with all that is fixed or moving, magnificent or minute, in the illimitable circle of this creation. Who can contemplate that mind, diffusing raptures pure as God's nature, and lasting as God's eternity, among the intelligences which swarm in worlds around the everlasting throne—who can contemplate such a mind in its infinite beauties, attractions, and glories, and not exclaim, with emotions of unutterable transport, "O the depth of the riches, both of the wisdom and knowledge of God?"

XV.

THE GOODNESS OF GOD.

"*There is none good but one, that is God.*" Matthew xix, 17.

THIS is, probably, the most interesting truth in the universe. It is interesting in all minds, and will be interesting in all eternity. Yet the thousands who accredit this truth are indifferent to its appeal, and resist its sanctifying influence. They confess it with the very lips which are accustomed to disparage and blaspheme Jehovah. Such persons are unhappy. "God is good;" his providence is merciful, his redeeming Son bears to them the blessings of the cross, yet they are unhappy. But it is not so in all places of God's dominion. There is another world, filled with life and intelligence, where this doctrine in its illustrations forms a perpetual heaven. And why does not that which is the parent of beauty and blessedness before the throne of God, imparadise this world? Has not the same Almighty goodness created earth and heaven? Are not men, as well as angels, the production of God's hand? Why, then, does this blessed attribute, shining in brilliant revelations upon both these worlds of life, inspire the one with overflowing rapture, and affect the other with painful and wrathful retributions? This question shall not escape our notice; but that we may approach it in proper order, and be prepared for its discussion, we will proceed to the following inquiries:

I. What is intended by the goodness of God?

II. What evidence is there of his goodness?

III. How may his goodness profit us?

I. By the goodness of God we understand, generally, his *benevolence, or good-will.* It consists of a disposition to promote the happiness of his creatures. This disposition is, by theological writers, called benevolence, and in the Scriptures is generally denominated goodness, or love. In the present discourse we shall, for convenience, and without regard to philological precision, use the terms goodness, benevolence, and love as synonymous.

That we may better understand the nature of this attribute, we will observe that God is *essentially good.* His creatures are some of them in possession of moral goodness. But their goodness is an accident. They can exist without it. They can reject it, and assume another and an opposite moral character, and still live. But God is essentially good; moral goodness is essential to his very being. It is a vital principle in the constitution of the Godhead. He must cease to be if he would cease to be good.

Again, God is *perpetually good.* If his goodness is essential it can not be subject to intermission, else his very being would be subject to intermission. Take away that which is essential to life, and you take away life itself. But the goodness of God is essential to his being; therefore, take away his goodness and you take away his being; that is, you annihilate him. But God is immortal, and, therefore, the universe professes in him a sovereign of perpetual goodness or love.

God's goodness is *blended with unerring wisdom.* Creature benevolence often fails to accomplish any thing toward the happiness of those whom it seeks to serve and to bless. Its aims are charitable, but its plans are indiscreet. But the goodness of God is as suitable in all its plans as it is generous in all its aims. It is said, "Cursed is the man that trusteth in man." Why cursed? Because the treachery of man renders him unworthy of confidence, and his ignorance incapacitates him for a safe and judicious exercise of even good intentions. It is said, "Blessed is he that maketh the Lord his trust." Why blessed? Because God always sincerely desires our happiness, and is infinitely wise to detect the means of promoting it. But the ultimate trust seems here more especially intended, of which infinite goodness and wisdom alone are worthy.

The goodness of God is always associated with his *power.* What he is disposed to do he can do. What his love prompts, his wisdom provides for, or his power executes. Not so with man. His goodness is often allied to impotence, and his yearning desire to avert evil or impart happiness may waste itself in empty wishes and regrets.

The goodness of God is *diligently active.* Creature benevolence is often unproductive. It is sometimes checked and smothered by base passions, and is often palsied by unworthy indolence. It says to the hungry, "Be ye fed," and to the naked, "Be ye clothed," and there pauses. But God hath a beneficent hand, as well as a benevolent heart. That hand is constantly employed in liberal ministrations to his creatures. It dispenses food to the hungry and vestments to the naked. It busies itself in a thousand enterprises to multiply and magnify the joys of all obedient creatures.

Once more, the goodness of God is *exclusive.* The text declares "There is none good but God." All the goodness or love in the universe is his. It flows from him as its source, and returns to him as its end. All holy affection depends on him for its motive and its inspiration. Blot out the moral goodness which is in God, and from God, and what would there be to inspire it? Creature goodness is constituted of streams from God, the infinite fountain. Destroy the fountain and the streams perish with it, and nothing of the nature of moral goodness remains in the universe.

II. Having considered, in a few words, the nature of this attribute, we shall proceed to notice some *evidence* of God's goodness.

And here let us commence at home. Man himself bears about him an impressive inscription of this truth, an inscription of such curious and wondrous execution, that the storms and ravages of six thousand years have not been able to efface it; an inscription wrought upon his body, written on his mind, and impressed upon his heart. How is it that this outward frame, composed with such delicacy, displays such strength? How is such apparent simplicity blended with such capacity for such various action, and posture, and suffering? Whence came unto it the power of the muscle, the sensibility of the nerve, the convenience of the members ; the ear, drinking in the melodies of the universe ; the eye, refreshed by its divinely penciled beauties ; the palate, regaled with its ten thousand sweets ; and all these blended with the breathing of its everlasting fragrance? Whence came the gift of sweet discourse, by which, in words, or anthems half divine, fancy sketches a thousand glowing scenes, and pours back upon the soul a new and reflex rapture? "Whence came they!" They are the mere dispersions of infinite benevolence.

But these are only the mechanism of the temple, with its decorated openings and outer courts. Enter its retreats and survey the occupant of the unconsecrated mansion. Here dwells immortal mind, and displays by its rich inventions and enchanting combinations the generous character of its Author. How comes it that this mind is not uniform, nor yet confused in its perpetual and unguarded actions? Wherein consists its strange capacity for blessing and for bliss? How is it that memory gathers joys from the past, that hope pursues and seizes those in prospect, and that these, joined to the fruition of the present, swell the raptures of the soul to overflowing? Is not this a benevolent economy, and does it not display affecting proof of the goodness of God?

But enter the most holy place of this temple. Approach the altar of human affections. O, could you have seen it in its original splendor! But as it is, polluted, profaned, and prostrate in the dust, it indicates the kindness of its Architect. Half concealed beneath the rubbish which profanes it, you may still trace the image of the Godhead in the constitutional structure, ardor, and high adaptations of man's affectional nature. How violent and raging are the passions of the soul! Contemplate the mighty energies of its love and hatred, its desire and aversion, its sordid covetousness, its soul-consuming envy, its restless vengeance, its towering ambition whose vigorous arm grasps earth, grasps heaven, and longs to hold in the vassalage of conquest the thrones below and the thrones above.

Do you say that passions, so base in tendency, and in vigor so infernal, betray the malice, not the love of the Creator? O sirs, you are now forgetting that God formed them "in the beauty of holiness," and gave to them a tendency as pure and blissful as he did a strength efficacious and ennobling. You are now forgetting how that purity was solicited by Satan and yielded up by man, or all the energy of passions, foul and base, and painful, would have been the energy of a Godlike virtue, pure, and blissful, and immortal. You are now forgetting that such they may become, through the power of the Gospel, and of that renewing Spirit which applies the Gospel to the heart. Remember this, and then say, what can more plainly indicate the goodness of God than to find in ourselves, fashioned in our very constitutions, channels deep, and broad, and abiding, supplied, if we solicit it, with streams of holy rapture gushing from the fullness of God's benevolence and love?

But pass to other scenes. Need we tell you that the whole visible creation bears impressive testimony to the Divine goodness? True, man's rebellion has provoked a curse from heaven to derange its order, to blast its beauty, and to draw a veil over its dazzling glory. But in its very fadings there is a charm, in its manifest disorder a purpose and an aim; and a veiled but awe-inspiring glory is forever seen beaming through the cloud. There are a charm, a purpose, and a glory in the light, which sets forth creation to the eye, in the still, or stirring air, which, through the several senses, pours rich perfumes and sweetly swelling harmonies in upon the soul, to entrance it as with visions of a heavenly paradise. There are a charm, a purpose, and a glory, in nature's changeful moods, which thrusts out the elder seasons from the family of time, and bring in by sure and faultless birth infant Spring, youthful Summer, and matronly Autumn, pouring their varied graces around, till morose Winter intrudes again, not to stay and frown forever, but to melt and fly at the return of vernal smiles and ardors. The cheerful day uttereth speech, and the gloomy night showeth knowledge of God's eternal love. For in action and in rest there is a blessing for the creature, and in that blessing there is a proof of God's benevolence.

But while traveling through creation for proofs of God's benevolence we alight upon a scene at which we pause—a scene which arrests not only man, but angel and archangel—a scene which attracts the seraph from his height, and the demon from his depth—a scene which fixes the gaze of every world but this—a scene which will forever challenge the devout or profane attention of heaven and hell. Approach and behold—while I draw aside the curtain and unveil the sacred mystery. See there! The altar, the victim, the agony of sacrifice, the sprinkling blood and water gushing from a heart all pure and palpitating in the writhings of death, the rays of God's benevolence circling and converging to intense and overpowering ardors till the victim is consumed! Creation groans! But on his bloody cross, and on his crimsoned vestments, and on his dripping hands, and on his gory heart, I read in flaming characters, "*God—so—loved—the—world!*"

III. Having offered some evidence of the goodness of God, we proceed to inquire *how his goodness may profit us.*

Do not suppose that because God is good we must inevitably be happy. Nothing is more evident than that God may be benevolent, and yet his creatures be inexpressibly miserable. If otherwise, if the benevolence of Deity is inconsistent with the misery of his creatures, then the doctrine of God's benevolence is false. If they are inconsistent, it is far less absurd to infer the malevolence of God from the misery of man, than it is to infer the happiness of man from the benevolence of God. If they are inconsistent, we must contradict the benevolence of God, for the misery of creatures can not be contradicted.

But they are not inconsistent. We know both from what we see and what we feel, that creatures are miserable. Of God's benevolence there is sufficient proof not only to convince, but to overwhelm us, and induce our cordial devotion to his service. And this is God's design in all the displays of his love toward us. His "goodness is to lead us to repentance," to rouse in us the same affectionate regard for him which he feels toward us. If it can accomplish this, if the love of God can beget in us a love for him in return, then it will have made us happy. But in no other way can the goodness of God affect us with any choice delights. His love can benefit us but little unless we reciprocate the sentiment. His goodness can profit us but little unless we reciprocate the principle.

How vain is it for the sinner to boast of the love, of the goodness of God! How vainly do any of us hope for any permanent advantages from that love, unless we love in return! By the constitution of our nature, if love be not reciprocated, if it awaken in us only enmity or disgust, or aversion, it becomes a source of disquiet and unhappiness. Especially is this the case when the rejection of proffered love involves a rejection of moral obligation. In such a case it needs no positive inflictions to produce wretchedness; it results from the laws of our being.

Did you ever chance to be loved by one of your peers, and feel your heart all chilled and pained by the unwelcome tokens of that affection for which you could return only silence and indifference? And was there to you any comfort of that love? Comfort! No. When that love sought you out; solicited your attention, craved your communion, and exhibited its sincere, and ardent, and deathless offerings, it was to you an irksome state. You were burdened and distressed by those offerings. Willingly would you have escaped from the society of your lover to the company of your bitterest foe on earth, and welcomed all his malicious persecutions. Now consider the eternal God in the place of that loving, but rejected friend. If such is the heart of man with man, such is the heart of man with God.

True it is that "God is good"—is pure and everlasting love. Even you, sinner, are an object of his intense concern. But mark the fruits of his love. If God will allow you the means of profane gratification, a gratification which implies perfect hostility toward him on your part; if he will keep himself aloof, never intruding upon you his claims, his presence, or his fellowship, you are well pleased with so convenient a love as this. In such circumstances you fully consent that God is good. But let the Almighty insist upon your tolerating his presence, and choosing his society and service, and his love will become the object of your utmost aversion. He will be to you like the discarded suitor, whose rich donations were highly prized and gracefully encouraged until he offered himself also, and then it was conceived that this incumbrance exceeded the value of all the gifts. Worse than this. You are like the unloving child of a loving parent. You loathe his presence and scorn his friendship, and requite hatred for his love. Thus do you entreat Almighty God. He of whose goodness and love you boast, presses himself on your notice by his Word, his ministers, his providence, his Spirit; but does his love delight and charm you? Alas! his love is to your soul bitter as death, whenever its expressions become near and intimate. If he will just keep himself out of sight, will afford to you the means of impure indulgence, will permit you to be a brute in the midst of pleasures, earthly, sensual, and devilish; if this, your "divine friend and lover," will never solicit from you the least attention or regard; if he will permit you to prosecute a course of treachery and rebellion toward his person and government without retribution or rebuke, you are charmed with such a love as this. But let him approach you, (as soon he must in one form or another,) and propose to you a pure and everlasting fellowship, which shall exclude all base and sensual delights, and you shall be miserable. Yes, the society of that God whose love you boast shall be to you, as a sinner, a sort of hell.

And now we are prepared to answer the question proposed in the exordium of this discourse. It was asked, "why the Divine goodness, revealed so brilliantly to earth and heaven, should inspire the one with overflowing rapture, and affect the other with painful retributions?" The reason may now be evident. Two things produce the choicest raptures of the heavenly state, namely, mutual love, and its resulting fellowships. In that happy world God loves and is beloved. This is what makes heaven so desirable. This is what renders it essentially superior to this world. But this world is painfully affected by the goodness, or love of God, because here God is not beloved. He is here. He displays his presence all around us. "In him we live." He makes us sensible of his presence and love. But he is not beloved. This surely is enough to curse and torture our sinful race. To be compelled to accompany with God, to see his everlasting beauty, and feel his everlasting presence, and yet not love, but hate him! It is a kind of hell. And such a hell is earth, for here God is not beloved. Not beloved! God infinitely lovely, yet not beloved! God infinitely loving, yet not beloved! God loving us in heaven, loving us on earth, seeking us, suffering, agonizing, bleeding, dying, rising, interceding for us, and yet not beloved! Be silent, tongue. Though all is true, it is truth too horrid to be uttered. O, sinner, its consequences will be too horrid to endure!

Let the Christian remember that God is good—let the Christian remember that God is love. Let the sinner, too, remember that God is love; but let him not forget that love unrequited, abused, scorned, *becomes only a "consuming fire."*

XVI.

CHRISTIAN BAPTISM.

FIRST DISCOURSE.

THE MINISTERS—THE SIGNIFICANCY—THE SUBJECTS.

"*Go ye therefore and teach all nations, baptizing them in the name of the Father, and of the Son, and of the Holy Ghost; teaching them to observe all things whatsoever I command you.*" Matthew xxviii, 19, 20.

"*And he said unto them, Go ye into all the world and preach the Gospel to every creature. He that believeth and is baptized shall be saved, and he that believeth not shall be damned.*" Mark xvi, 15, 16.

OUR aim, in this discussion, will be practical utility, and we shall invite your attention to the ministers, the significancy, and the subjects of baptism, and

I. THE MINISTERS OF THIS ORDINANCE.

This has become important on account of the views recently inculcated by a gentleman of respectable talents and acquirements, and a public teacher of religion. It has been urged, as you very well know, that all the baptized are qualified and authorized to baptize others—that the Christian ministry belongs in common to all the members of Christ's visible Church. Nothing, then, but a loose and changeable policy forbids the most ignorant disciple to act as a public proclaimer of the Gospel and administer its sacred ordinances. In opposition to this disorderly opinion and practice, I array the language of the text. It contains the commission to teach and to baptize. This commission was not delivered to the body of the disciples. The narrative represents Jesus as in the midst of the eleven apostles, and of them, only, saying, "Go ye into all the world."

By consulting all the evangėlists the reader will be convinced that the commission was limited to the apostles, and to such others, in subsequent ages, as should be sent by Jesus, especially moved by his Spirit. The method by which our Savior preserves in the Church an authorized ministry is exemplified in the case of Paul. He declares that God, counting him faithful, "*put* him into the ministry." From that day to this, God has continued to call some to this arduous service. They, like Paul, can vindicate their apostleship by declaring that God met them in the way, and by appealing to the *fruits* of their labors—the visible seals of their ministry. Christ is now the only source of all authority to teach and baptize. It flows *not* from his Church or others of his ministry, though it may and should be recognized and accredited by them. The lofty claims of some reputed ministers to confer this authority are unfounded. The commission in the text warrants the exercise of no such functions as of Divine right, and when they are exercised it should be considered, as in our own Church, a matter of discreet ecclesiastical policy, and not by a Divine warrant. The commission in the text does not read go, teach, baptize, and confer on men of another generation authority to do the same. No such provision is made by the commission to preserve a line of apostolic succession, and found and edify hierarchy, prelacies, sees, or papacies. Neither Peter, nor any one of his fellows, is endowed by this commission with any peculiar prerogatives. The commission sends them all to one work, and dismisses them on terms of equality. When Paul joins them, he is their peer. As this is the perpetual commission of Christ's ministers, how could the meekness of sanctified minds infer from it the essential imparity of those ministers, so that while some are to go and baptize, others are to sit in the seat of Christ and make apostles for the service of the Church. I am aware that some in favor of so gross a heresy urge those words—"As the Father hath sent me, even so send I you." But from these words they might as well infer that as the Father sent Christ to be crucified, so *they* must be crucified.

The heavenly oracle will guard the docile on this point against both extremes. It will show us the folly of that religious plebeianism which puts the vessels of the sanctuary in every man's hands, yet it will betray the unfounded pretensions of lofty dignitaries, who, by a reckless torturing of Scripture, have originated distinctions among Christ's ministers which subserve no other end than the gratification of an ambition so profane that it stops not to glut itself upon the sacramental provisions of the sanctuary. We insist, then, that none are authorized to minister baptism but such as are called and sent of God.

But here the question may arise, "Suppose I have been baptized by one not sent of God, is the baptism valid?" I answer, not if the fault was yours. If you were of age, and sought baptism from an administrator who did not bear along with him the credentials of his office, you are guilty, and your baptism is invalid. You are bound to use due discretion in seeking, both for yourself and for your children, a minister of the ordinance who you had reason to believe was duly authorized by Christ. You may ask by what rule you are to judge? I answer, the Church is to be his voucher to you. You are to seek that minister, in some branch of the Church, which holds to a divinely authorized ministry. For where Christ by his Spirit calls and moves a man to his work, he generally moves the Church to recognize him as a laborer in the vineyard. When, therefore, you apply to such a one for baptism, you have used your best discretion, and are acquitted of all blame. "But suppose, after all my precaution, it should turn out that I was deceived, and that the administrator was not an authorized minister of Jesus Christ?" I answer, while you remained in ignorance of this fact, your sincerity and good intention would be accepted of God in lieu of legal formality; but, upon better information, it would become your duty to seek baptism according to the due form and order. David's first attempt to remove the ark to Zion was not accepted, though done in good intention, because they did it not "after the due order." 1 Chron. xv, 13. The sin of ignorance brings no guilt while the ignorance remains and is involuntary, but when knowledge of the fault comes, then instant reparation must be made, or guilt fastens upon the conscience. In the law of Moses, in such cases, "where the sin was known," (Lev. iv, 14,) the offender was required to bring his sacrifice of expiation.

But if you go into communities (called Churches) which deny that there is a divinely appointed order of ministers in the Church, and where baptism is administered (as it often is in a society of recent origin) by laymen, or lay-children, (as for any principle among them which forbids it,) and submit to the ordinances among them, your baptism is doubtless invalid, and of no more religious virtue than the Summer ablutions of playful boys.

Christ's institution gives baptism its validity. It must be administered, therefore, by such as he appoints. The water and the words of the sacrament are of no more importance than the authority of the administrator. The conclusion is, therefore, that none can lawfully administer the sacrament of baptism except those who are called and authorized as were the apostles.

II. The significancy of baptism.

Baptism is a sacrament, and as such it has two intentions or uses. It is a *sign* and a *seal.* As a sign it indicates that inward cleansing, which is accomplished by the blood and Spirit of Christ. Thus we read in Hebrews x, 22, where the blood of Jesus is represented as a purifier of the conscience, and is connected with baptism. And again, Titus iii, 4–6: "But after the kindness and love of God our Savior toward man appeared, not by works of righteousness that we had done, but according to his mercy he saved us, by the washing of regeneration, and the renewing of the Holy Ghost which he shed on us abundantly through Jesus Christ our Savior." Here is an allusion to baptism by water, and its signification is declared to be the purification of the soul by the Spirit shed on us abundantly through Jesus Christ.

Again, Isaiah, in a strain of evangelical prophecy, chapter xliv, says, "I will pour water upon him that is thirsty, and floods upon the dry ground; I will pour my Spirit upon thy seed, and my blessing upon thy offspring." The first clause of this text is a plain reference to the emblem, water baptism, the second unequivocally promises the inward cleansing or the baptism of the Spirit.

Of the same import is Ezekiel, chapter xxxvi: "Then will I sprinkle clean water upon you, and ye shall be clean. And I will put my Spirit within you and cause you to walk in my statutes." The blood and the Spirit of Christ—that to cleanse from guilt, and this, from corruption—are always spoken of as the agents of man's moral purification. Both were prefigured in the Jewish ritual, and both are signified in the sacrament of baptism. Hence the exhortation, "Arise and be baptized, and wash away (that is, symbolically) thy sins, calling on the name of the Lord," (that is, that the thing itself, shadowed forth by that emblem, may be accomplished.) Here baptism is certainly viewed as a sign of remission by the blood of Jesus Christ, which cleanseth from all sin. We think this sufficient to show the candid hearer that baptism is significant of inward purification by the blood and the Spirit of Christ.

But we said that this sacrament is a *seal* as well

as a sign. What, then, is its sealing efficacy? We answer, unhesitatingly, that in receiving it by faith, and in a due regard to the obligations which it imposes, the receiver, or subject, is secured of the blessings which it shadows. A seal implies a covenant, and is the confirmation of the covenant by its parties. When thus confirmed, the obligations of the covenant are sacredly binding on the parties, and can not be unfulfilled but by a tortuous breach of the covenant. God will not break that covenant which is sealed by the sacrament of baptism. If from thenceforth the baptized person "renounces the devil and all his works," and unreservedly "takes the Lord to be his God," the blood and the Spirit will be applied to his heart. The consequence is, that baptism invariably insures the blessing which it signifies whenever it is partaken in faith, and its obligations are sacredly regarded. The only reason why the spiritual regeneration is not always experimentally connected with the symbolical—the baptism of the Holy Ghost with the baptism of water—is because the water baptism is not mixed with faith. When the Eunuch received baptism he believed with all his heart. What was the consequence? He was so blessed that he "went on his way rejoicing."

We do not doubt, however, but it is with baptism as with prayer—its blessings are often held in abeyance, or are reserved awhile, being confirmed indeed, but not immediately conveyed to the possession of the baptized. In multitudes, also, the great blessings shadowed by the sacrament are first sought and obtained, and the sacrament is received by the applicant, in token of a purification already accomplished. So it was with Cornelius and his associates, of whom Peter said, "Can any man forbid water that these should not be baptized, who have received the Holy Ghost as well as we?" As to the sealing efficacy of baptism, then, we repeat that it *insures* to the Scripturally baptized, who believe and who keep the covenant, all the blessings which the sacrament shadows forth.

This, however, is the *invisible* efficacy of baptism. It has besides a visible use. As it shadows inward purification, which is a prerequisite of admission into the invisible Church, so it very properly stands in the Christian system as an open initiatory ordinance, introducing its subject into the visible Church, and making him, in the sight of men, no longer an alien, but "a fellow-citizen with the saints and of the household of God." Then, as a citizen of Zion, he can claim all its privileges. He is subject to its laws, must yield to its discipline, must treat its economy, and the ministers of that economy, with due regard, and watchfully subserve its interests, as knowing that they are his own interests, and that the covenant which he sealed with his God in baptism demands this at his hands. And, above all, he must embrace all opportunities to partake of the remaining sacrament, the Lord's Supper, so that, as by baptism he was born, *emblematically*, into the holy kingdom, he may, by feeding *mystically* upon the blood and body of Christ, grow up into him in all things. For by these symbols, two covenants, the one for our birth and entrance upon life, the other for our growth and the perfection of that life, are sealed; and if we proudly and wantonly despise the covenants and its seals, our pride and wantonness may prove our undoing.

III. THE SUBJECTS OF THIS SACRAMENT.

The subjects of baptism are plainly indicated in the New Testament. "All nations," and "every creature," are the two phrases designating these subjects. These phrases, it will be perceived, are of *great*, and, indeed, of universal extension. They include every thing that hath the form and the attributes of humanity.

But great efforts are made to narrow it down to a portion of the human family. We shall, for the sake of an immediate approach to a point of so great interest, lay down the following proposition:

The commission warrants the ministers of Christ to baptize, as well as to teach, men, women, and children. From the language of the commission, by which the ministers of Christ are directed to bestow the ordinance upon "all nations," and upon "every creature," one would think it impossible to question this proposition. And yet it *is* questioned, and they who embrace in "the nations" little children are deemed, by some true Christians, derelict in doctrine and in practice. As men and women are admitted by all to be embraced in the commission, we shall not speak of them, but will proceed to consider the claims of *children* to the sacrament of baptism.

1. We urge their claims from various Scriptures: (Matt. xxviii,) "Go ye, therefore, and teach all nations, *baptizing* them"—"*teaching* them." It has been

objected to infant baptism that in this text the disciples are commanded to teach all nations, and then to baptize them; and, as infants can not be taught, they must not be baptized. This difficulty is easily disposed of. Whoever will obtain a Bible with marginal translations, or philological notes on the common translation, will find that the text reads thus: "Go ye, therefore, and *disciple* all nations, baptizing them," etc. This is the correct rendering from the Greek. The English reader, who finds the verb "teach" before baptize, and the participle "teaching" immediately after it, would conclude that the same word was used in the Greek Testament in both places. This, however, is not the case. Go ye, therefore, and "*disciple*" — (in Greek, *matheteusate*,) — or "*initiate* as pupils," all nations, baptizing, etc. Then "*didaskontes*," "teaching," not *matheteuontes*, as it would have been if the same thing was to be done after as before baptizing them; but "*didaskontes*"— teaching them. The word, improperly rendered teach in the first part of the text, means to admit as a pupil; that in the middle of the text means to *instruct* the pupil thus admitted. How exactly is this direction suited to the condition of infancy? "Go and disciple them," "*matheteusate*," "put them into Christ's school," then "*didaskontes*," teaching them the science of that school. That is, as the minds open and enlarge, occupy them with the truths of the Gospel, and give every rising thought, as far as possible, an inclination toward the cross. No language could be invented better suited to convey the impression that children are the objects of the apostolic commission, are to be initiated as pupils by baptism, and then be taught the lessons of Christ's school. If the term nations does not embrace children, we would ask what generic term in the language does embrace them?

Another text from the Gospel by St. Mark xvi, 15, 16: "Go ye into all the world, and preach the Gospel to every creature. He that believeth and is baptized shall be saved, and he that believeth not shall be damned."

The terms of the commission embrace "every creature." As to the objection so often raised by the opponents of infant baptism, that inasmuch as infants can not believe they must not be baptized, there is this to be observed. The language does not propose faith as a condition of baptism, but it proposes faith and baptism as two conditions of salvation. Analyze the proposition: "He that believeth and is baptized shall be saved." Here is not a series of conditions and promises. It is one promise with *two* conditions. The text does not read, "He that believeth shall be baptized, and he that is baptized shall be saved."

To illustrate the independence of baptism as it regards faith, suppose a teacher should say to his pupil, "Get a lesson in geography and a lesson in arithmetic and you shall have a medal." The medal would depend on both lessons, but the lesson in arithmetic would not depend on that in geography. Nor need the child get the lesson in geography first because it happens to be mentioned first. Now, faith and baptism are to salvation what the two lessons are to the medal. You may say that baptism, then, as well as faith, is essential to salvation. I answer, he who denies infant baptism is accountable for that. They *are* necessary to salvation on his principles, not on mine. His principles carried out, will send all that die in infancy to hell; but mine will not. Mine will admit them to heaven, and, of course, will admit them to baptism; but his excludes them from baptism, and, much more, from heaven. If he shrinks from the inevitable consequences of his own principles and says, "These words only mean that the *adult* must believe in order to be saved"—I rējoin, these words mean that the adult only must believe in order to be baptized. And he must not use this text to guard the font of baptism against little children, unless he will use it also to guard heaven against little children. If it shuts them out of any thing, it is certainly heaven. What! when one speaks of baptizing infants, shall I seize this text with polemic greediness, and forbid him, because the child has not faith? And again, when he talks of children being damned for want of faith, shall I reject this text as the greedy do a scalding mouthful, and insist that it has "nothing to do with infants?"

> "We all agree
> To call it freedom when ourselves are free."

Surely you may perceive, without any severe study, that if these words subject any person, young or old, believing or unbelieving, to any loss, it is the loss of salvation much more than of baptism. The pupil might get his lesson in arithmetic without getting his lesson in geography; but without both lessons he could not receive the medal. So in regard to this text, (and we now speak of this without reference to other Scriptures,) an infant might be baptized without faith, even though he could not be saved without it. How much more may the infant be baptized without faith, when without faith all agree that it may be saved! And here I have the best opportunity which my brief compass will afford to apply the principle contained in this text and its exposition to many portions of Scripture. The principle is this: Faith is a Scriptural condition of baptism and of salvation in all adults—in all who are capable of believing—but it is no condition of either baptism or salvation in infants who are incapable of believing. Take this principle along with you, and apply it to any example in the New Testament, and it will clear up all objections to infant baptism. For example, Philip said to the Eunuch who sought baptism, "If thou believest with all thine heart thou mayest." To whom did he say this? To an adult. And because he was an adult, and was capable of believing, he could say no less, according to the principle which we have laid down. But would you infer from this that infants may not be baptized because they can not believe? Then consider another case, and see how you will maintain consistency. On a certain occasion the jailer who had kept Paul and Silas, being roused by an earthquake, fell down before them and said, "Sirs, what must I do to be saved?" They answered, "Believe on the Lord Jesus Christ and thou shalt be saved." Now, would you infer from this that *infants* must believe on the Lord Jesus Christ in order to be saved? If you urge the objection to infant baptism in the former case, you must admit the objection to infant salvation in the latter case. These examples serve to illustrate the satisfactory result of applying the principle laid down above, namely, that "faith is a condition of baptism and of salvation, in adults, but is not a condition of either baptism or salvation in infants." Now, as "*all nations*" and "*every creature*" are the terms which denote the objects of the apostolic commission, you must find some language in Holy Writ to exclude infants specifically, or you are bound to consider them as embraced in that commission. Who ever heard it questioned that infants were a part of the nation to which they belonged? Did not God consider them a part of Nineveh, when, mostly on their account, he spared the whole nation? Were they not considered a part of Israel when God entered into covenant with that people in the land of Moab? (Deut. xxix, 10–12.)

2. This leads us to argue the validity of infant baptism, secondly, from the fact that in all the leading covenants made with mankind, infants were embraced, and shared in all the benefits of those covenants. The first covenant was with Adam in his state of innocence. It secured to him and to his posterity the Divine blessing on condition of obedience. We find the blessing recorded in the first chapter of Genesis: "And God blessed them, and God said unto them, Be fruitful and multiply," etc. This with the subsequent prohibition as a condition of retaining the blessing, formed a covenant between Adam and his Creator. That covenant had a seal or sacrament, namely, the

fruit of the Tree of Life. This was consecrated by the will of God to some very sacred use. It was not like the other trees of the garden, for the common purpose of reflection. That it was sacramental we learn from the fact that it was too pure and excellent for the profane to approach and feed upon; therefore, after this fall, the sinning pair were driven from the garden, lest they should partake of its fruit and live forever.

A second covenant was made with Noah before the building of the ark. (Genesis vi, 18.) And the ark itself, which Noah built by the direction of God, seems to have had a sacramental import and to have been the seal of this covenant. (1 Peter iii, 20–22.) Another covenant was made with Noah after the Flood, and its sacrament was the rainbow. It pledged security from a second deluge. To this very day that covenant is of binding force; and to this very day nature in one of its aspects is a holy sacrament for the eye to feast upon. Never should we gaze at that celestial sign but we should view it, not merely as the most beautiful phenomenon in nature, but also as a perpetual seal of the bond which secures to us an immunity from the horrors of a universal deluge.

The next was the covenant made with Abraham, which was a covenant of grace, the very covenant under which we live, and by which we receive all the blessings of the grace of Jesus. The sacrament of this covenant was circumcision.

The next covenant which we shall mention is that which spared the first-born of Israel when the angel of death passed through the land and slew all the first-born of Egypt. Its sacrament was the Passover. And now, to go no further, from which of these covenants are children excluded, and which of their seals or sacraments was not designed for them? If Adam had remained obedient in Paradise, would his children have been excluded from the sacramental Tree of Life?

Were the children of Noah excluded from the ark, and from the benefits of the covenant? They were admitted for Noah's faith. Genesis vii, 1: "And God said unto Noah, Come thou and all thy house into the ark; for thee have I seen righteous before me." Were the children of Abraham excluded from the covenant of grace, and from the sacrament of circumcision? Genesis xvii, 10: "This is my covenant which ye shall keep between me and you, and thy seed after thee: Every manchild among you shall be circumcised." Were the children of the Israelites excluded from the Passover? Certainly not. So far from this, that every child who was of sufficient age to partake of food, was compelled to observe the Passover. This was the command of God: "Seven days shall there be no leaven found in your houses. For whosoever eateth that which is leavened, even that soul shall be cut off from the congregation. In all your habitations shall ye eat unleavened bread. And ye shall observe this thing for an ordinance to thee and to thy sons forever."

But we invite your attention, more particularly, to the passage already referred to in Deuteronomy xxix, 10–15: "Ye stand this day all of you before the Lord; your captains of your tribes, your elders, and your officers, with all the men of Israel, your *little ones*, your wives, . . . that thou shouldst enter into covenant with the Lord thy God, and into his oath, which the Lord thy God maketh with thee this day. . . . that he may be to thee a God. . . . Neither with you only do I make this covenant and this oath; but with him [children as well as others] that standeth with us this day before the Lord our God."

Whatever men may say, one thing is conclusively proven by the history of God's covenants with mankind; namely, that infants can stand in a covenant relation to God by the act of their parents. In the last instance, they did assume such a relation, for the fact is unequivocally asserted by God himself. So also in regard to the Abrahamic covenant, God commands that the seal of the covenant shall be imposed on the infant at eight days old. If the circumcised infant could not be a party to the covenant, this was as improper as it would be to write a deed on one sheet of paper, and in executing it, affix the authenticating seal to a different and to a blank sheet of paper. Or to change the illustration, it was like drawing up a covenant between A and B, whose names are inserted in the instrument, and then, in executing it, using the name of F, who is not a party to the covenant.

Would it be proper to use the royal seal of France on parchment which records a treaty between the United States and the Russian Autocrat? No more proper would it have been to put the seal of the covenant with Abraham upon the children of the family, when these children were not parties to the covenant.

Circumcision was the seal of a covenant which was fundamentally and essentially *our* covenant—the covenant of grace. This is positively affirmed by Paul in Romans ii, 17–24: "And if some of the branches be broken off, and thou being a wild olive-tree, wert graffed in among them, and with them partakest of the root and fatness of the olive-tree: boast not against the branches. But if thou boast, thou bearest not the root, but the root thee. Thou wilt say then, the branches were broken off, that I may be graffed in. Well; because of unbelief they were broken off, and thou standest by faith. Be not high-minded, but fear: for if God spared not the natural branches, take heed lest he also spare not thee. Behold, therefore, the goodness and severity of God: on them which fell, severity; but toward thee, goodness, if thou continue in his goodness; otherwise thou also shalt be cut off. And they also if they abide not still in unbelief, shall be graffed in: for God is able to graff them in again. For if thou wert cut out of the olive-tree, which is wild by nature, and wert graffed contrary to nature into a good olive-tree, how much more shall these, which be the natural branches, be graffed into their own olive-tree?"

What could more strikingly exhibit the unity of the Church and the identity of its covenants, from Abraham to the times of the apostle? The Abrahamic and Christian covenants are one olive-tree. The falling away of the Jews is the excision of a branch from that tree, and the conversion of the Gentiles is ingrafting them into the same stock from which the Jews were broken off. The Church and its covenants are one in the days of Abraham and of Christ, and as in the days of Abraham, so in the days of Christ and his apostles, children are to be brought within the purview of that covenant by the imposition of the sacramental seals; namely, by circumcision then, and by baptism now.

But if the identity of the Abrahamic and Christian covenants be denied, it matters not. Infant baptism, even then, stands on an immovable foundation. If the Christian covenant be a new covenant, differing ever so much from the Abrahamic, it contains the same provision in regard to children as did the Abrahamic. In proof of this, consider the language and behavior of Jesus toward children. He declares them to be members of the Church, Mark x, 13–16: "For of such is the kingdom of God." The kingdom of God, among the Jews, meant the Church on earth, or the Church in heaven. If Christ meant the Church in heaven, that was no reason why he should say, "Let them come unto me;" for it implied no attraction in their present character that those among them who died in infancy, or were converted in old age, would occupy seats in heaven. No. He meant that the Church on earth was composed of little children. The children which he then took in his arms bore in their bodies the token of his covenant. They were the children of the promise made to Abraham. The language, "Of such is the kingdom of heaven," must have been remarked by all of you, as implying that the kingdom of heaven is composed exclusively of children. Now, this is not the case with the beatific heaven, but it was a declaration which assorted most perfectly with the kingdom, or Church, on earth in our Savior's day. Then the subjects of that kingdom all assumed their citizenship in it by circumcision at eight days old. None of the children of Israel could defer their token of fealty later than this. To do so was fatal, and excluded them from the congregation of God's people. Now, in saying, "Of such is the kingdom of heaven," he does not mean that all in the Church are infants, but he means that all were infants at their entrance into the kingdom of heaven. He refers to their initiation, which always (except in some few instances of proselytism) occurred in their infancy. As if the husbandman should say to his servants, take care of the tender blades, for of such is the harvest; or as if the fruitist should say, guard and train the young shoots of the nursery, for of such are the fruits of the orchard. In the Church were none but such as had taken their membership therein during their earliest infancy—and infancy, therefore, was the hope of the Church. Well might Jesus rebuke those who proposed to shut out these infant disciples from his notice, and veil these budding honors of his vineyard from his eyes. Well might he say, "Suffer little children to come unto me, for of such is the kingdom of heaven." So far as I have read, this is a novel exposition of this passage; but it is certainly the most natural exposition, and strong reasons must be urged to set it aside.

Now recollect, that at the time Jesus uttered these

words, and claimed for the circumcised children the immunities of the Church, or kingdom of God, whatever in the Abrahamic covenant was (as some will affirm) contrary to, or inconsistent with, the Christian covenant had passed away. John, the forerunner of Christ, had accomplished his work, and the kingdom of Immanuel was then being set up. If the dispensations essentially differed, the Abrahamic was expiring, and the Christian was assuming its place. Yet, just then, to his own disciples who were to follow his words and example in their future ministry, he most solemnly, and in opposition to their apparent wishes, confirms the membership of little children in the Church. He rebukes their unadvised interposition, takes the children in his arms, and, laying his hands on them, pronounces the blessings of the covenant, sealed by circumcision, upon these infant disciples. Turn now to these very disciples who, in regard to children and the treatment they were to experience under the regimen of the Gospel, had received a lesson which they were most unlikely ever to forget. The vivid recollection of Christ's displeasure, when they rebuked the parents who brought their children to Jesus, would be likely to remain with them forever. If Peter, that rash man, who was so apt to commit indiscretions, was the offending disciple, as is probable, he would remember an occurrence which had so displeased his Lord, and he would remember, too, the saying of Jesus after the resurrection: "Feed my sheep and feed my lambs." Let us go forward, then, to the day of Pentecost, when Peter preached his first sermon, and see if there are any indications that these circumstances dwelt upon his mind. Should a Baptist minister, as has been the case, discover his error concerning children, and find that, like Peter, he had been laboring to keep them away from Christ, when Christ himself was striving to call them to him, he would make amends by preaching infant baptism in every sermon. So does Peter. The very first sermon contains provisions, not only for the sheep, but for the lambs: "Repent and be baptized, every one of you, in the name of Christ, for the remission of your sins, and ye shall receive the gift of the Holy Ghost. For the promise is to you [here is food for the sheep] and to your children" [this is for the lambs.] Doubtless, at that moment, the scene recorded in Mark was before him. In his mind's eye he saw Jesus hold the infant disciples in his arms, and with the authority of Godhead vindicate their claim to the covenant by which the Church had its very being. If you will substitute covenant for promise, and seed for children, in this language of Peter, you will have the declaration of an inspired apostle concerning Abraham and his children: "The covenant was to Abraham and his seed." So under the preaching of Peter: "The covenant is to you and to your seed;" for covenant and promise, as well as children and seed, mean the same things.

Now consider that God directed the seal of circumcision to be extended to infants because the covenant extended to them. The seal and the covenant must be coëxtensive, and as the covenant was to Abraham and his seed, both must be circumcised. But under the Gospel, Peter declares, "The covenant is [still] to you and to your seed." What, then, would be the inference? If the Gospel covenant is to our children, (would the Jew say,) then the Gospel seal (baptism) is to our children also. For where is the validity of a covenant without a seal? And who would ever think of inserting the name of a person in the body of a covenant as one of its parties, and then refuse that person's seal in executing the instrument? That baptism is the Christian circumcision, that is, performs the same sealing office in the covenant of grace now as circumcision did formerly, is plain from the language of Paul, in Colossians ii, 11, 12. Here baptism is expressly called the circumcision of Christ, that is, the circumcision instituted by Christ—the Christian circumcision.

3. Our last argument in favor of infant baptism is the example of the apostles, as illustrated by sacred and ecclesiastical history.

(1.) Sacred history is principally that portion of the New Testament called the Acts of the Apostles. There we have several baptisms recorded. If you will carefully examine them you will find that about one-third of the whole are family baptisms; that is, baptizing men and women, with their households or families. In Paul's ministry with one Church (Corinth) the proportion between the individual and family baptisms is not as stated above, namely, one-third, but two-thirds. He baptized at Corinth, Crispus and Gaius, and the household of Stephanas. But we learn from the Acts that the family of Crispus, also, was baptized. Now we must judge of the apostles' unrecorded acts by what are recorded. If there are twelve baptizings noticed in Acts, and four of the twelve are family baptisms, then we may calculate that in 1,200 baptizings 400 would be family baptisms. Some of these families are said to have heard the Word and to have believed, but of other families it is expressly declared that the parent believed, and all the family was baptized. See the case of Lydia, Acts xvi, 15. I have no dry criticisms to make on these facts of sacred history. There is a surer way to understand them and apply them in argument. The apostles were missionaries. As they went from one heathen city to another some were converted. In the Acts you have a brief register of things that transpired in their missionary tours. Now we have missionaries abroad, and so have Presbyterians, Episcopalians, and Baptists. Suppose now it were announced that a missionary from abroad would give an account of his labors in the First Presbyterian Church to-night. Suppose you should go, and on the way should learn that he is not a Presbyterian minister, but is either a Baptist, an Episcopalian, or a Methodist, you know not which. Suppose he should go on to state that there had been a glorious revival in the field of his labor, in which thousands of poor heathen cast away their idols, and were baptized into the Christian faith. "I will give you," he says, "some examples of the conversion of heathen. The work commenced in such a city. Myself and my colleague commenced preaching there without any special encouragement, and, to our surprise, thousands who gathered around and listened to us, became so affected that they drowned our voices. We directed them to the Lamb of God, and before night 300 of them were baptized. This great work was noised abroad among the heathen all about the country, and, when we left that city, go where we might, the poor heathens were full of curiosity to see us, and many among them were disposed to listen to our instructions. For example, one day on a journey a man overtook me and invited me to ride with him. He had heard about the strange upturning in the city, and began immediately to question me. I explained to him and presented Jesus as a Savior. He listened and wept, and, as we happened upon a place where there was water, he wished to be baptized, and I baptized him on the spot. On another occasion, a savage wretch, to whom I spoke a few words, became so infuriated that I was in danger; but a sudden change came over him: the Holy Spirit found way to his heart, he became meek as a lamb, took me to his house, called all the family together, and, after a short exhortation, I baptized the whole family. On another occasion I found a company of women on the bank of a river, where I had been accustomed to seek retirement and pray with the converts. I took advantage of it and preached Jesus to them. One respectable woman was converted, and I baptized her and all her family, and afterward found a very pleasant missionary's home at her house. Another very interesting family in the same neighborhood I also baptized, and its members have been devoted Christians ever since."

Here he finishes his narrative. As you turn away from the Church would you take that man to be a Baptist missionary? If you have been accustomed to read the reports of their missionary from foreign lands, you certainly would not. They give no account of baptisms performed the very day that the persons were struck under conviction, nor scarcely any of the baptism of families. We do not believe that you can find ten instances upon record among all the Baptist missionary reports, where a whole household or family is reported to have been baptized either with or without conversion. The language which describes baptisms by the apostles is just such as might be expected from a Methodist missionary in giving an account of conversions among the heathen. Now we have in this form of narrating baptisms, which embraced whole families, strong presumptive proof that the apostles baptized infants.

(2.) But we do not rest on presumptions, however violent. We have confirmation strong. Ecclesiastical history pours a flood of light upon this subject. It renders the baptism of infants by the apostles just as certain as it is that the apostles baptized at all. We can trace the practice of infant baptism up to the first century, and find it was then spoken of as a universal practice which had never been called in question.

Justin Martyr is our first witness. He was born during the first century. He doubtless conversed with old persons in his youth who had seen the apostles themselves. He speaks of disciples who were then sixty or seventy years old, and says they were made disciples in their infancy. If made disciples they were baptized in their infancy.

Irenæus was born in the year 97. Polycarp, who

was a disciple of the Apostle John, instructed Irenæus, and doubtless informed him what John himself had said and done in regard to infants. When you hear Irenæus speak, then you hear his teacher Polycarp; and when you hear Polycarp you hear *his* teacher, John, the beloved disciple. But this Irenæus says: "Christ came to save all persons who by him are born again unto God; infants and little ones, and children, and youths, and elder persons." By "being born again," Irenæus shows in others of his writings that he means being baptized.

Clement of Alexandria was born about fifty years later, and he says, "If any one be a fisherman let him think of an apostle and children taken out of the water." Clement is here directing Christians what sort of images to engrave on their seal rings, and directs fishermen to choose the image of an apostle baptizing infants.

Tertullian was the first person who ever urged the delay of baptism in the case of infants. He was contemporary with Irenæus, and the manner in which he urges the delay of baptism proves that the common practice was to baptize them. He does not pretend that the apostles did not baptize them, and, of course, implicitly grants that they did. For if they did not it was as well known to him, as it is known to us whether or not Mr. Wesley baptized them. Tertullian's language on this subject proves that the apostles and their immediate successors baptized infants *very young*, for he does not speak against baptizing children, but urges that it should be *delayed*.

Origen, who was the most learned of all the

fathers, was born 184 years after Christ. He says, first, "that infants are baptized for the remission of their sins," and, secondly, "that the Church has received the tradition from the apostles that baptism ought to be administered to infants."

Cyprian, who lived and wrote at the same time with Origen, says that "sixty-six bishops, being convened in a council at Carthage, had the question referred to them, whether infants might be baptized before they were eight days old, and decided unanimously that no infant is to be prohibited from the benefit of baptism although but just born."

Now, consider for a moment the testimony of these two men. Their writings are in our hands, and are just as well authenticated as the writings of the New Testament. That is, we are as certain that they wrote what passes for their writings as we are that Matthew wrote one of the Gospels, or Paul the Epistle to the Romans. It was impossible for them not to know with moral certainty whether infant baptism was practiced by the apostles. They lived much nearer to the times of the apostles than we do to the times of Luther, and Calvin, and Knox. Now, is it possible for us to be ignorant of Calvin's views on the subject of infant baptism? It is not possible. Yet Origen and Cyprian lived one hundred years nearer to the apostles and to the Savior than we do to John Calvin. And one of them has left it written with his own hand that infants are baptized for the remission of sins, and that the Church has received the usage from the apostles; while the other testifies that a council of sixty-six bishops, when the question was put to them whether infants might be baptized before they were eight days old, decided without one dissenting vote, that no infant is to be prohibited from the benefit of baptism, although but just born. A man who can get rid of this proof of the apostolic origin of infant baptism can get rid of dying.

Now let us come down the stream of ecclesiastical history, touching at different points, and see how the Church in different centuries stood affected on this subject.

Gregory Nazianzen was born 330 years after Christ. He exhorts parents to offer their children to God in baptism.

St. Augustine, whose name as a writer of prodigious industry and of great eminence is familiar to many of you, was born about 354 years after Christ. He says: "The whole Church practices infant baptism; it was not instituted by councils, but was always in use." Another remark of this celebrated father should be inscribed in the memory of every Christian parent. He says that he does not remember ever to have read of any person, Catholic or heretic, who maintained that baptism ought to be denied to infants. This baptism, he says, the Church has always maintained.

Pelagius, a contemporary and learned antagonist of Augustine's, says that "he never knew a heretic so impious as to deny that infants are to be baptized." This testimony was from one who denied the doctrine of native depravity. And when Augustine inferred an argument in proof of that depravity from the baptism of infants, Pelagius, instead of avoiding the argument by denying infant baptism, which he would have done, if possible, declares that he never knew one so impious as to deny baptism to infants. You will readily perceive that he did not live in our day.

In the first four hundred years of the Church, Tertullian was the only solitary person who objected to infant baptism generally, and he only wished it delayed. For nearly 1200 years after our Savior's crucifixion, the baptism of infants was universal and uninterrupted, and not a society or an individual, except Tertullian, suggested its inutility, nor did he dispute its lawfulness or its apostolic origin.

In the year 1120 a small sect of Waldenses opposed it, but they soon came to nothing, and for 400 years there was no opposition. Then, at last, in 1500 years after our Savior's death, and after infant baptism had been so long an undisputed usage in the Church, the settled opposition arose, and for three hundred years past has produced no little opposition to this practice.

And now, if, as we have seen, the commission given by Jesus to his disciples embraces all nations and every (human) creature; if infants are capable of their sustaining a covenant relation to God, by the act of parents; if they have been embraced in every leading covenant which God has made with mankind; if the seals of these covenants have always been put upon them; if Jesus Christ pronounced them members of the Church, what presumption is it in mortals to shut the door of the Church, which he left so wide open, saying, "Suffer them to come unto me!" Do they who take on themselves this responsibility imagine that they will succeed? When the millennium shall have come, and all nations shall be gathered in—when all the ends of the earth shall turn to the Lord, and all shall know him, from the least unto the greatest—when the earth shall be full of the knowledge of the Lord as the waters cover the seas, and all the kingdoms of this world shall become the kingdoms of our Lord and of his Christ; shall infants alone be then excluded from the visible kingdom of God? Without baptism they must be excluded. None can enter that kingdom without being born of water as well as of the Spirit. And while all the world is admitted, shall the innocency of childhood be excluded? Shall all be permitted to approach the tree of life—shall all be permitted to survey with holy exhilaration the splendors of that goodly scene—shall all be the seed of the promise and the circumcised of the Lord except little children? Was it left to the Gospel alone—that Gospel which was intended to be the most expanded and catholic covenant of God with man—that Gospel which was intended to break over the contracted bounds of all former covenants, and embrace a world—was it left to this Gospel of mercy to do what none of the partial and exclusive covenants had ever done before, namely, shut out from its purview and sacraments the sinless portion of our race—those that were unfortunate, but not actually guilty—those whose natures are defiled but whose wills have not transgressed? Is it true that the good news announced at the advent, embraced the disfranchisement of helpless and suffering infancy, which till then had been embraced in every covenant of mercy? Is it true that the Star of Bethlehem stood over where Immanuel was, to warn the nations that the slumbering babe whose birth had just awakened the jubilee of the universe, (like the dragon which drew the third part of the stars of heaven and cast them down to the earth,) was about to sweep from the spheres where the God of Abraham had placed them, constellations upon which at that moment his own infant glory shed a new and unfading luster? Blessed Jesus! thou who hast sanctified infancy by passing through all its stages and assuming all its weaknesses and prerogatives! have mercy on those who would select the objects of thine unconditional complacency, as the only beings in this redeemed world, who may not share in thy covenanted smiles, who may not claim those exceeding great and precious promises which were intended as crowning tokens of thy universal and everlasting love!

XVII.

CHRISTIAN BAPTISM.

SECOND DISCOURSE.

THE CEREMONY.

"*Go ye therefore and teach all nations, baptizing them in the name of the Father, and of the Son, and of the Holy Ghost; teaching them to observe all things whatsoever I command you.*" Matthew xxviii, 19, 20.

"*And he said unto them, Go ye into all the world and preach the Gospel to every creature. He that believeth and is baptized shall be saved, and he that believeth not shall be damned.*" Mark xvi, 15, 16.

IN our former discourse we spoke of the ministers of baptism, its significancy, and its subjects; we come now to invite your attention to the *ceremony of baptism,* or to the manner in which the element should be applied. Here the difference which exists between us and our opponents should be understood. It is briefly this: We believe that the word *baptize* is generic, or directs the application of water to the person in any convenient form, especially by sprinkling, pouring, and immersion. They believe that the meaning of the word is specific, or directs the application of water in one form only, namely, immersion. We shall endeavor to vindicate our views from the following considerations:

I. THE ANALOGY OF GOSPEL ORDINANCES.

II. THE EMBLEMATIC SIGNIFICANCY OF BAPTISM.

III. THE MEANING OF THE WORD BAPTIZE.

IV. THE EXAMPLE OF CHRIST'S APOSTLES.

I. We vindicate our views, first, from the *analogy of Gospel ordinances.*

The Jewish rites were burdensome. An apostle declares that neither they nor their fathers were able to bear them. Christ intended to introduce in the place of onerous ceremonies, a yoke which is easy and a burden which is light. But if he commanded his disciples to go and *immerse all* nations, he laid on them a more embarrassing service than any which belonged to the priests of the tabernacle, or temple. He imposed on the people of many nations a greater outward burden than any Jewish ceremony from which the Gospel relieved them. Remember that there are nations toward the poles, and in the deserts, as well as in temperate climes, and in watered and fertile regions ; and as the millennium dawns, all these dwellers at the poles, and in the deserts, are to "catch the flying joy." Are *they* to be *immersed?* It is impossible, and, therefore, the command would be unreasonable. In Labrador, Winter continues nine months in the year. During six of these months the streams are congealed to their bottoms, and a minister of the Gospel could scarcely collect wood from the scanty shrubs of the country to thaw ice enough to immerse a penitent. Could he do this, the water poured from a kettle into a font would freeze faster than he could heat it. Without a miracle his baptistery would congeal before he could fill it and prepare for the ceremony. In parts of Asia and Africa whole tribes wander in Saharas, and make the sands of the desert their homes. Their whole country would scarcely accumulate a fountain large enough to bathe the person. There, if the religion of the wanderers require ablutions, the ceremony is often performed by using the sands of the desert, sprinkling it over them instead of water.

To such, has Christ left a command which obliges them to be immersed? You may say that in the Polar regions they must baptize in Summer. I answer, the apostles did not delay. They almost invariably baptized their converts on the day that they were struck under conviction. One waited a few days and was reproved for doing it. "And now why tarriest thou? Arise and be baptized," etc. Again, our opponents can not delay baptism through our short Winter, and how can they expect others to delay two or three times longer? Will you say, again, that the desert tribes must travel into well-watered regions for baptism? I answer, how would it suit *our* poorest people to travel with their families from fifty to one hundred miles to obtain baptism? Is this the "easy yoke" of Christ? Is this the spirit of Christ's declaration to the woman of Samaria—"The time is coming when neither at Jerusalem, nor in this mountain shall men worship—but they that worship the Father shall worship him in spirit and in truth."

You may say, again, that all the people of Jewry went to Jordan, unto John, to be baptized of him. I answer, that was the baptism of penance, or repentance, and not Christian baptism; whereas, after the resurrection of Christ, no man or woman is represented ever to have moved one step from the spot where they were converted to obtain baptism. Now, as the command to immerse the nations would have been unreasonable, because often impossible, every presumption is against it.

But presumption is not proof. It only prepares the way for proof. It inclines a judicious mind to receive and to be satisfied with proof when it comes. And yet this presumption approaches near to proof, for this reason. All other Gospel ordinances, except this, are easy and attractive. The sacrament of the Supper is so. It does not consist of costly feasts and flowing libations. A few ounces of bread and a gill of wine will serve a man in this sacrament, for his life-time. If all other Gospel ordinances are so easy and expenseless, if the other sacrament is so well adapted to every condition and every clime, analogy claims that baptism, the sister sacrament, be equally facile and accessible to all—to the dwellers at the Equator and at the poles, in the desert and on the seas; to the strong and active, and to the timid, the sick, and the dying.

II. We vindicate sprinkling and pouring by referring to the *symbolic significancy of baptism.*

On this point we shall say but a few words. We introduce it to relieve ourselves of one or two objections frequently urged against aspersion or affusion. One is founded upon Romans vi, 3, 4: "Know ye not that so many of us as were baptized into Jesus Christ were baptized into his death? Therefore we are buried with him by baptism into death; that, like as Christ was raised up from the dead by the glory of the Father, even so we also should walk in newness of life." The second is Colossians ii, 12: "Buried with him in baptism, wherein also we are risen with him, through the faith of the operation of God, who hath raised him from the dead."

They who urge these texts in opposition to pouring and in favor of immersion, suppose that by descending into the water and rising out of it again, they copy the blessed Savior's burial and resurrection. How strange it is that they do not pause to look at the history of Christ's burial and resurrection, and thus correct an impression which has no other foundation than their own fruitful fancies! How, I pray you, was our Divine Redeemer buried? Have you supposed that the earth overwhelmed him; that the clay, like waters, closed over his sacred person? His burial was much more like our repose in a chamber, than it was like the usual interring of the dead. We are told in the history that Joseph wrapped the body in linen and *laid* it in a sepulcher. This sepulcher was so spacious that, on the morning of the first day of the week, it was occupied by two angels, who were sitting, the one at the head and the other at the foot, where the body of Jesus was laid. What is there in immersion which bears the least resemblance to such a burial? The resemblance is just as striking as it is between immersion and crucifixion, or immersion and planting, in the next verses. The apostle represents us as *buried* with, as planted in, and as crucified with Christ, by baptism. If immersion resembles Christ's burial, how does it represent the planting or crucifixion?

Suppose I should undertake to prove sprinkling from these texts of Scripture, by seizing on that particular passage: "Knowing this, that our old man is crucified with him," etc. When our Savior was crucified, his blood, pouring from his wounds, was sprinkled upon his own raiment. The crown of thorns, the nails in his hands, and the soldier's spear, stained his limbs, and countenance, and vesture. This was probably the very baptism to which he referred when he said: "I have a baptism to be baptized with, and how am I straightened," etc. Much more plausibly may I plead for sprinkling, then, because it resembles the crucifixion of Christ, than for immersion, because it resembles his burial, that is, his reposing in a spacious sepulcher.

You may ask what is the meaning of these texts? I answer, if you insist, that baptism represents certain states in which the body of Jesus was at different times, as his crucifixion, death, burial, etc. I should conclude that some of the Romans were immersed, some were sprinkled, some were poured upon, and some stood in the water while the ceremony was performed. Those who were immersed, you may say if you choose, were *buried* with Christ—though that is the most awkward comparison of all. Those who were sprinkled were *crucified* with him by water aspersion, resembling the blood from the wounds inflicted by the thorns and the nails. Those who stood in the stream to be thus sprinkled were *planted* with him in the likeness of his death, like the roots of a tree planted in the soil. Thus the baptisms in the Church at Rome must have been as various, if this is the meaning of these passages, as they are among the Methodists. But, although we doubt not that their baptisms were various in mode—though all one in regard to the name into which they were baptized, as it is said, "one Lord, one faith, one baptism"—yet we do not believe that these passages have any regard to external mode. They teach us simply that in our baptism we profess to be dead and buried to sin and to the world, and to be alive to holiness and to God. This is the foundation of a special claim upon us to "walk in newness of life." The import of the words is much the same as those in Galatians iii, 27: "For as many of you as have been baptized into Christ, [that is, by water and the Spirit,] have put on Christ"—that is, have put on the profession, and have assumed the tempers of love and loyalty to Christ.

Having disposed of these objections to pouring and sprinkling, I infer from the signification of water baptism as an emblem, the propriety of these modes. The signification of baptism, as a religious ordinance, is *purification*. In almost all religions, washing with water, to signify inward purity, was thought a suitable preparation for sacrifice and worship. Purifications, under the law of Moses, were multiplied; and these were not for the cleansing of the body; for, however free this might be from defilement, there were legal cleansings, which had no other aim than to shadow purity of mind. In the times of John the Baptist it was expected that the Messiah would baptize, and that his baptism would be an emblem of purification.

We find that a question arose among some of John's disciples and the Jews about "purifying," and from the conversation which immediately followed with John himself, (John iii, 25, 26,) we learn that this purifying was baptism. Here, then, all disputes about the emblematic signification of baptism are at an end. *Baptism is an emblem of inward purification.* But inward purification is procured by the blood and the Spirit of Christ. If, then, we can ascertain how the blood and the Spirit are applied to the soul and the conscience, from their application we can infer a strong presumption in regard to the mode or modes of water baptism. As to the blood of Christ, it is represented, first, as "*sprinkling*" our hearts, etc., second, "unto Him who hath loved us and *washed* us from our sins in his own blood." The Spirit is represented as "*poured out.*" From the *sprinkling*, and *washing*, and *pouring*, we infer that either of the three modes is warranted and is perfectly satisfactory.

III. But we proceed to consider the meaning of the word *baptize*. If, as immersionists fondly insist, it means, in the New Testament, to *immerse*, and nothing else, then all argument for any other mode is good for nothing. This is a point which involves philological criticism, but if the speaker were prepared for this, his audience is not prepared to go along with him. There is a more instructive and a surer method. It is an appeal to Christ, and to the inspired philologists. They sometimes used Greek words and phrases in a sense in which they were never used before. How else could they have spoken truths which had never entered into the conceptions of Greeks, or other Gentiles? Even Nicodemus could not, at first, receive the sublime import of the

Savior's use of the Greek words "born again." As the New Testament doctrines and ordinances have a higher and often different significancy from any thing known to the heathen world, so the New Testament writers must have used the Greek language often in a higher and even distinct sense from what native Greeks assigned it. The question for the Christian, and the Christian minister, is not what is the classical import of a word, but what is its Biblical and evangelical import. The question is not how Homer, and Plutarch, and Sophocles used them, but how did our Savior and the sacred writers use them? And we shall always find that the Bible explains its own use of terms.

If there is no occasion to change the meaning of words, and the Scriptures do not require any change, they are to be used in their usual and classical sense. But if there be undoubted tokens that the inspired penman, or the Divine Redeemer, used a word in an unusual or unclassical sense, to array proofs to the contrary from the ancient usages of speech is irrelevant, skeptical, and profane. The only question for us, then, is what Christ and his disciples mean by the word baptize. These baptisms are spoken of by John. These are distinguished by the elements with which they are performed. The first is by water, the second is by the Holy Ghost, the third is by fire. Two of these, water and fire, are symbolical, and are merely designed to shadow forth or signify what is real and substantial. Now we can determine the meaning of the word baptize, in the Scriptural sense, if we can ascertain how either of these baptisms was performed. In each case, an element is applied to the person of the baptized. We say to the person, for the soul and body both belong to the person. How, then, is the element used? Water is one element. The Scriptures are examined to ascertain how it was used, and a controversy arises. Some say it was used in one form, some say in another. Nine-tenths of the Christian world insist it was applied in any convenient form and quantity; one-tenth, more or less, say it was applied only by *immersion.* Who shall settle the question, and, how? Any one may settle it by traveling on through the New Testament and ascertaining how the other baptisms were performed. What was the mode of baptism by the Spirit? To ascertain this, you must go to Peter's sermon on the day of Pentecost. After the company of the apostles had been baptized by the Spirit, and were filled with the Holy Ghost, Peter stands up, and says to the wondering multitude, who accused them of wine-bibbing, "These are not drunken, as ye suppose; but this is that spoken by the prophet Joel, And it shall come to pass in the last days, saith God, I will *pour out* my Spirit upon all flesh; and your sons and your daughters shall prophesy. And on my servants and on my handmaidens I will *pour out,* in those days, of my Spirit, and they shall prophesy." Acts ii, 17, 18. And this is repeated in another form, verse 33: "Therefore [Jesus] being by the right hand of God exalted, and having received of the Father the promise of the Holy Ghost, hath *shed forth* this which ye now see and hear."

There are two other portions of Scripture which

we wish you to connect with these passages, and we are sure that you can scarcely again, without great weakness, not to say irreverence, doubt whether pouring is valid baptism: The first is in Matthew iii, 11: "I indeed baptize you with water unto repentance; but he that cometh after me is mightier than I, whose shoes I am not worthy to bear. *He shall baptize you with the Holy Ghost and with fire.*" This is an early announcement of Christ's future office, when he should ascend upon high to give gifts unto men. The other is in Acts i, 5: "For John truly baptized with water; but ye shall be *baptized with the Holy Ghost,* not many days hence." This is the language of Christ himself, uttered after his resurrection. And just as he was about to ascend into heaven, he said as his last words, "It is not for you to know the times and the seasons which the Father hath put in his own power; but ye shall receive power after that the Holy Ghost is *come upon* you." Thus, three years before our Savior's crucifixion, John says that Jesus shall baptize with the Holy Ghost and with fire. Then, only ten days before Pentecost, Christ says: "Ye shall be *baptized* with the Holy Ghost, not many days hence." And then, again, in the eighth verse, Christ signifies the form of that baptism, which was so near: "Ye shall receive power after that the Holy Ghost is *come upon* you"—not when it has immersed you. Ten days after, Pentecost arrives, the promised baptism comes, and Peter, in the language of the prophet Joel, says that this baptism is the "*pouring out*" of the Spirit—that "Christ, having received of the Father the promise of the Holy Ghost, has *shed forth* this which you now see and hear." In these passages we have the testimony of John, of Peter, and of Jesus Christ, to say nothing of the prophecy of Joel. Jesus was to baptize. His baptism was to be spiritual. He never did baptize with water in any one instance. If he did not baptize with the Holy Ghost, and with fire, he never baptized at all. But, unless *pouring* is baptizing, he never did baptize with the Holy Ghost. Every prophecy and every narrative in all God's Holy Book, that speaks of any manner or mode of giving the Holy Spirit, uses language which signifies the descent of the Spirit upon the subject.

Now, did Christ, or did he not, baptize? If he did, his only mode of baptizing was by *pouring*. And while he *thus* baptizes we shall be glad to follow his example. The efforts of our opponents to escape the force of this argument are enough to relax the muscles of grave logic into a smile. We will notice two of them:

First, they say that the disciples were really immersed in the Holy Ghost, for the narrative states that the Spirit filled all the house where they were sitting. This is a mistake. "The sound as of a mighty rushing wind filled all the house where they were sitting;" but the Holy Ghost is not mentioned till the second verse after. The order of events was as follows: 1. The miraculous "sound as of a rushing mighty wind," as the precursor of the baptism; 2. The appearance of the "divided tongues, as of fire, sitting upon each of them," as the symbol both of the mode and the reality of the baptism: the mode "*sitting upon*"—the reality, *spiritual purifying*, symbolized by "*fire;*" 3. The plain, historic account of the meaning and the effect, "they were all filled with the Holy Ghost."

The other evasion is, that this is a mere figurative baptism. A figurative baptism! And who drew the figure? The Lord Jesus Christ. And he pictures himself as *shedding down* and pouring out the Holy Ghost on the people to baptize them! How do our opponents sketch the same scene? Instead of the element being poured out from above, they insist that we must drop the baptized into the element beneath. As they picture it, all flesh is poured out into the Holy Spirit, instead of the Holy Spirit being "poured out upon all flesh." Christ says the Holy Spirit shall *come upon* the disciples, but they will have it that the disciples come upon (into) the Holy Spirit. Now, whose authority shall we prefer, theirs or their Savior's? Indeed, we will not hesitate. If our Savior's baptism be a figure, we thank him for a figure which reveals the true mode of baptism, and sets our hearts at rest forever. But it is not a figure. It is the prototype, the substance shadowed forth by a figure, and that figure is water baptism. This doctrine is carried out upon the face of all those announcements of John Baptist and Jesus, above noticed, whose baptism by water and by the Holy Ghost are conjoined. And if spiritual baptism is the thing signified, water baptism, which signifies it, should conform to it in mode as well as idea, in order to be a perfect type.

There is another baptism mentioned by John and narrated in Acts. That is by fire. "Ye shall be baptized with the Holy Ghost and with fire." And what is the mode? "Cloven tongues like as of fire *sat upon* each of them." They were not immersed in fire. If our opponents insist that the baptism of the Spirit was a figure, they ought to yield that the baptism of fire was not. Here, at last, the element was material. The form of human tongues which the fire, or the semblance of fire, took, symbolized the many languages in which they were to proclaim the Word of God; also the new power of the tongue, now to be imparted for the general preaching and teaching of the Gospel. The fire symbolized the intensity of that spiritual purification which they were now to receive, and also the energy and searching power of the words which their tongues should utter. But the manner of this baptism by fire was identical with that of the Holy Ghost. Here, then, we should expect that controversy would end, and that the meaning of the word baptize, as used by our blessed Savior, would be settled forever. I would as soon think of carrying a Greek Lexicon up to the throne of God, to teach the Almighty Savior what he does not understand, as to trifle with his holy Word and example by opposing the classical meaning of *baptizo* to his perpetual baptizing by pouring.

This example of our Savior's baptizing has less weight with weak minds, because the Holy Spirit is invisible. But we should consider that the action of the Spirit is as exactly described as though we saw it visibly descend like rain from the cloud. His emblem, fire, was visible. Suppose you could see it descend like falling light, or like gentle showers on an assembly of Christ's worshipers, and, at the same moment, should hear the voice of Jesus, like the sound of many waters, proclaim, "I baptize you with the Holy Ghost," would you meet the Son of God with a contradiction? Would the voices of those who plead for immersion break out amidst the pauses of the Redeemer's benediction, and say, "Stop, Savior. Thou art mistaken. This is not baptizing. This is what we call on earth *rantizing*, or sprinkling, and thou art wrong, either in thy deed or in thy word." O how often, in the midst of revivals, may this folly have been committed!

In a communication narrating a revival of religion, I have found a man writing in one clause, "God has *poured out his Spirit* in showers, and numbers have been converted," and in the next clause he has thoughtlessly added, "I have baptized thirteen, while our pedobaptist friends have *rantized* [sprinkled] twenty-five." Did this brother perceive how that word *rantize* bore on his own description of the baptism of the Spirit? He had just said, "God has poured out his Spirit in showers." This was *Christ's baptism.* Then, a moment after, he ridicules the sprinkling or pouring of another branch of the Church, and denies it the name of baptism, though it is the very act which he ascribes to Jesus in baptizing with the Holy Ghost. We lament the ways and means which good men sometimes take to guard indefensible positions. If the baptism of the Holy Ghost is indeed by immersion, let our opposing brethren adapt their phraseology to that fact. Let them always say, "God has immersed a multitude in the Holy Ghost, and we have immersed so many in water." If they will thus adhere to their opinions, we will adhere to ours, and describe our revivals by saying, God *poured out* his Spirit on the people and baptized them with the Holy Ghost, and we poured out water on the people and baptized them for admission into the Church. This would hold up our several views in undisguised features before the world, and all men could discern what is attractive and what is repulsive in each. But I close this head by remarking, that after all the efforts of our opponents to prove that baptize means nothing but immersion, in almost every notice of revivals of religion, they yield the point and make that word mean pouring. They do this just as often as they say, "God has poured out his Spirit," and revived his work.

IV. Lastly, we infer sprinkling or pouring as valid water baptism, from the practice of the apostles. It seems most remarkable that it should be necessary to resort to the example of the apostles to vindicate pouring, when we have, without the least dispute, the example of Christ himself. That he *always* baptized by pouring—by no other method—we have clearly seen. And if Christ and his apostles differed, if he baptized by pouring and they by immersion, we should unhesitatingly follow the example of the Savior. But I believe that the apostles generally, after the crucifixion, baptized by pouring.

There is a foundation laid by our opponents themselves to prove this point very satisfactorily. This you will learn from the sequel.

In arguing for immersion exclusively, it is customary to resort to the ministry of John, and show from the circumstances that he must have immersed. The circumstances are supposed to be such as would not have existed without painstaking; and such as would have provoked no pains but for the fact that John wished to immerse. For instance, the Evangelist informs us that "there went out all Judea and Jerusalem, and all the regions round about Jordan, and were baptized of him in Jordan, confessing their sins." This, our opponents say, was by immersion; else why did they go all the way to Jordan? If they were sprinkled or poured, a bowl of water would have answered, and this could easily have been procured without resorting to Jordan. Now recollect this comment, for it is of great importance in the remarks which follow. It embraces two reasons for resorting to Jordan to baptize. One is that there was water in Jordan to immerse, and the other is that there was *not water* in the cities for that purpose. Very well, so let it be. We are content to have it understood that John immersed, and that he went to Bethabara, beyond Jordan, because he could find water there for that ceremony; and that he was also in Ænon, near to Salem, for the same reason, namely, because water could not be found in the cities to immerse, but was abundant in Ænon. All we ask is that our opponents will abide by their own positions.

But, finally, John is beheaded, and Christ is crucified. The office and the baptism of Christ's herald, or forerunner, are superseded. The baptism of Jesus Christ by the Spirit is introduced, and in one day three thousand who have received that baptism by the shedding of the Holy Ghost upon them, believe, and wish to be received into the visible Church. This is done, and on one afternoon three thousand are baptized and admitted.

But where is this wonderful scene laid? It was undoubtedly the greatest "baptizing" ever witnessed in one half day. John baptized for months, but probably he never baptized so many in any one week as were baptized on that occasion. Suppose it had been done in Jordan. This would have been very convenient. The place where John dipped the multitudes was known to many, and this would have saved some hours of searching after a good place where the minister and candidates could get down the steep bank, find still water and good bottom. But here are difficulties. First, Jordan was twenty miles distant; and, secondly, one man could not baptize three thousand in half a day. And if all the disciples helped, they would want a great many places—some say a hundred and twenty. Now, it would puzzle any man to find places on the Ohio in one afternoon where one hundred and twenty ministers could baptize at once. And Jordan was less convenient still, being a small stream, with bold banks, and generally rocky bed, and rapid. Even in Jordan, then, the baptism of three thousand by immersion would have been difficult, at least for the time allowed.

But this occurrence was not at the Jordan, nor among the many waters of Ænon. It was at Jerusalem itself that the three thousand were baptized, and this *fact* is alone a moral demonstration that they were not immersed. We *know* as well as we know any thing that *can not be* otherwise, that they were not immersed.

First, there is not a city in America where three thousand persons could, in the same time and circumstances, be immersed. To convince you of this, we will suppose Cincinnati to be the place of trial. Say, then, that it was now Conference time, and a meeting had been appointed in one of the churches at nine o'clock in the morning. Soon after the meeting commences a great excitement takes place among the people. The city is aroused, and thousands, mostly strangers, flock to the chapel, and fill it, and crowd around it. Suppose the sermon is finished by ten o'clock, and then, while the people are crying out in every direction, "What must we do to be saved?" the preachers begin to exhort them to repent, believe, and be baptized. At twelve o'clock it is ascertained that a great many wish to be baptized, and in the end they prove to be three thousand in number. How shall we proceed? If we send for water and shed it forth upon them as Jesus shed his Spirit on their hearts, by the aid of eleven ministers they may be all baptized by twelve o'clock at night. But if we go to the river and immerse, then the case is different. Then it will take three times as long to prepare for the baptism as it will to perform it. If we all start to the river together, and go to one spot, not more than from one to a half dozen ministers could officiate. Then it would take about twenty hours to baptize three thousand, allowing three minutes for a baptism. If we stop to take the names of the three thousand converts before we start to the river, that will occupy at least two hours. But if one hundred ministers are to baptize, it will be necessary to divide the three thousand into one hundred equal companies, and give each minister his quota, and that will take till sundown. You could not in two hours divide the congregation into one hundred such companies.

Suppose, then, that the three thousand be reckoned out, as some suppose the Pentecost converts were, to the one hundred and twenty disciples, twenty-five persons to a minister. Now, if each minister had a separate place to baptize, all would do nicely, and the business could be gotten through with in a short time. But where shall we find one hundred and twenty baptisteries, in churches, or brooks, or canals, or rivers, or reservoirs? We scarcely know where to go for *one* good place to baptize these persons, and, after examining a day, have scarcely succeeded. But, having divided the three thousand into one hundred companies, by sundown, suppose ten, or fifty, messengers are sent out to seek one hundred and twenty places to immerse. Water flows all around our city, and they have a fine chance. But I will venture to say, notwithstanding, that they will not in three days find the one hundred and twenty places. What, not in Cincinnati? No, indeed! If we had known a week beforehand, that such an exigency would have happened, we might have been prepared for it; but in an occurrence so unexpected as was that at Pentecost, even here, we could not, if all the ministers in the Conference were to assist, immerse three thousand persons in the fragment of a day. But why do I talk of this city? It was in

Jerusalem that the three thousand were baptized! And how unlike this city is Jerusalem! This is one of the best watered, that one of the most thirsty cities in the world.

It had one small brook in the valley of Jehoshaphat, near to the east wall of the city, called Kidron. In addition, it had the fountains of Siloam and Gihon, and the pools of Bethesda and Hezekiah. In the rainy season these were about equal to Deer Creek, the reservoir, and one small bath-house. But, on the day of Pentecost, they were not half equal. The brook Kidron had no water but in the rainy season. The rainy season closes, in Palestine, in March, soon after the Passover. The feast of Pentecost comes fifty days after the Passover, at the beginning of wheat harvest. The channels of the Winter torrents were dry, the grass upon the hills of Judea brown from heat and drought, the fountains already began to run low, and the people were thrown back upon their artificial cisterns and tanks for supplies of water for the use of man, and for irrigating their gardens and vineyards. Kidron, therefore, was dry. The fountains of Upper Gihon, Siloam, and Bethesda, were a mile apart. Besides, the sewers of the temple and east part of the city emptied into Kidron, and made it unfit, at any time, for baptism. These statements are from various and unimpeachable sources. Ancient history and modern tourists confirm them. Siloam, Gihon, and Bethesda, then, were the chief waters that were available. The waters of Bethesda could not have been extensive. It was a pool near the "sheep-gate," now called the "St. Stephen's-gate," of the city, at the north-east corner of the temple. It was under the control of the priests, for temple uses, and its few porches crowded with sick people. It is not likely the priests would have conceded the apostles the use of this pool for baptism. Siloam and Gihon were each about a mile distant. Indeed, such was the scarcity of water in the city, that one of Solomon's greatest works was taking supplies by an aqueduct from Bethlehem, and one of the distinguished acts of King Hezekiah's reign was to turn the waters of Upper Gihon fountain, by a subterranean channel, inside the city wall, and stop the outer fountain, so that a besieging army should not find supplies of water, while the city might still sustain itself against a siege.

But our opponents talk of private baths as being very numerous and very convenient for immersing. It is all fancy. There is not the least evidence that Jerusalem was remarkable for private baths. Luxuriant fancies have built them, and easy imaginations have conveyed the three thousand to their brink and dashed them in. We have historical proof that the more eastern cities had numerous baths. The voluptuous Persians, for example, abounded in them. But it does not follow that what is mentioned as a luxury in a voluptuous city, situated on both sides of the ample waters of the Euphrates, must also have been a characteristic of Jerusalem, an inland city, nestled among the mountains, with inadequate natural supplies of water, and with rarely a shower of rain from the last of March till the first of October. It is true that the houses generally, according to the ability of the owners, or occupants, were supplied with private cisterns, or tanks, which were filled in the rainy season, (between October and March,) and used to patch out the supplies of stern necessity for the year. But these were all absorbed by the actual demands of animal and vegetable life, and not constructed for the convenience of immersion. But suppose they were as numerous as some fruitful fancies have imagined, were the disciples of the abhorred and crucified Jesus likely to find ready access to the privacies of citizen's houses? If the Mormons were to meet a vagrant multitude in this city on some public festival, and were to succeed in making some hundreds of converts, would our citizens admit them to their bathing rooms? If not, remember that whereas we might pity as well as censure the Mormons, the citizens of Jerusalem looked with unmingled abhorrence upon Christ, his doctrine, and his disciples. They not merely despised, but hated them with a fierce and bloody hatred. And the converts on the day of Pentecost were not citizens, but mostly strangers, who had no dwellings in the city to resort to.

Such was Jerusalem, and such the circumstances of the apostles and their converts. And now, if, with all our brooks, canals, and rivers, it is rather difficult to immerse a few, with days and weeks of previous preparation, imagine three thousand here, all convicted and converted in one day, and all to be baptized the same day. Then imagine Deer Creek, and Mill Creek, and the canal, and Licking, and the Ohio to be dried up, and all the city to be in an uproar, and its citizens crowding upon us in a rage, mocking us, and railing at us, as a company of drunkards, telling us that even the ministers are full of new wine, and you have a picture of that scene amidst which the apostles baptized their three thousand recruits. And now, if you can believe that the baptism was by immersion, you can easily believe in the story of the golden bible and the promised land.

But could you believe that all these persons were immersed? I do not see how our opponents can believe it, according to their views of John's baptism. They tell us that John left the cities of Judea and returned to Jordan, because there they could find water to immerse. Now it seems to me that a place where three thousand can be immersed in six hours, or thereabout, and that, too, in the dry season, when water was always scarce, could not have been so badly supplied with water as to render it necessary for the whole city to go twenty miles to be immersed.

If one hundred and twenty disciples could find one hundred and twenty baths on the day of Pentecost, how happens it that John could not find one? A few minutes since, this John was said to be baptizing in Jordan because there was not water in Jerusalem; and all Jerusalem went twenty miles to Jordan for the same reason, to find water deep enough to be immersed. But now all Jerusalem seems to be turned into a pool, and one hundred and twenty disciples can not go amiss for places to immerse in. Strange that John could not be admitted to baptize the owners of these baths, and yet the hated disciples and the three thousand strangers found ready admission!

Strange that John, the most popular public teacher that Judea ever saw, whom "all counted as a prophet," and to whose baptism all resorted, should not find one baptistery in all the pools and mansions of Jerusalem; but these drunken disciples, as the Jews represented them, should find one hundred and twenty, and that without any time to search for them! But I can not pursue the theme. My heart sickens while I trace the logic by which it is proved, first, that John went to Jordan to baptize, because he could not immerse in Jerusalem; and secondly, that the apostles immersed in Jerusalem, because John immersed in Jordan. These circles of convincing sophistry will not always pass for genuine argument. Men will, sometime or other, read their own Bibles, and not trust to neighborhood commentaries.

And now, my brethren, if the baptism of three thousand on the day of Pentecost was by pouring, if it was performed, first, by the descent of fire, secondly, by the descent of the Spirit, and third, as we think we have shown, by the effusion of water, thus copying the example of the baptism by fire and by the Spirit, we invoke these examples as a perpetual vindication of our own catholic practice. These examples are our sufficient warrant. While they stand on record, men must busy themselves in vain to convince us that our baptisms are invalid. To all objections we make but one reply. Pointing to the day of Pentecost, we present the baptized thousands, and say, by the mouth of two or three witnesses, are we vindicated? First, the apostles effused the water. If you deny this, then we affirm what none will or can deny: Jesus effused the fire and the Holy Ghost. He still *pours out* his Spirit on the nations to baptize. "It is sufficient for the disciple to be as his Master, the servant as his Lord."

As to other baptisms recorded in Acts, we need not examine them. If the Eunuch was immersed, we have no objection. If Paul and the jailer were sprinkled, it is equal. If the rebaptized, mentioned in Acts xix, were poured; if, as the apostle effused the water, he dropped his hands on their heads, and the Holy Ghost came upon them, there was a very beautiful analogy between the shedding of the water and the shedding of the Spirit upon them.

And now the question may arise in the minds of some persons whether the speaker is opposed to immersion. I answer, no. I am not opposed to it on the ground that it is not valid baptism. It is exclusiveness that I oppose. We argue this question, not to oppose others, but because we are opposed. We merely vindicate, not impugn. We do not say immersion is wrong, but we do say effusion is right. We believe that Christ prescribes *no* definite ceremony in baptism, and does not oblige us to infer any definite ceremony, either from his own or the apostles' examples. God is not wont to suspend the interests of the soul on an external form, and leave that form so uncertain as to expose the sincere to mistakes. Had he intended baptism to be performed with an outward exactness of this sort, he would have prescribed the form as cautiously and definitely as he did the furniture and ceremonies of the Jewish tabernacle.

How different from this is the Christian ritual!

It was intended to dismiss from the Church of Christ a minute carefulness about ceremonies. And yet some of its teachers will exact precision in forms which our Savior has left in designed uncertainty.

But I must not forget that there are those in this house who are expectants of the sacrament of baptism this day.* I lament, my friends, that it should be necessary to argue such questions before you this morning. It is a poor preparation for a service which God designed should be eminently spiritual. It is like accumulating weights upon the racers in the games. But it is on our part an imposed service; imposed by the uneasiness of your own minds on a subject which, we pray, may never invade and vex another mind in this assembly.

Do you say, nay, we ought to investigate this obscure subject? No, you ought not to investigate. Do you ask why? I answer, because it is obscure. If to know it certainly were of any importance, Christ would never have left it obscure. Some things need to be investigated. But outward forms are not those things. The moment these are uncertain, you may dismiss anxiety, for God attaches no importance to them. If *important* they are *plain*. As complex and multiplied as are the ceremonies of the Jewish ritual, not one tittle can be mistaken. Must you study hard to know how to place your hands or incline your person in prayer? how much bread and wine you must partake in the Lord's Sup-

* This sermon was preached at Wesley Chapel, Cincinnati, in the morning, and in the afternoon Mr. Hamline baptized, by immersion in the Ohio River, about twenty candidates for this solemn ordinance.—ED.

per? These things are indifferent, and therefore not to be sought in the Bible. So with the ceremony of baptism. How much water you shall use, how it shall be applied, in what position you shall stand, or kneel, or incline, are things indifferent and therefore not prescribed. Were they not indifferent they would have been commanded in language which none could possibly mistake. No man ought to read the Testament but once to prepare for baptism. And then he should read it to get the baptism of the Holy Ghost, and to be persuaded to receive the external token that the Holy Ghost is given. You may ask whether you are not to inquire at all about the mode. I answer, when you seek the baptism of the Holy Ghost, do you think about the *mode?* Would you in prayer be fastidious on that point? Would you tell your Savior that you wish to be baptized with the Holy Spirit, and add, "Blessed Jesus, my conscience is tender. I have doubts about having thy Spirit *poured* upon me. I am a great sinner. It will take much to cleanse me. I fear that the pouring out of the Spirit will be a superficial work. I must be immersed in the Holy Ghost." Say, my friends, have you ever offered such a prayer? If not, if you are thoughtless about the mode of the spiritual baptism, why do you perplex yourself about the symbolic? You fear in regard to that which is the least important of all. You care more for the shadow than for the substance which must fashion the shadow.

Ah, my beloved friends, go now to the place of baptism, but carry not one thought along with you about the manner, as though it were of the weight of a silken fiber. Be henceforth as thoughtless of the mode as you are of the mode of the Spirit's operation, when you feel his healing virtue like balm upon your wounded consciences. To study the *mode* of the Spirit's operation is one sure method to grieve him from the heart. So to study the mode of applying water to the person, since Christ has not prescribed it, is sure to rob you of the sacred benefits which the baptismal seal was designed to convey and confirm to you forever.

May he who has received the promise of the Father, shed down his Holy Spirit, causing you to "grow as the lily, and to cast forth your root as Lebanon!"

XVIII.

THE SOUL AND THE WORLD.

"*For what shall it profit a man, if he shall gain the whole world, and lose his own soul?*" Mark viii, 36.

"'WHAT shall it profit?' Nothing!" you exclaim. "There is no ground for such a query. At least its terms should be wrought into a suggestion of loss, and not of gain; for who can associate the idea of advantage with a contract in which the soul is to be exchanged for a world?"

Your theory is orthodox; and were your life as rational as your moralizing, I might pause, your Christian friends might dry their tears, and our humble expostulations might be superseded by grateful songs and praises. But do you really esteem the soul to be worth more than the world? Is this your firm conviction? Does it agree with what your friends observe in your behavior? Is there no discord between your language and your life? Alas! while you affect surprise at the query of the text, does not your own conduct suggest that query? We fear your life is an example of that folly which, in words, you seem so willing to reprobate? Whatever you may now profess, as to the value of the soul, you have in practice contemned it; and with mad ambition have pursued this fleeting world. And now, to moderate this madness, we invite you to consider,

I. THE INTRINSIC VALUE OF THE SOUL AND THE WORLD.

II. THE ESTATE WE MAY ACQUIRE IN THEM.

III. THEIR USUFRUCTUARY BENEFITS.

IV. THE CONSEQUENCES DEPENDING ON OUR USE OF THEM.

I. As to their intrinsic value, we shall be brief. It is a very familiar topic, and nothing new can be said upon it. The soul is a spirit like unto God—intelligent and active, endowed with strong emotions, capable of the very holiness of Deity, and of his happiness, constituted with tendencies as deathless as the Godhead, and destined to an equal term of being. Who can pretend to estimate the value of such a soul? God alone can set a price upon it. Nothing short of infinite intelligence can survey its rich capacities, can forecast its destiny.

We ask you to turn and glance a moment at the world. Is the soul a spirit, subtile and indissoluble as the essence of the Godhead? The world is gross in all its elements, and, in its fairest forms, is doomed to foul corruption. Is the soul intelligent and active? Has it an eye to search for truth, and a wing on which to soar, in its pursuit, to the very throne of God? Earth has no eye nor hand to employ in a work so ennobling and delightful. Is the soul rich in heaven-inspired affections? Does it feast on created and uncreated beauty? By its pathetic powers does it reach after and appropriate the very joys of Deity? The world is unconscious. It has no capacity for happiness. It can neither smile nor weep. Is the soul immortal? The world is even now the victim of gradual dissolution, by fires half-concealed within its tortured bosom. Soon those fires must rage throughout its melting mass, till it forms a universal conflagration.

The history of creation presents man in an attitude of glorious preëminence. It advises us of the commencement of the work without any note of deliberation on the part of the Creator. No stage of its progress appears to have been of sufficient moment to induce delay, till it approached its consummation. It was prosecuted with unfaltering assurance till the heavens and earth were finished, and all the irrational host thereof. It seemed a trifling work to reduce chaotic ruins into order, and lift the everlasting curtain which concealed them from the light. To build up earth and heaven, and beautify and garnish them, was scarcely a serious enterprise for an Almighty hand. It was the pastime of Omnipotence.

When it was accomplished—when the sun was stationed to diffuse his splendors all abroad upon creation; and the moon to shed her silvery beams upon the night; and the stars to repose like diamonds in their airy, ocean beds—when earth commenced her course around the spacious heavens, and bore aloft her verdant vales and hills, her flowery charms and forest glories, her flowing streams and crystal fountains, her ocean depths and terrene heights, and, last of all, her animated tribes in all the fresh glowing beauty of their first natal hour—then, indeed, the morning stars sang together, and all the sons of God shouted for joy. Then, too, God looked forth to survey his handiwork, and pronounced it "very good." Yet all these required no pause—no formal counselings between the persons of the Trinity. They were the unstudied efforts of an unhesitating mind, apparently engaged in a familiar avocation. But how different when man was created! This was a work of such signal interest as involved a consultation between the persons of the everlasting Trinity. Mark the Scripture record of this mysterious procedure: "Let us make man in our own image, after our likeness;" so "God created man in his own image." Observe, first, that the soul of man, unlike any thing besides, has the likeness of the eternal Spirit; and second, to form the soul with such divine features, was a work so momentous that it was preceded by a pause, and was prosecuted by the Trinity in counsel, and in concert. So great was the difference between the soul and the world. The world was merely a residence for man—a house which God did build and furnish for his use. Its soil was his footstool—its appendages his furniture—its living tribes his servile ministers. Its darkness was the curtain of his balmy midnight hours—its light his harbinger, announcing to creation the appearance of its elected and its anointed lord. Man was to the world like the sun to the system which he cheers, and binds, and regulates. That world was destined to receive beauty and blessings from his presence and his smile. From man the world derives its value, and without him has no excellence. To him it is like the stage to the actor—like the canvas to the colors which combine in enchanting imitations of what is seen or fancied. Let man be exiled from the world and it may be buried in the profoundest abysses of the universe, and none will lament its everlasting ruin.

II. We proceed to consider what estate we may acquire in the soul and in the world. Two things constitute riches; namely, great possessions, and a liberal tenure. And now, although in themselves the soul is so precious and the world so worthless, yet, if we reflect, our relation to them may reverse their values—may make the first last, and the last first—the precious vile, and the vile precious. Ten acres of land in fee simple are worth a thousand by lease, with heavy and consuming rents. A shilling of one's own is worth thousands deposited with us for an hour. One loaf of bread is of more value to a hungry man than a crown of gold to the dying. Thus do circumstances increase or diminish the value of objects around us.

In our second division we use the word estate in its legal acceptation, to designate the interest a man has in that which is his by just possession. This interest depends on covenant engagements, or on the law of the land. The most valuable estate is termed, in legal phrase, a "fee simple." This is where property is assured to a man and his heirs forever. It is conveyed in the strongest terms, and is intended to be like the Median and Persian laws—unalterable. If a man were to gain the whole world, he could expect no more than to hold it by this tenure, and must rest in the security of a mere human warranty.

But the grant is sure to be defeated; first, by the failure of the warrantor, or, second, by the death of the warrantee, or, third, by the destruction of the thing warranted. How vain is that security which is derived from man! He pledges to his neighbor an estate "forever," and writing it on parchment, drops the pen and dies; or he who takes the pledge gains a title to that which is worth very little, except it be as a purchased burial spot, where it is doubtful if his bones will be permitted to repose through two generations. But were the parties to survive, and were death itself destroyed, the world would perish. Then where would be the mountain which seemed to stand so strong? What is a fee simple in that which is doomed to dissolution? Man can not properly thus convey nor take, because the world will be subject to no such disposition. The lofty word "*forever*" is unsuitable to every thing but that which is inscribed with the characters—*eternal.*

Again: As we can not have a fee simple in the world, so neither can we hold in it a "life estate." While we journey through the world, we need its ministrations. But these are not secured to us. Millions die without them. How often, by the malice of a foe, or the envy of a friend—by some popular convulsion, or by some unexpected providence of God, do we lose, in one brief hour, what an impotent conveyancer had assured to us forever! We can not have a life estate in this fading world.

What, then, can we have? Nothing but the lowest estate of all, namely, an estate at will. And the law recognizes no other interest so worthless. Originally it was so insignificant as not to be the object of covenant provision. It was an estate dependent on the mere will of another. To omit its modern qualifications, we hold all we have on earth by this humble tenure. Multiply your warranties to infinity—hold them with ever so firm a grasp—spread them on the public parchments, that they may evidence your rights, and defend you in the undisturbed enjoyment of them, and after all you gain nothing but a mere estate at will.

Whose will? His who claims the world—who "raiseth up one, and putteth down another." God has said, "The world is mine and the fullness thereof." He waits to take its reversion at our hand. He teaches us to look for no extended term—for no warning of its termination. He tells us to be always ready to resign to him his own; because his claim is absolute, and his seizin will be sudden. Thus God controls our fortunes. What we bind on earth he does not bind in heaven. Should we gain the whole world, it is a mere estate at will, too cheap for wise ambition to covet or pursue. The technical precautions which a thousand years have furnished, can secure to us no higher interest. We might as well hold the winds and vapors in fee simple, as the world in its most stable, solid forms. The rainbow hues which deck the shaded skies, are an emblem of the fitful fortunes of poor mortals.

But what estate may we have in the immortal soul? I answer, more than an estate at will. A covenant, faithful and unchangeable, secures to us a higher interest. More, also, than an estate for life.

The soul survives the ravages of death. At that awful hour we must resign our worldly interests. But the process which ejects us from all temporal treasures will only consummate our seizin of those inward energies, of which we now possess the mere germinating seeds. At death all the moral tendencies of the soul will be retained—all its aptitudes strengthened—all its powers invigorated—all its efforts liberalized, by its escape from the clay which did enshrine and incumber it. These will form, thenceforth, our everlasting treasure of weal or woe—of curses or of blessings.

This leads us to say that our estate in the soul will be strictly a fee simple—assured to us "forever"—not by the covenant of feeble man, but by the warranty of Heaven. This estate will be indefeasible by the act or wrong of others, and will be to the holder an inalienable property. It seems, then, that an interest in the world is of the cheapest kind, and an estate in the soul of the very highest nature. The former is contingent, may terminate at any moment, and must, at all events, soon yield to the stern demands of death. The latter is certain—has for its security the pledge of God's own covenant, and will last while God shall live. We proceed to notice the soul and the world in regard—

III. To their usufructuary benefits. By this law term we mean the *advantageous uses* to which both may be appropriated. The world is useful to us. Its ministrations we much need in probationary life. We must breathe its air, bask in its sunshine, drink at its fountains, and feed on its fruits, or we wither like the seared leaf. Yet we need but little, and all beyond that little is a mere incumbrance to us, because it imposes care, and can impart no real satisfaction. But, more particularly, the world is not subject to man's actual, but only to his constructive or nominal possession. We divide society into the rich and the poor; but how great is the difference between them? Has not the poor man air to breathe, and food to eat, and shelter and raiment to protect him? What else do riches furnish? Can the "whole world" supply any satisfactions but such as it pours in upon us through the senses? There was one to whom history ascribes the conquest of the world. And what did he derive from his vast acquisitions? Could he possess what he had conquered? Could he "with one hand touch the east, and with the other the west?" and breathe at once the odors of every clime which his sanguinary hand had seized and trodden under foot? Could "he set his right foot upon the sea, and his left foot upon the earth," and spread the folds of his royal garments over their broad wastes? Were the regions which confessed his prowess, and yielded to his sway, transformed, as by enchantment, into Edens, to cheer and imparadise the conqueror? Could he carry Persia into Egypt, or convey both into India, or transfer them all to Greece, and there eat them, or teach them how to sing or dance, or shine like suns, and entertain him? No. He held, by actual occupancy, the spot on which he stood, or sat, or slept, and all else he was compelled to resign to the vagrant multitudes whom Providence might present to the vacant benefice.

As with the great so with the little. He who has one hundred acres of land, well tilled and innocently appropriated, possesses all he can possess; for actual seizin is by the senses. What we see, and hear, and feel, and taste, and smell, we properly possess, and nothing more. Man has no capacity for the world. He may claim, but can not hold it. And where, then, is its value? He may also point to the moon and all the planetary worlds, and call them his; and these would be as useful to him as the world.

Not so with regard to the soul. Here our possession is not nominal or constructive, but actual and intimate. Here every element, pure and impure, blissful and painful, alluring or repulsive, is so held by us as to be a portion of ourselves. In the soul are no wastes unoccupied, no desert unfrequented and forgotten. We are related to our souls as God is to the universe which is pervaded by his omnipresence. With regard to our souls, we are omnipresent. Consciousness, as an all-pervading spirit, dwells and breathes in all its chambers, attending it in all its outward excursions, and returning to watch its secret retirement. What God possesses he eternally pervades. He dwells in the bright and the obscure—in the low and the lofty of his vast dominions. So do we in regard to our souls. Do we fly backward and hover over the graves of buried scenes? Consciousness is there. Do we soar upward on the wings of expectation and gaze at reversionary treasures? Consciousness is there. Do we unloose an excursive imagination, and yield it to the pastime of a thousand unrestrained wanderings? Consciousness is there. Consciousness dwells amidst all the powers, and intermingles with all the elements, and flows in all the affections of the soul; sees all, and reports all to the reflecting mind. Thus intimately do we possess the soul.

But there is a difference, not only in regard to the intimacy, but also in regard to the constancy of these possessions. The world is capricious. She gives and takes away by turns. Her modes are mutable as the lunar phases. At one moment the world is all love and beneficence. She can scarcely bestow enough upon her children. Her ministrations seem as they began to be toward unsinning Adam in Paradise. She sends to caress us all her sweet and smiling ministers. She shines upon us with her light, warms us with her fires, and fans us by her gentle breezes. She spreads before us the verdure of Spring; feasts us with Summer dainties, and enriches us with Autumn harvests. She waters us from her cloudy canopy, wreathes the gloom with rainbow charms, and spreads over us the bow of the covenant to assure us that her love is everlasting. But we soon find her in another mood, and experience from her another dispensation. She yields up her smiles and meets us with frowns. She puts out her lights and blinds us. She quenches her fires and freezes us. She rekindles them like a furnace, and scorches us. She blots out the beauties of Spring, snatches from our lips the fruits of Summer, and consumes from our garners the stores of Autumn. She converts her dews into frosts, her calms into storms, her temperate ardors into torrid heats, and, from caressing, frowns upon and persecutes us.

The soul is not thus affected. If we seek aright,

we shall find it overspread with a perpetual calm, and cheered by constant sunshine. We shall feel the refreshing dew, and dread no blighting frost. We shall find its climes all temperate, its aspects all fair, its moods all amiable. The charms of a moral Spring, and the sweets of a moral Summer, and the riches of a moral Autumn, all blend in its Divine constitution. And no morose Winter will come to despoil it of these glories, and chill and freeze the spirit. Christ is become a sun to the sanctified soul, and his beams will always cheer it—Christ is become its shield, and he will guard it—Christ is become its food, and he will fill it—Christ is become its heritage, and he will enrich it with everlasting treasures. Thus, all that belongs to the soul may be possessed without interruption. The apostle says, "Rejoice evermore."

Again: The world depreciates—the soul improves by use. The world does not bear acquaintance. The more we have to do with it the less it satisfies us. At first its novelty attracts and entertains us. Familiarity diminishes these attractions, and spoils our entertainment. In the mean time Death is on the way to dismiss us from these scenes of hope and disappointment, and transfer us to the judgment, and to an eternal retribution. We hold the world as the lessee does his premises. The term is every day approaching its close, and, of course, every day lessens its value. But in the soul we have a reversionary interest, whose value is increased in proportion to the depreciation of the leasehold. Let the sinner lay it to heart, that all he has, and all that he can obtain, is of less and less value every day and every hour.

Each moment steals a jewel from his treasures, and soon time will take all. Let the Christian realize, that while the world depreciates, the soul may every moment enrich itself by fresh acquisitions.

The soul is formed for improvement. It is projected for an everlasting progress—if holy, a progress upward toward God and the heights of his throne—if unholy, a progress downward into the depths of sin and misery. Rising or sinking, it must advance, in the vigor of every faculty, in the reach of every thought, and in the measure of every capacity for ecstasy or agony. All may see that the powers of the mind are feeble in the morning of life. A ray of light first flits in its tabernacle. The breath of God fans and kindles it. At last, from a spark of intelligence, without system of thought or effort, it becomes a vigorous spirit, aspiring to the heights of the eternal throne, and watching the developments of its lofty administrations. Do you seek for evidence? Watch the prattler in its playful moods, and then the youth in the glow of opening genius, and then the man in his maturity of wisdom, and you shall find the evidence.

If the soul improve on earth, it will improve in heaven. There it will be free from a thousand embarrassments which now check its pursuit of truth, and detain it in its march through the fields of science. A glorious destiny awaits it. Sanctified by grace, it will journey on forever, through floods of light and fields of bliss, still nearing the throne of God, and happier still in the sweet approximation. Each discovery will become a new point of enlarged observation more entertaining than the last. And she will pass from one point to another—from the summit of one discovery to another—forever extending the range of her vision, and forever increasing her raptures by the rapid ascent and enlarged survey. Thus the soul improves and the world deteriorates by use. If they were now of equal value, it would be madness to choose the world. If the world be silver, it will depreciate to dross—to sordid dust. If the soul be as iron, it will, by transmutation, become as silver—as gold—*a diamond* so precious that Christ will delight to set it in his everlasting crown.

Again: The world is useful only in certain conditions—the soul in all conditions. The world suits the caprice of childhood, the gayety of youth, and the cheerfulness of bright and prosperous states. It answers not in declining age, or in the hour of death. Take the whole world to the dying man, and tell him all is his. Can the world allay the rage of fever? Can it assuage the pains of dissolution? Can it anoint for burial, and animate him with the joys of eternity? No. When man needs help, when he seeks support for a sinking frame, and demands cordials for a fainting spirit, then the world falters and forsakes him. But these are the times for inward triumphs to the soul which spurned the world in anxious care for its own choice interests. Now that soul hath a light within, and beareth through the vale of death sweet and reviving cordials, and maketh music as it passes along, leaning on the rod and staff of the Almighty.

Having glanced at the usufructuary benefits of these estates, we shall,

IV. Consider the consequences depending on our use of them. These are summed up in the "gain" or the "loss" of the soul. Here we doubt some may object that the soul can not be lost. We reply to such a suggestion, that the soul is lost already. If not, why came the Son of man to seek and to save it? The soul whose security you boast, is not only in peril from future events, but is already forfeited to justice; and by God's unerring sentence is doomed to punishment. "He that believeth not is condemned already, and the wrath of God abideth on him." We are not to rest in security already acquired, but we are yet to acquire security. The soul is to struggle from darkness into light, from slavery into liberty.

The Gospel is a system of recovery, not of preservation. It seeks to change, not to confirm. It bears a commission to effect a new creation, not to proclaim the beauty and excellence of the old. It descends to be our angel guide from darkness to light; from midnight glooms and perils to midday calms and splendors. Let this be granted, and does it not follow, that to recover what is lost requires greater effort than to preserve what is already safe? And heaven has, with correspondent effort, commenced the work of our salvation. We, in the same spirit of effort, are to prosecute and consummate it. And it leaves no time to pursue the world. Heaven is to be gained not by the conquest of this world, but by victories over our own hearts, and their affections, by cleansing the base and impure, and seeking in prayer the gracious sympathies of a renovated, heaven-born nature. To accomplish this, so great a work, much need we have to let the world alone, and resign it to those who seek no greater good. Much need we have to follow His example, who, absorbed in the glorious enterprise of man's redemption, so earnestly prosecuted it that he lacked food to stay his hunger, and couch to rest his weary frame. He saw the world only as an object of God's wrathful indignation, which he longed to rescue and to save. So we must see it. In the same spirit we must live, and toil, and die. In our zeal for salvation the world must be forgotten. If we waste our energies in digging for its treasures, we shall inevitably lose our souls.

What is it to lose the soul? To lose the world is to be deprived of it. To lose the soul is quite another thing. The loss of the soul is not deprivation. It is not the loss of perception and reason, and memory and consciousness. It is infinitely worse. It is the perversion of all its faculties, moral and intellectual. It is not the destruction of the noble edifice—vacating its site to the rose, the lily, and the fragrant air. It is the desecration and pollution of the temple, till it becomes a scene of loathsome and abhorred abominations, which none can bear to look upon.

But we must abruptly close. Turn back to the commencement of this sermon, in which we present you—as if startled at the language of the Savior—insisting that the interrogation of the text is preposterous—that its suggestion should be of loss, and not of gain, in a contract where the soul is to be exchanged for the world. Review that opening paragraph. Consider well whether, at some former period, the sentiments therein expressed were not your own. If, as we supposed, you deem the query of the text unfounded, then we entreat you, in the spirit of your theory, live, and act, and die, and live for ever. Steadily survey these objects till the value of the soul appears in striking opposition to this fleeting world. Set the former, in all its grace and durability, against the latter, in all its corrupt and wasting forms. But why should we exhort you? We persuade you that the soul is superior to the world, and you acknowledge it. You confess that the soul is a diamond, precious as God can make it, and the world a mere bed of dust on which that gem reposes, till God shall select it from such unworthy rubbish, and set it, in all its sparkling beauty, among the jewels of his crown.

But, alas! "While your tongue talks of wisdom, your hand dealeth foolishly." And that immortal soul, enstamped with God's own image, and made to "drink of the river of his pleasures," is each hour exposed to sale, and the most trifling earthly good is buying all its interests. Satan would fain possess it. He strives to outbid the Son of God; and with some he does succeed. Jesus has paid his blood, and offers heaven to purchase it. Satan holds up the world, and says, "This will I give thee, if thou wilt fall down and worship me." Do it. Take the price. Serve the world. And that jewel which Jesus intended to ornament his crown shall soon grace the coronet of the triumphant prince of hell.

XIX.

JESUS REVILED.

"He saved others; himself he can not save." Mark xv, 31.

NEVER was there more of truth and falsehood uttered in one sentence than in this. Of truth, because in its letter it asserts the necessity of Christ's suffering; of falsehood, because in its spirit it denies his omnipotence. Let us consider,

I. THE TRUTH OF THE TEXT.

II. THE FALSEHOOD.

I. First, then, it is wholly true that "Christ saved others."

1. He saved them from *temporal calamities.* It is common for infidelity to charge Christianity with apathetic indifference to the sufferings of this life. It questions the purity of that benevolence which busies itself in anxieties for the soul, but overlooks the pains of the body. It denies the sobriety of that faith which impels us to seek the treasures of another world, while we seem indifferent to the comforts of this.

The genius of infidelity addresses Christ's disciples thus: "You talk of two worlds, the present and the future. When you speak of this, your terms are intelligible, for this world is visible. By a thousand influences it impresses on the soul sensations of pain and pleasure. But what you say of a future is altogether mystery. That world is invisible. It has no beauty for the eye, no harmony for the ear; no fragrance or sweets to charm the waiting senses. If there be such a world, man is placed without the sphere of its soul-affecting influences. You plead for a religion which is said to be compounded of truth and love; but, alas! it has no eye to see, no heart to feel, no hand to relieve the sorrows which now assail the victims of misfortune. Its Quixotic zeal anticipates evils which may never come, and guards against ills which probably are visionary. Such charity is graceless. It shows no credentials of its virtue and utility. It hinders, rather than promotes the bliss of man, by diverting his attentions from the means of real happiness, to seek fictitious joys which he hopes to seize hereafter. This religion will not answer. Its charities are reprobate. It wants the proper evidence of sincerity and worth, namely, *consistency*. True religion must breathe a love whose deeds shall be suited to the exigencies of this present suffering life, and not to a future and an uncertain state of being."

Such are the expostulations of infidelity. And what can an accused religion answer to the charge? She can propose a prompt denial; and among a host of witnesses summoned for her defense she can point, first, to him who gave her being; who nursed her helpless infancy; whose tutelary doctrines and precepts and example fashioned her fair form, and molded all her manners—to Him whose meek and loving spirit has possessed, impelled, controlled, all her legitimate, unwavering disciples. Religion can silence such complaints by conducting her accuser to the fields of Palestine, and pointing to those scenes which rise as sacred monuments, or spread like shaded canvas, to commemorate the Savior and his deeds of healing mercy. Judea's hills and brooks and groves, her battle-heights and plains, her fissured rocks, her very dust, could it become reanimate and vocal, would join to vindicate our faith, by proclaiming the history of its Patron and its Lord.

That history informs us that Christ was never weary in his works of saving mercy. "He went through all Galilee," not only to teach in their cities, but "to heal all manner of sickness and disease among the people." His pity for the distressed spread abroad his fame, and "they brought unto him all sick people that were taken with divers diseases and torments, and those possessed with devils, and those who were lunatic, and such as had the palsy; and there followed him great multitudes." The maimed, the blind, the dumb, the halt, the bowed together, waited his healing mandate. Nor did they wait in vain.

He did not stay till friendship sought him out, or flattery courted him from his retreats. He preferred not the mansion of the magistrate to the cottage of the poor, or the hovel of the vile. He did not spurn abject misery, and seek the sickly victims of luxury and pride. In a word, his charities were not human, but divine, and therefore divested of all partiality; falling upon the wretched like rain upon the field, or like sunlight upon the bright meridian. All, from the wisest to the simplest, from the courtly ruler to reprobate publican, from refined and queenly delicacy to the seven-times cursed Mary, were welcome to approach, and sound, if possible, the depths of his compassion. Childhood, youth, and hoary age, were alike precious to the Savior of a world. His word calmed the rage of madness—his look rebuked the demon's fury—his touch restored unclouded vision to the eye of melancholy blindness—his Ephphatha waked the ear of deafness to listening, joyful life—his mandate roused the dead, and despoiled the frighted sepulcher. But these were not his fairest trophies. He performed a work of still greater glory, however the world may view it.

2. He saved others *from the curse of ignorance.* When Christ appeared on earth, the light of useful knowledge had fled to other worlds. That which was called philosophy served no other purpose but to render darkness visible. With sighs and lamentations the best of heathen teachers held up their glimmering tapers, trimmed them with anxious care, fed them with watchful diligence, and invoked the wandering multitudes to come to them for guidance through the glooms and storms of life. But, alas! the light was too feeble to attract the multitude, and too obscure to guide them. The guides themselves grasped it with an uncertain hand, watched its fitful gleamings with alternate hopes and fears, and paused, at last, to doubt, despair, and die. At the advent, darkness covered the earth, and gross darkness the people. The world was not insensible to the wide, withering curse. It felt the blasting scourge, and was groaning for deliverance. It even showed the signs of a near

regeneration, in the piteous throes and wailings of some approaching birth. Then the heavens revealed the tokens of a glad deliverance. The Savior was announced. He came as a light to bear witness to the truth, and "enlighten every man that cometh into the world." His doctrine was from heaven, and he impressed it with convincing energy on the conscience. He lifted up the veils which conceal the worlds invisible, and displayed to human vision scenes of death and retribution. Man was no longer left to the guidance of an obscure or erring light. The Sun of Righteousness arose, and mortals were permitted to bask and triumph amid enchanting scenes, which rose like paradise beneath the first bright sun of Eden. Go up to patriarchal ages, then turn down the stream of history, and see how the light of saving knowledge grows dim and dark in all your course, till you reach the time of Jesus. Then pause and wonder at the gloom. Do you say it was an era of scientific splendor? Alas, the splendor shone from hell! It was an intense reflection from the fires which light perdition. It was the science of falsehood, not of truth—of that which pains, not comforts—of that which kills, not revives—of that which brutalizes and damns the soul, not purifies and adorns it for the supper of the Lamb. The Son of God alone could supplant this baleful science, extinguish these false lights, and diffuse that saving knowledge which has half transformed the world, and is leavening its moral mass into holiness and bliss.

3. But Christ saved others from *sin.* He saved them from *its guilt.* He redeemed the race from the

curse pronounced on Adam. He procured for helpless infancy, in every age and clime, judicial innocence. As his justified subjects, defiled but not condemned, polluted but not malicious, he received children to his arms, pronounced them blessed, and confirmed their sacred title to an inheritance in heaven. He also saved from guilt acquired by actual transgression. Millions in heaven and on earth, like the thief upon the cross, have enjoyed by faith this sweet deliverance. With a voice of benediction, Christ has announced their sins forgiven.

He saved from *its power.* Sin defiles the heart, and renders it a fountain of corrupt and painful passions. What base desires and purposes proceed from within this fountain! No creature power can cleanse it. Its stains are like the leprosy till Christ commands, "Be clean." He cures the vile disorder. He is anointed to heal the broken-hearted, and release the dying captive from sin's most cruel bondage.

He saves from *the punishment* of sin. Where its guilt is remitted and its pollutions are cleansed away, nothing hinders the free and full effect of Mercy, which may then work as pleases her, for Justice will not hinder. Hence her power is redeeming, and transfers the immortal spirit to the paradise above. Thus, as the text declares, Jesus Christ saved others.

But while he ministered thus to others, what befell himself? While he healed others, did he not heal himself? While he ruled the winds and calmed the seas, and roused the dead, did he not defy his enemies? In conscious self-security, did he not scorn their wrath? No. In a sense most moving to the heart of humble piety, "himself he could not save." He must not evade the terrors of the cross. He could not for three reasons. *Covenant*, *prophecy*, and *charity* forbade him.

First, his *covenant* forbade it. He had conferred with the persons of the Godhead, and the work he was then accomplishing was necessary, as the execution of what he had stipulated in concert with the Father and the Holy Ghost. He had pledged himself to justice as a sufficient victim to satisfy her claims, secure her holy interests, and exhibit all her sacred excellencies to the view of heaven, and earth, and hell. He had for four thousand years been receiving upon credit the travail of his soul; and now the travail of his soul was upon him in all its horrors, and he might not turn away from the passion and the agony. The covenant he had made and partly executed, rendered it impossible for the true and faithful Jesus to contradict its claims, or annul its plain provisions. He must fulfill its fixed conditions, and bleed upon the cross. The taunting multitude might cry to him and say, "If thou be the Son of God, now come down from the cross, and we will believe." The reviling scribe might say, "He saved others, himself he can not save." The Savior, taunted and reviled, must, to prove his Godhead, remain upon the cross, and yield himself to death. Having covenanted, he ought to have suffered all these things, and then have entered into his glory.

Second, Christ could not save himself, because *prophecy* forbade it. The covenant to redeem had been published to the world; and that which was at first a stipulation in heaven between the persons of the Trinity, had become a covenant on earth, between Jehovah and his creatures. The world, accursed as it was, corrupt and guilty as it was, could demand this deep humiliation of the suffering Son of God. The pledge was in the hands of his crucifiers; for they held the types and promises which constituted a record obligation upon Jesus to "pour out his soul unto death." This obligation, self-assumed by the blessed, bleeding Savior, now bound him by bonds strong as the truth of Jehovah, to hang, and bleed, and die.

Third, Jesus could not save himself, because his *love* forbade it. His love of holiness and righteousness prompted him to do what should honor all their principles, and maintain their sacred and supreme dominion. This required their vindication in the punishment of man, who had aspersed and contemned them by transgression. His love of man impelled him to an effort to deliver him from those eternal pains, which the vindication of these principles would inflict upon him. To accomplish both these objects, he becomes man, vindicates his law, and saves the rebel subject, by enduring in his own sacred person the agonies of the cross. And his love for the righteous law ot God, and for the race which it condemned, never once forsook him. It moved him to form the covenant to redeem. It bore him on the wings of mercy to our degenerate world. It urged him on, in the midst of all his labors, to their final consummation. It swelled and overflowed his bosom in the hour of final conflict, pouring forth its aspirations in the memorable words, "Father, forgive them!" This love for man warmed his heart in death; and the sneers of the profane and the weapons of ungodliness did not restrain, but feed it. The more corrupt and demon-like the world he came to save, the more his bowels yearned to effect its renovation. The depth of its debasement and completeness of its ruin were the fuel of his pity, so deep, and pure, and glowing, that it bound him to the cross with force indissoluble. "Love is stronger than death," is a truth illustrated in the crucifixion of the redeeming Son of God. Thus it is true that Christ "could not save himself."

II. In the second place, let us consider the *falsehood of the text.*

Its falsehood lies in the *intention* of those who uttered it. How blind were these foul scoffers! What tokens could they covet of Christ's divine mission—of his proper Godhead, which his deeds did not afford them? Well might some of them exclaim, "When Christ appears, shall he do greater miracles than these which this man doeth?" Yet with sacrilegious blasphemy they stand around his cross and say, "Let him now descend, that we may believe!" Why believe? He had invoked dead Lazarus from the grave, while they stood gazing; yet the miracle only served to exasperate their hatred, and provoke crucifixion. Could they, without satanic instigation, believe that he who, by a word, had healed Judea of its sicknesses, fed thousands on five small loaves, calmed the stormy seas, and restored the dead to life, was the helpless victim of their malice? But their labored incredulity was a service to religion. Little did they dream that their malicious taunts contained in them the virtue of a most convincing testimony to prove what they denied. Behold, boasting infidelity, an example of thy folly, and of God's mysterious wisdom! The seers of ancient times had announced the striking truth, that Christ should be a Savior, but yet himself should suffer. And it is even so. He comforts all around him, but is himself a man of sorrows. Healing all, himself is wounded. The sword aimed by force immortal at a world of graceless sinners, diverted by his arm, is bathed in his own blood. He chose this lot of grief for the joy that was to follow. Little did the crafty scribe and plotting priest suspect it, or they would not have declared the prophecy fulfilled, which, because it was unlikely, required the attestation of enmity to prove it. Why did they not perceive that Jesus chose to die, otherwise death had no dominion over him? Had he not throughout his ministry mocked all the rage of death, defied its fatal weapons, and reseized its trembling victim from its frightful, cold embrace? Had he not entered its dark domains and borne back to life and loveliness the profaned and putrid tenants of its most secret chambers? Yes, and they were witnesses. Why, then, do they exclaim, "Himself he can not save?" The Lord insnares the wise in the net of their own craftiness, and this is an example. The malice of his foes is the Savior's testimony—their contradiction his credentials, their reproach his honor, their slander his bright fame, to live, and spread, and bless the world till it burn and sink forever.

Having considered the truth and falsehood of the text, we urge the application of its doctrine:

1. The necessity of Christ's sufferings affectingly appeals to the sinner and the saint. To the sinner, because transgression occasions that necessity. Had not man sinned, Christ had never died. Sin brought the blessed Jesus from the skies. Sin enrobed him in weak and suffering flesh. Sin imposed on him hunger and thirst, nakedness and weariness. Sin drove him to the mount for prayer, to the field or the wilderness for dwelling and for shelter. He must be tempted, persecuted, denied, and betrayed, because we had sinned. He must endure the garden agony, must be buffeted and spit upon, must be crowned with thorns and dragged with thieves to shameful crucifixion, because we had sinned. And shall we sin still? Behold him in his glory before the world was, and trace him in his passage to the garden and the cross, then say—*shall we sin still?*

2. This subject contains an appeal to Christ's disciple. Why could not Jesus save himself? Because he loved you, Christian, with an everlasting love. Let this melt your heart into humble, contrite thankfulness. Rejoice with tears, that in the hour of deepest anguish his love for you was stronger than death. Rejoice that he held to his gracious purpose of redeeming you. With anthems, let heaven and earth celebrate that hour. Let both concert eternal melodies in memory of the cross. Let the taunts of crucifixion form the chorus of that song. Let it echo and reëcho—HIMSELF HE CAN NOT SAVE.

But if the blessed Jesus, for your sake, could not

save himself from the ignominy of the cross, can you, who hear his name, and profess his doctrine and spirit, shun that same cross hallowed by his death? If your salvation could be wrought out in no other way, can you now be saved in any other way? Has he died upon the cross that he might release us from the cross? Nay, he has said, "If any man will come after me, let him deny himself, take up his cross and follow me." O let these words and this example of Christ reverberate their solemn tones through all the chambers of the soul of every worldly minded disciple of the suffering Lamb of God!

He died, and all is well. 'T is well on earth—'t is well in heaven. 'T is well for you, sin-sick soul, burdened, faint and dying—well for thee, suffering pilgrim, who, like Mary, watchest beside his sepulcher—well for you, backslider, who, like Peter, bewail the denial of your Lord—well for you, faithful soul, leaning, like John, upon his bosom—well for you, aged disciple, who hold him, like Simeon, in your trembling arms! Well was it for you, ye spirits of the just made perfect, whose robes are washed in his blood—and well for you, ye angels that excel in might, desiring to look into these holy and blessed mysteries—well for thyself, Father, Son, and Spirit, whose covenant and word, and love are now assured and everlasting, that Jesus could not save himself and come down from the cross!

Glory be to the Father, and to the Son, and to the Holy Ghost, as it was in the beginning, is now, and ever shall be, Amen!

XX.

THE SABBATH OF THE WORLD.

"They shall not hurt nor destroy in all my holy mountain: for the earth shall be full of the knowledge of the Lord, as the waters cover the sea." Isaiah xi, 9.

THIS prophecy is very significant. It is worthy to be inscribed on all the high places of Zion, that her eye may see it, and her spirit receive strength. It presents to the mind images of the world as it has been, as it shall be, and in its progress from the past to the future. I shall invite you, therefore, to survey the world—

I. IN ITS MORAL RUIN.

II. IN ITS MORAL RENOVATION.

III. IN ITS TRANSIT FROM THE FORMER TO THE LATTER.

I. For six thousand years this world has suffered the curse of Heaven, and bears, even now, the deep impress of crime and reprobation. It is replete with sin, and shame, and misery. It is the theater for the display of the basest passions and rankest crimes which pollute and deform the universe of God.

It is vexed by the fury of diabolical passions. It is the seat of pride. Unfitting as this passion is for man, he not merely indulges, but cherishes it. He accounts it not his shame, but his honor. He wears it as a robe, and displays it in all the walks of life, as though it possessed some divine attraction. That abomination which heaven could not tolerate—which roused to flame Almighty vengeance—which doomed angels to chains of darkness, is esteemed the beauty and the glory of this world. Earth grasps with eagerness what heaven repels with loathing.

In close alliance with this passion is envy, its eldest born. Envy is a sort of famine in the soul; nothing but universal misery could relieve it. It matters not what it has devoured, it is in agony because its capacity is filled ere it has consumed all the bliss of conscious being. From envy springs slow-moving malice, with the genius both of the serpent and the tiger, and with more methods and instruments of mischief than man can reckon up.

Pride, envy, and malice are among the prominent evils of the heart. Their malignity must be ascertained by their effects. No analysis can expose it. It could not have been conjectured by any finite mind, that pride and envy are so potent as to produce revolution first around the throne of God, where all was pure and stable, and then in this fair world, which came a paradise from the hand of the Creator, and was designed a residence for new-born, holy spirits, to repair the breach in heaven. And yet, by the energy of these malicious passions, the beauties of Eden became a frightful desolation, heaven itself was blemished, and its choicest moral riches were transformed into the elements of a new, infernal world.

But let us confine our vision to this world, and

examine more minutely its enormous crimes and miseries. Could I skillfully portray the tragic scenes of all its sanguinary ages, your hearts would recoil. Let your imaginations summon from the grave the dead of sixty centuries. From the hundred thousand millions select, first, the disciples of true wisdom. They form so small a portion of the whole, that their subtraction will not sensibly affect the vital mass. Next proceed to separate that mass. Give to these millions a discreet classification, into the moral, who concealed and restrained their vicious appetites; and the profligate, who indulged and exposed them. The former never suffered their base passions to transform them into demons; but glossing into decency the grossness of their vices, acquired the esteem and reverence of mortals. What relation do these bear to true moral excellence on the one hand, and to extreme moral turpitude on the other?

As to moral excellence, charity itself would confess their alienage from all its attributes and charms. Their seeming virtue was an accident, not the intention of any purity of heart. It resulted from the peculiar combination of their vices, which, like blended shades, produced a hue of character unlike any of its elements. What, then, is the real value of that character? It depends on its constituents, and these were impure and destructive. It is a character which the world has treated with some equity in baptizing it morality, thereby denoting an outward form as distinct from inward sentiment, as is the garnish of the sepulcher from the foul abominations contained within its bosom. To moral excellence, then, these persons are related as is the putrefaction to the polish of that sepulcher. On the other hand, to extreme moral turpitude, their relation is like that of the egg to the serpent, which crushed, breaketh out into a viper. Development alone was necessary to constitute them destroyers—murderers. Latent energies of a most pernicious tendency slumbered deep within, and were harmless, like the tiger in its cage, because they were controlled by other vices, or by the restraints of Providence or circumstance.

From the devotees of virtue and the decently depraved, let us glance at the flagitious. Spurning all restraint, and surrendered up to appetite, they become the interpreters of the human heart—the expounders of corrupt human nature. These are not a small minority of mankind. We are not to judge of ages past by what we now behold, nor of what we now behold without careful observation. Hasty judgment would decree to more than half the world the meed and praise of virtue; whereas the true history of the world would be a history of crime, and the recital of its virtues would scarcely form an episode. Is it extravagant to affirm that half the adult world, throughout its generations, is involved in the guilt of heinous crimes? God himself shall be the judge, "Being filled with all unrighteousness, fornication, wickedness, covetousness, maliciousness; full of envy, murder, debate, deceit, malignity; whisperers, backbiters, haters of God, despiteful, proud, boasters, inventors of evil things, disobedient to parents, without understanding, covenant-breakers, without natural affection, implacable, unmerciful."

Here is a picture of the nations, sketched not by man, but by Him who can not err. It presents them in an attitude of murderous rage and murderous deeds. Let your fancy behold them reënact the tragic scenes of their guilty, living hours. Come up, ye blood-stained tenants of the grave! As sands of the sea for multitude, disspread yourselves over a thousand hills and a thousand vales. From terrene heights and ocean depths, and whithersoever the winds and waves have borne your scattered dust, come ye murdered—mingle now as once ye mingled, to curse and kill, to shriek and die! What sights! what sounds! what a fearful blending of fury and dismay, of curses and entreaties, of reeking hands and gory hearts! The rage of six thousand years swells like angry oceans in yonder mass of life. The collected blasphemies of six thousand years are now floating on the breeze, and ascending up to heaven. Millions of faces writhe distorted; millions of eyes glare fury. Every lip is compressed by the power of stern and bloody resolution. For an instant all is wild confusion, and death gleams o'er all the scene. His victims quail. The winds of heaven are burdened with their groans, and earth sickens as she drinks up their blood!

Here is a faint picture of the crimes and miseries of past generations. It reveals half a world murdered in your presence, while the agents and accomplices in this infernal work survive in agonies of conscience, to curse both their being and their Maker.

But you may wonder that we dwell on past generations, and not rather on the present state of things. My friends, cease to wonder. In its essential features, the world remains unchanged. Just around us its bitter waters have been sweetened. But while a few small fountains have been cleansed, the seas and oceans are full of putrefaction. Of eight hundred millions of souls now on earth, one hundred millions have been slightly tamed by the Gospel. Of these, perhaps one-fourth have submitted to the restraints of Gospel principle from conviction and servile fear. A twentieth part may have been radically changed, and blest with the purity and consolations of Christian life. But where are the seven hundred millions that remain? They inhabit regions gloomy and repulsive as death and hell. Bloodshed is the fashion of their lives. It is not a fashion of mere revenge, or even of pastime; but O, blasphemy! it is used for religious sacrifice and worship. With them, bloodshed is not rare. Nature in their bosoms does not abhor it. There are nations in which scarcely an adult could be found whose hands are unstained, perhaps with blood of child or parent! We rejoice that in Christian lands there is commenced a renovation. It points us to that period which is usually termed millennial, which is the theme of the second head of this discourse.

II. It is believed and declared by many persons that these prophecies were uttered under the influence of ardors which were unfavorable to exact description, and that fancy, rather than sober vision, moved and guided the prophetic pencil. We object to this hypothesis. It depreciates too much the prophetic character; it reduces to scorn the Scripture revelation; and last of all, it reproaches God himself. To mention these objections is sufficient. They will bear in every impartial mind the force of irrefutable argument. The chapter which contains the text refers to the millennium. In the first five verses the Messiah is described in the same glowing style as obtains throughout the chapter. And are we to assume that this description of the Savior is also a fancy-piece? that the prophet in his ardor exaggerated the beauties and glories of Immanuel? The thought is profane. In speaking of this "rod from the stem of Jesse," crowned with the wisdom, and girded with the strength of Godhead, we agree that the prophet uttered sober truth. And why should we suppose that he who spoke with such sobriety concerning Zion's King, became a prophet of mere fancies in speaking of Zion's kingdom? We believe that the philologist as well as the prophet was inspired, and that the phraseology employed in this description is intended to shadow forth a perfect moral state.

In this the prophet confirms us. He teaches us that the world will suffer so great a change as to be worthy of a name of honor utterly unsuited to its present character. In expectation of that change, God calls it "his holy mountain." The appellation is high and glorious. It could scarcely be applied to that which bears the slightest impress of sin and suffering. It would form a proper designation of heaven itself, with its glorious hierarchies and its everlasting thrones. When applied to less than heaven, it must at least point to objects in which all pure and lofty attributes possible to creatures are made to concentrate, and from which all others are excluded. And such shall be this world.

It is called *mountain*, which indicates that God will place it high in his affections, will exalt it among the worlds, and will station around it the guards of his omnipotence. It is called *holy*, and that in a sense not negative, but positive—not merely to indicate its freedom from defilement, but as a dwelling-place of holiness—as the home of spotless beings who will adore their Maker with seraphic ardors, and will extol him with everlasting anthems. It is called *God's* holy mountain, not merely to designate his property therein, but in token of his purpose to dwell and reign there, and make it glorious as the place of his rest.

The language indicates that the whole earth will be sanctified, and will become the mountain of God. The islands and continents; the rivers, seas, and oceans, shall aspire to this Divine honor, and shall not aspire in vain. God will impress a comely uniformity upon every thing terrestrial—a uniformity not of outward aspect, but of moral, spiritual grace. The inequalities which now obtain between nations, civilized and barbarous, Christian and heathen, will disappear. The "Sun of Righteousness" will rise on all the nations. Every valley shall be exalted, and every mountain shall be brought low; the crooked places shall be made straight, and the rough places plain. The state of the world will then be one of perfect innocence. There shall be *nothing to hurt or destroy.*

What a picture is this of the happiness of a renovated world: a picture without one gloomy shade, fair as light and comely as heaven! Now, almost every thing is charged with some malignant influence. Whatever may attract us, we approach dreading some latent evil. When we pluck the rose, we watch for the thorn; when we recline in bowers, we dread the serpent; when we gather sweet fruit, we select the salutary from the poisonous; when we breathe the most fragrant atmosphere, we are apprehensive of the wandering pestilence. Human associations, which seem to promise security and rapture, are found to be both perilous and painful. Even friendship deceives us. It invites our confidence, betrays our weaknesses, and triumphs in our agonies. The strongest, purest love, such as glows in the maternal bosom, has been known to turn back its streams, or to be dried up in its fountains. In fine, every thing, animate and inanimate, rational and irrational, is less our friend than our foe—is more to be dreaded than to be desired—is more to be avoided for its probable malignity, than to be sought for its possible advantages. So true is this, that experience teaches us to assume a repulsive attitude toward every thing around us, and either bid defiance to the world, or yield ourselves its despairing victims.

Such a world as this God has adopted as his own, and has purposed by regeneration it shall become the seat of unoffending innocence and of universal love. After a few more generations, ours will become a sanctified race. All will be holy. Not a thought, a sentiment, or an agent of evil, will be found in all these regions of terror, pain, and death. Where all will be holy, there can be no need of suffering, for the purposes either of discipline or punishment. Every bosom will then overflow, not as now, with malignant passions, but with charities pure as the love, and refreshing as the mercy of Godhead. Frequent and joyous, then, will be the communion between earth and heaven. No more will angel messengers bear from paradise commissions of vengeance. They will descend as ministers of mercy, to adore Immanuel in this, his holy habitation, and to salute with pure embraces the redeemed of his love. No more shall pestilence and death go before Jehovah; but he shall lay his hand upon the nations to bless them, and from his rainbow smile shall distill diffusive rapture, to crown the bliss of this new-created world.

While earth and heaven will be so intimately blended, powers infernal shall dread the holy concord, and quake at their affiance. Earth and hell shall be divorced. Their league against Jehovah shall be broken, and all their ancient covenants shall be dissolved. The devil and his angels shall be exiled to the pit, and not come forth to vex the nations. The omnipotent dynasty of Zion's King will guard the approaches to that holy mount, which will then be the seat of an empire secure and impregnable as the barriers of heaven.

And now, can you scarcely anticipate the approach of these scenes? Do you deem it almost too much to be believed, that out of materials so unsightly as the world now contains, there should arise a beauty so perfect? that from such vile discord there should arise such harmony? that from a universe of groans and tears there should arise a universe teeming with bliss and flooded with rapture? We know it is a matter in which doubt is facile and faith is difficult; yet we have at hand a cure for skepticism. God has pledged this blessedness to the world, and his covenant is begun to be fulfilled. The testimony of his lips and the evidence of our senses are a sufficient confirmation. Whoever suspects his naked word, his covenant, his oath, may behold the world in its gradual transition from a lower to a loftier moral station. He may witness the working of meliorating influences, or, rather, of regenerating energies, which, from their effects, are known to be of sufficient force and virtue to complete the new creation.

But we shall amplify this thought as we proceed—

III. *To consider the world in its transit from a ruined to a renovated state.* On this topic we shall confine ourselves to the *power*, the *mode*, and the *instruments* of its renovation.

1. The power is Divine. The same Almighty energy which reared the stately fabric is engaged to reëdify the whole. This truth must never be forgotten. On it we must build our high expectations of the coming grace and glory. Faith would be folly did it look to any arm but that of Omnipotence to effect so great a change. Our labor to advance it would be almost profane, were it not bestowed in reliance on God. The enterprise is his own. All its parts bear the impress of his hand. Every new-born soul is begotten by his word, and can trace its heavenly life to the quickening influence of his Spirit. At that moment when the world shall be wholly sancti-

fied, it will form a richer illustration of his wisdom, power, and love, than when the "morning stars sang together, and all the sons of God shouted for joy."

2. Although Divine power will effect this new creation, it will not be by miracle. It will be a gradual, not an instantaneous work. It will be, not like the springing up of worlds from chaos, but like the stealing dawn or the cautious tread of Spring, its march will be clandestine, and its gentle, noiseless conquests will be almost unobserved among the nations. And thus the text presents it. The knowledge of God, or of his truth, diffused throughout the earth, is to transform it into holiness and beauty. The Bible is the source of Christian knowledge. This blessed volume, attended by the Holy Ghost, is charged with energy divine. The power of God is in it. You may perceive, then, that the world is now suffering transformation and improvement.

Within half a century the Bible has been translated into a multitude of languages. It is now rendered accessible to a hundred tribes and nations, which were lately excluded from all its hopes and joys. And more than this, the *preaching* of the Gospel is ordained to give it impression and effect. And its ministers are multiplied. Many are running to and fro, and knowledge is increased. The world, which had for centuries looked with nausea upon the proffered Word of life, now displays a craving appetite for its teachings and its blessings. Once the heathen waited for the Gospel to search them out; but now, like the hungry multitudes which followed after Jesus, they come to seek the Gospel. Their sighs, borne on the breezes of the wilderness, die away upon our ears, and fall like death-sounds on our hearts. They traverse arid plains and ocean wastes, and, like the Athenian messenger from Marathon, sink, faint and dying, at our thresholds. But in their agony they raise their withered hands, point us to their country, and whisper *the "name of the Christian's God!"*

What mean these tokens? They admonish us that God, by his Spirit, has created a universal thirst among the nations, and that they are turning everywhere to find the springs of life. The whole earth is convulsed by the movement. An earthquake shakes the globe—not to bury in its ruins the dwellers on its surface, but to rouse their sleeping consciences, to display God's awful power, to reveal the reeking wonders of the Cross, and to impel its streams of healing mercy to a universe of broken, bleeding hearts. Then earth shall be like heaven.

3. But in the regeneration of the world there are not only power and method, but instruments. Such is God's plan of working, that the *instruments* are as indispensable as the *power.* Without them God will not exercise his power. His chief instruments are the ministers of Jesus, and the members of his militant Church. To his ministers he says, "Go ye into all the world, and preach my Gospel to every creature." The Church he warns to pray for his ministers, to reciprocate temporal good for spiritual, and, more generally, to "distribute to the necessities of the saints."

The preachers of God's Word are his instruments

in executing the most beneficent enterprise ever conceived by infinite wisdom. This is enough to overwhelm them. To think that they, frail earthen vessels, are made the depositories of the treasures of Gospel truth, and are commanded at their peril to distribute those treasures, not to a few, nor to many, but to *all*, is enough to raise the dead. It may well allay their worldliness, chasten all their pleasures, annihilate ambition, root out pride, and blot from their hearts the love, and even memory of every thing but duty.

Their condition is embarrassing. Moved by the high behest of Heaven, they take on them the ministry; yet they feel that to accomplish its full purpose, the Church must minister to them also. In the name of a disciple she must bestow a crumb of bread and a cup of cold water. She must freight them on shipboard, and send them forth as wanderers, to pray, and preach, and die, in barbarous climes. She must furnish them with copies of the Scriptures, that they may sow the seeds of truth in pagan soils, and leave it to a happier generation of Christ's servants to reap what they have sown.

We say their position is embarrassing. And do you ask why? Because it involves both responsibility and dependence. God commands them to visit all the world. He enjoins it on the Church to empower them to do it. They depend on the Church. But if she prove craven, her dereliction is no excuse for them. If the Church will feed them, they can go and live and labor; if she will not feed them, they must go and suffer and die.

And now I am at that point of this discourse which appeals to the Church's sense of duty, to her humanity, to her ardent Christian charity and sympathy. To preserve unity in this appeal I will reject all other topics, and press on your attention the sufferings of the missionary. You know that many of the ministers of Jesus are turning their faces from the delights of home and country, to the arid wastes of paganism. Some are already enshrouded in its gloom, some are buried in its bloody soil. Some are on the ocean seeking for, and hastening to, the deserts which are to drink their flowing tears, and expose their bleaching bones. Some seek the equator, some the pole; some bear the standard of the Cross into the heart of bleeding Africa; some unfurl it on the shores of Ceylon, others at the bases of the Andes, and others still on the plains of Oregon.

"From shores where freedom dwells, and Gospel light—
Where holy Truth unveils her radiance bright,
Glides the proud vessel to the distant strand;
With eager footstep, on that stranger land,
Alights the messenger of peace—his eye
The index of his heart's philanthropy.
How changed the scene! The savage, nursed in blood,
Impure, and treacherous as the changeful flood,
Circles his exile home; enslaved to sense,
Degraded outcasts from intelligence."

While he suffers in cold exile, you dwell at home. You greet your friends by day, and your own hearth becomes a paradise by night. You have found the blessed Savior. His presence cheers your dwelling, sanctifies your joys, calls forth aspiring hope, will guide you to the tomb, and will transport you to heaven. Consider all these circumstances of comfort, hope, and joy, then turn to the wandering minister of Jesus. Array your ease against his toil, your joys against his sorrows, your sweet associations in the midst of Christian life against his frightful solitude, or his more frightful fellowships. Set your means of comfort, your competency, your wealth, against his destitution, his poverty, his vagrancy. Place the pictures before you in their shades of striking contrast, and then, for the sake of Jesus Christ, spare him from your abundance one little morsel. I ask not your dwellings, or furniture, or treasures—I ask no more than you give in one short year to gew-gaws and sweetmeats for your children. They for whom I ask it are holy men of God. Their names are written in heaven, and they will shine as the stars forever and ever; yet they will gladly eat the crumbs that fall around your tables. Surely you will not spurn them; you will grant them this poor privilege. But as you can not send them fragments of bread and flesh, bestow a little silver in their place. A dollar from your hand may relieve the hunger of an apostle of the Lord, and purchase for him the privilege of pointing the savage eye of some proud, expiring pagan to the bleeding Lamb of God!

XXI.

THE IMMUTABILITY OF CHRIST.

"*Jesus Christ, the same yesterday, and to-day, and forever.*" Hebrews xiii, 8.

IMMUTABILITY belongs only to God. It is claimed by him in the Scriptures of truth as one of his distinguishing attributes—an attribute in which he differs from all creatures, and by which he is elevated infinitely above them. To the immutability of his nature he teaches us to trace the stability of his purposes, and the moral uniformity of his government over the world. To his immutability we must ascribe that deliberation of his providence which neither his friends nor his foes can disturb—a deliberation which prevents all haste to reward and to punish, and which accomplishes the work of moral correction, and of ultimate retribution wisely, both in regard to their methods and their periods. "I am the Lord, I change not, therefore ye sons of Jacob are not consumed."

The text ascribes immutability to our Lord Jesus Christ. Of course, it presents him as clothed with an incommunicable attribute of Jehovah. No language can be found, in the Jewish or Christian Scriptures, which less equivocally or more forcibly asserts absolute and eternal unchangeableness, than does the language of the text—"*Yesterday—to-day*—and *forever.*" Yesterday denotes eternity past; to-day designates the present; forever points to eternity future. In these three states, embracing with an impressive particularity and emphasis a *whole eternity*, Christ is declared to be the same. And the declaration proceeds from authority which it were impious to discredit, and profane to contradict.

The inevitable inference is, that Christ is the "true God." This is the conclusion to which the language of the text would naturally conduct the mind of a docile disciple. Can we apply its affirmation to creatures the most exalted? Enoch, and David, and Paul were very eminent men. Substitute either of those names, or that of Michael or Gabriel, for Jesus Christ, in the text, and you can better determine the propriety of reducing our blessed Lord to an equality with angels, or to a level with mere man.

The apostle inculcates patience under trials, by an argument drawn from the unchangeableness of Christ. Let us briefly dwell on this encouraging theme, by considering,

I. What is implied in the DIVINE IMMUTABILITY.

II. The peculiar support which the believer derives from THE UNCHANGEABLENESS OF CHRIST, as blending in himself the Divine and human natures.

I. Let us inquire what is implied in the Divine immutability. On this point we must be cautious, and not include in the idea of Christ's immutability that which does not properly belong to it. When we say that he is unchangeable, we do not mean that whatever may be predicated of him is unchangeable. Action may be predicated of Christ. But his actions are not invariably the same. He employs his agency in new scenes of creation and providence, and with variations adapted to the purposes of his infinitely inventive and benevolent mind. To speak more plainly, he begins to do things which he had never done, and ceases to do them when his work is finished. He *began* to make this world, and having accomplished it, as the history declares, he "rested from all his work." The time will come when he will begin to destroy this world, and having done it, he will cease. It is evident, then, that there are variations in Christ's agency. And such variations we shall find to be in perfect harmony with his immutability.

The immutability of Christ does not imply an *unchanging providence.* His government must always suit the moral states—the holiness or the sinfulness of his creatures. If his subjects are immutable, his providence must be so; but if *they* change, his dispensations toward them must be varied. His creatures have changed. The holy have become sinful, and the sinful holy. Therefore, his providence toward them has also changed. The Divine smiles, which originally constituted the bliss of the unsinning pair, have been turned into frowns. Curse has succeeded blessing at the mouth of the Lord. Paradise, with its charms, has been blotted out, and earth has become a depository of plagues and curses, to distress and to destroy her rebellious children. This is an example of the innumerable variations of providence toward capricious moral subjects. Christ's immutable rectitude requires that his providence should be thus varied, and adapted with infinite skill to the moral states of his creatures.

Christ's immutability does not require that he should so adjust his providences to the moral states of his creatures, as to render their harmony apparent to us in this life. He is pledged to the ultimate vindication of all his actions. But the time is not now. At present he permits his ways to be involved in much obscurity, so far as man is concerned. We are left to wonder at the sufferings of the innocent, and the prosperity of the guilty; and must wait until "every secret thing is brought into judgment," for the clearing up of the mysteries which are involved in the Divine administration. To us it would seem that there is partiality in the controlling energy which sends the Gospel to one nation and not to another—which produces a revival in one city and not in another—which bears present conviction to the conscience of one sinner and not of another. Without the Bible to guard us, and without faith in its assurances, we might infer from such dispensations that God is exceedingly capricious, and that he is as free from the control of firm and righteous principle as the most unstable and unreasonable of his creatures. But all these temptations to misconceive and misjudge the Divine administration grow out of our ignorance, which God will sometime disperse, and show us, to our admiration, that he was unchangeably wise and righteous in his government of mankind.

Christ's immutability does not imply a circumstantial uniformity in the revelations which he makes of himself to his creatures. His countenance may change—may be veiled and unveiled by turns, while he remains the same. He, therefore, appears and disappears among men, as suits the purposes of his infinite wisdom. In ancient times he exhibited the tokens of his presence to the senses—as to Adam, to Jacob, to Abraham, and to Moses. He revealed himself in the groves of Paradise, in the pillar of fire, and in the lightnings of the stormy mount. Sometimes his presence was a form exhibited to the eye, sometimes a sound falling on the ear, and sometimes an impression resting on the soul, and overwhelming it with the tokens of his anger or his love. He came also as angel or as man, to hold converse with his degenerate children. But he did not always walk in Eden, nor glow in the burning bush, nor thunder on the mount of terrors, nor shine amidst the tents and tabernacles of Israel. Yet veiled or unveiled, seen or unseen, revealed in fire, in thunder, in the form of man or angel, or not revealed at all, Christ himself is the same.

But *how* is he the same? He is the same in his *attributes*, in his *purposes*, and in his *promises*.

He is the same in his *attributes*. He is unchangeable in his omnipresence, his omniscience, and his omnipotence. These are involuntary and necessary attributes. He can no more dispense with them than with his being. They are his yesterday, to-day, and forever. They were employed in the creation. In originating and cherishing the forms of universal life, they *will* be employed forever. He is infinitely and unchangeably wise. He knows the end from the beginning, and makes an infinitely equitable use of his knowledge. He is infinitely and unchangeably holy. This is a voluntary attribute, in which he exceedingly delights, and which flows in streams of ceaseless beneficence to the myriads of his creatures.

He is unchangeable in his *purposes.* These have always existed under the influence of unmingled benevolence, and thus they always will exist. It is now, always was, and always will be, his purpose to punish sin, and to reward obedience. Never for a single moment has he relaxed this holy and righteous purpose. It is as inflexible as the pillars of his throne. When that purpose changes, Christ will cease to be Jehovah.

Lastly, he is unchangeable in his *promises.* His promises are mere records or publications of his purposes, and as these are stable, those must be sure. All his promises, both to the good and to the evil, will be fulfilled in showers of blessings or in storms of wrath. He has said that heaven and earth may pass away, but that his Word shall not pass away. He has added oaths to promises, that, doubly assured, we may be warned or comforted—warned, as obdurate sinners, that there is no hope of escape; and encouraged, as contrite believers, that no wrath awaits us. Thus is Jesus Christ, in the language of the text, "the same yesterday, to-day, and forever." In his essential attributes, in his holy purposes, and in his unfailing promises, he is the unchangeable Jehovah.

II. The doctrine of Christ's immutability affords support to believers under trials. The unchangeableness of Jehovah, viewed separate from Christ, can not comfort—can not strengthen. It is when Divine immutability blends with the condescending sympathies of humanity in the person of Christ, that it becomes available to our support.

That we may appreciate our Christian privileges, we must consider that in Christ we have a new manifestation of Jehovah. We have noticed the various forms in which he formerly revealed his presence to mankind. In ancient times, these revelations were made to select individuals or communities. But when Christ came in the flesh, the revelation was intended for the *world.* He who blessed Abraham, wrestled with Israel, and talked with Moses face to face—he who associated with Shadrach and his brethren in the furnace, and guarded Daniel among the lions, came at last on a visit less transient, and far more public, and gracious, and merciful. For four thousand years, a mysterious sympathy for our fallen race had occasionally brought the Holy One of Israel into the midst of us. At last he comes to fix the "habitation of God amongst men." But he does not appear in cloud or in flame—in the vesture of lightning or of storm. Nor does he come in the form of angel, or with the mere countenance of man. His last advent of mercy is *in the flesh,* and is assumed by ordinary forms. Like any of his creatures, he goes to the wardrobe of nature, seeks his attire, casts it around him, and presents his humbled humanity to the world. Why was not that humanity assumed by some open and attractive miracle? Because he would not avert its reproach, and invest it with a dignity not properly its own. He chose to appear in servile form, uncomely as a root out of dry ground. To the eye of ambition his was a repulsive, not an attractive presence. Whatever was exotic to human nature, he seemed resolutely to exclude; while all that was indigenous — except its moral taint—he seemed resolutely to claim. Nativity, infancy, childhood, youth, and mature age, were his chosen states. He practiced submission in domestic and social life. He had the innocent appetites of man, and sought their sinless gratification. His lot was poverty and reproach. Privation, with its hunger and thirst, its houseless vagrancy and weariness and painfulness, was his heritage. Can we contemplate him in these aspects of depressed humanity, and accredit him as the immutable God? While we look upon his visage, "marred more than any man," can we *feel* that we look upon Jehovah?

We often derive false impressions from outward show, even when we know that show to be deceitful. Virtue in a ragged livery is slighted, while vice in princely robes is half adored. So it is with persons. Royalty enthroned is feared and obeyed—in exile, is pitied and despised. When David issued his mandates from the palace, they were obeyed with diligent dispatch; but in reproach and exile his royal order was forgotten, and his wretched son was slain. We are strongly moved by outward appearances, and slightly affected by objects of faith—unless that faith be of the operation of God. In our views of Christ, the text should correct this tendency. From the manger and the cross, it should direct our attention to the glory which Jesus "had with the Father before the world was." In his humiliation his judgment is taken away—his character is misconceived, unless from the point of observation which discloses the scenes of his suffering, faith looks upward and surveys his forsaken throne. In his mere agony, can we perceive any thing to impress us with reverence or adoration? Is there dignity in a crown of thorns? Is there honor—is there glory in the Roman cross? Alas! unrestrained by a divinely wrought faith, how promptly does nature rise up in us, as we take our station at the cross of the sufferer, and demand—"If this Christ be God, where now is his Deity? Where is his wisdom—where his strength, that he eludes not—resists not his sanguinary foes? If this Christ be God, whence these throes, these convulsive pangs—the wail bursting from a spirit overwhelmed with terrors, and confessing its *exile* from the Father?"

Faith must respond to these interrogatories. They rise in the minds of all, and sometimes to the disquiet of the sincere. It must be settled in our hearts, that in his humiliation the divine glories of Christ—like the sun behind the clouds—are not quenched, but *veiled.* And do we not see his Godhead now and then beaming through the concealment which surrounds him? Sometimes the tokens of his humanity and his Deity blend in most convincing concert. Consider his birth. At the mention of it, do the manger and its rude associations suddenly present themselves? Do you seem to behold the ejected parent, driven out, like Adam from Eden, to implore from nature a shelter for its exiled God—or with the embarrassment of meek-eyed modesty, seeking to fraternize him with the tenants of the stall? While you remember these things, do not forget that other events belong to the history of his birth. No prince or potentate was ever honored with such rare pageantry as attended the natal hour of the Son of God. Earth disregarded, but heaven was moved—all its harps were strung, and untried melodies flowed to other worlds:

> "Swift through the vast expanse it flew,
> And loud the echo roll'd;
> The theme, the song, the joy was new,
> 'T was more than heaven could hold.
> Down through the portals of the sky
> The impetuous torrent ran;
> And angels flew with eager joy,
> To bear the news to man."

The nativity of Jesus was heralded by the prophets of four thousand years, and by messengers of God out of heaven.

Our Savior's life, as well as his birth, displays both his Godhead and his manhood. True, as man, he suffers the pangs of hunger; but as God, he feeds thousands upon a few loaves. As man, he seeks fruit from the tree; but as God, his word blasts the tree from its root. Does he ride into Jerusalem on an ass? He also rides upon the wings of the wind, and makes the waters his pathway, transporting himself from the mountain to Gennesaret, and walking on its stormy waves. Was he derisively robed in scarlet, and crowned with thorns? At his transfiguration he was clothed in raiment white as snow, and his face did shine as the sun. Did he yield to the power of death, and give up the ghost? Even the grave was his empire, and he held its keys. In his own good time he spurned its dominion and cast away its cords.

Such are some of the tokens of Christ's supreme Divinity. And now, standing by the cross, and watching the scene of his deep humiliation, let us realize that we behold the true God. Let us never forget that the expiring Nazarene is infinite in glory. Those very eyes which pour out floods of sympathy at the grave of Lazarus, look through heaven, earth, and hell. Yonder victim of human impotence formed the worlds, marked their courses, and impels them in their flight. He who cries, "I thirst," laid earth's broad foundations, reared its massy mountains, delved its vales, and hollowed the beds of its seas and oceans. Is it so? In that weary sufferer are there concealed the energies which impress this fair creation with its charms? To that fainting form may we trace the hidden source of all that ever *was*, or *is*, or *shall* be? Yes. He who is now gasping out his life, once breathed on chaotic ruins and marshaled them in order. He breathed again, and earth forsook her chambers to greet the new-born light. He breathed again, and verdant charms and flowery graces curled and waved upon her surface. He breathed again, and from her teeming bosom sprang all that animate her dust, shelter in her vales, or flood with life her watery depths and airy heights.

Deem not these views of the character of Jesus irrelevant to my theme. They will prepare us better to appreciate the doctrine which the text inculcates. Immutability, of itself, has no value. Its excellence as an element of character depends on other associated attributes. Let *wisdom, power,* and *benevolence* be stamped with the seal of immutability, and they constitute infinite perfection. In Jesus Christ we have all. But we have them, too, in forms of revelation, which assort most strangely with our own state. That God in all his persons is unchangeably wise, strong, and good, we might possibly have perceived without their manifestation by Christ as our incarnate Redeemer. But whether without Christ we could have availed ourselves of that knowledge for saving purposes, is more than doubtful. In such a case we should have regarded God's wisdom as strictly judicial, his power as the minister of stern equity, and his goodness as the almoner of bounty and of bliss to those only who yield a sinless and perpetual obedience to his declared will. We should have inferred from these attributes of Jehovah, the inevitable destruction of all moral offenders, and the preservation of the unsinning, in states of perfect enjoyment. If, as sinners, we had in such circumstances fondly looked for the favor of God, it would have been an unreasonable, because an unwarranted expectation.

Who now can fail to perceive the nature of our gains, as sinners, by the sufferings of Christ? He is not only wise, but he has become *our* wisdom. He is not only righteous, but he has become *our* righteousness. He is not only holy, but he has become *our* sanctification. And to draw us by the sweet violence of a subduing faith to these, his treasures of wisdom, strength, and beauty, he makes out to us the evidence of three things: First—that he hath borne in himself our weaknesses and woes, and of course feels a quick sympathy for our sorrows, and a deep concern in our destinies. Second—that these benevolent sympathies are armed with the strength of omnipotence, in our behalf. Third—that these sympathies of his manhood, and this energy of his Godhead, are immutable; so that we can fear no change in the blessed Savior's willingness and ability to bring "off conquerors, and more than conquerors," all who enlist under his banner, and cleave to him as the Captain of their salvation. This last is the doctrine of the text.

How can the believer indulge a servile fear, when he is taught thus to apprehend Christ? Entering his closet, he bows down between the cross and the throne. *There*, are pledged to him the sympathies of the humanity, and the energies of the Divinity. He pleads with him who not only occupies the throne, but with him who also reposed in the manger—with him who not only commands the winds and waves, but with him who also wept over Jerusalem—with him who not only will judge the worlds, but with him who also felt the agonies of dissolution, and bowed himself submissive unto death.

In the language of the context, then, *consider* him who is "the end" of the believer's "conversation"—Jesus Christ, the same yesterday, to-day, and forever. Consider him in his states of humiliation and exaltation—of weakness and of power—of suffering and of triumph. Especially, when grief and temptation, with all their waves and billows, go over thee, keep thy steadfast eye on him who has made the passage of this sea of sorrows before thee, that he might, as an experienced voyager along its stormy passes, keep thee from harm, guide thee in safety, and bring thee to the haven:

> "While he is intimately nigh,
> Who—who can violate thy rest?
> Sin, earth, and hell, thou mayest defy,
> Leaning upon thy Savior's breast."

Finally—if we would know what Jesus is, let us search the records of his life. From his condescension while on earth—from his tender solicitude for his followers, from the compassion with which his bosom overflowed toward the sick and the suffering, and from the prompt exercise of his power to relieve those who believingly and reverently sought his mercy, we are to judge of his present character. How many and how wonderful were the examples of his charity! Whose hunger did he not relieve? Whose infirmities did he not bear? Whose sickness did he not heal? And has he divorced himself from pity? He bore his *humanity* to heaven, and has he left his sympathies behind? No. We have not an High Priest who can not be touched with the feeling of our infirmities. He will still bear our weaknesses. He was already ascended when the apostle said, "Cast all your care upon him, for he careth for you." Blessed be his holy name, he still knows, as in the days of his flesh, "*how to succor them that are tempted*," and still he speaks to us, and says: "*I will never leave thee nor forsake thee.*"

XXII.

CHRISTIAN PATRIOTISM.

A DISCOURSE OCCASIONED BY THE DEATH OF PRESIDENT HARRISON.

"*Pray for the peace of Jerusalem.*" Psalm cxxii, 6.

WE are brought just now to a solemn pause. An unexpected and deplored event assembles millions in the temples of religion, to humble themselves devotionally before God, and to consider the meaning of his providences. Thus we are assembled. The tenor of the proclamation which convenes us must govern our meditations. It calls us, not to pronounce eulogies on the illustrious dead, but to offer prayer to the supreme Governor of nations for our country—for its government, so much the object of our solicitude and prayers—for its surviving rulers, burdened with such delicate and vital trusts, and for ourselves, under God the sovereign guardians of its integrity and welfare.

Prayer is helped by meditation. To contemplate the good which our prayers are intended to secure, will feed the fervor of our devotions. Let us, then, while performing acts of national humiliation, glance at those social interests whose perpetual preservation we anxiously implore. The genius of our Federal

Constitution demands that we institute frequent and solemn inquisitions to assure us of the integrity of its ministers and of its beneficent operation. And it is in harmony with the event which has convened us, and with the patriotism which glowed in the bosom of our lamented Chief Magistrate, that our thoughts and sympathies should travel forth, and be busied in devices for the welfare of the nation. Assembled as we are, to implore blessings on our country, how meet it is to inquire what will make that country blest!

I shall invite your patient but brief attention to the following questions:

I. WHAT BLESSINGS SHOULD WE SEEK FOR OUR COUNTRY?

II. WHY SHOULD WE SEEK THEM BY PRAYER?

I. Among the national blessings which we should seek for our country, I will enumerate

1. A *beneficent form of civil government.* Government is necessary. This is implied in the Jewish and Christian Scriptures, and has been confessed in all ages. A few years since it could not have been believed that an American would rise up and denounce all human government. It remained for recent times, with its unprecedented ultraisms—its neological advances in religion, in philanthropy, and in social improvement, to commence crusades against all political institutions. It has been justly held that the worst government is better than none, because without it society could not exist. Let religion reach the point of perfect and universal sanctification, and it would not render civil government unnecessary or inexpe-

dient. It would modify our political constitutions by relaxing the rigor of their provisions and rendering penalties useless. But national distinctions would remain, and would perpetuate the bonds of civil compacts. Before government can be dispensed with, men must be infallible in understanding as well as immaculate in purpose. I repeat, therefore, that civil government is necessary, and its worst form is better than none.

But all forms are not of equal utility. Some governments are evil, though less evil than anarchy. *Good* government is among the choicest donations of Providence. It is good in itself, and it enhances the value of every other gift. Whether government shall be a blessing or a curse, or both by turns, or both with subtractions and mitigations, depends much on the provisions of the civil constitution. By constitution I mean those written instruments, or those cherished usages which create the depositories of civil power. The constitution prescribes that the supreme power shall be in one, in many, or in a majority. It dictates how much power public officers shall sway—whether they shall be elective or hereditary—whether the legislative, judicial, and executive departments shall be blended or severed, and other cardinal principles of equal and of vital moment.

The constitution, then, has much to do with the prosperity or adversity of any nation. It is true that under the worst constitution the people may enjoy prosperous periods. In an absolute monarchy, where the will of the sovereign is law, and where the most cruel mandates are unquestioned, tyranny can not always occupy the throne. It will now and then leave an interregnum to be filled by a gentler spirit, under whose generous scepter the oppressed may breathe. But these are only accidental or providential intervals in the career of tyranny. Government should *secure* something to its subjects. Men should so fashion it as to *enforce* its contributions to their peace and happiness. God has nowhere commanded us to erect thrones, invest them with the indefeasible prerogatives of tyranny, and yield them to the possession of whomsoever the issues of war or stratagem may place thereon. Nor has he called us to construct governments whose principles shall subject us to the ministry of mercy or of malevolence, according as good or evil men shall chance to ascend the seats of power. So far from this, we are morally obliged to secure, if possible, forms of government which shall not only yield brief periods of prosperity, but which shall secure to us unremitted thrift and happiness—forms which shall not render tyranny facile and protection difficult; but such as shall make equity and clemency inevitable, and oppression, as nearly as may be, impossible. Under the influence of such governments, society assumes new and attractive forms. Where they exist, they should be cherished with almost as much solicitude as was the fire upon the Jewish altar.

In all these respects no government excels our own. Its prominent features are so nearly what we might desire, that there is small chance for improvement. It places the supreme power in the hands of a popular majority, who exercise it through representatives of their own enlightened choice. It extends the franchises of the citizen to the utmost limits of safety, and guards his acknowledged rights by the strongest possible defenses. Under so benign a regimen we have prospered beyond example, and have reason to be satisfied with our national compact. We should desire no radical change in our federal or state constitutions. As to the former, Heaven forbid that it should yield to any substitute! Let its slight blemishes be cured, but in its essential features may it endure forever.

It is easily inferred that we have no acquisitions to make on this score. Yet there is something for us to do. Our office is to preserve, not to create. This last our fathers did. Sacred be the work of their hands! Heaven grant us the wisdom and the grace not to destroy what they constructed!

2. Another blessing which we should covet for our country is a *righteous and skillful administration*. For the time being, the best administration makes the best government. Despotic officers can render the mildest and most guarded polity tyrannical; for against the cunning and unmerciful, no constitutional guards can prove a perfect and sure defense. But clemency in rulers can render the worst form of government tolerable.

I use the word administration in its generic import, as embracing the legislative, the judicial, and the executive functions. These should be exercised in harmony with the Constitution, which must be sacredly guarded at whatever sacrifice. The Constitution is supreme. It is above the magistrate—it is above the judge—it is above the law and the law-maker; and, finally, it is above the people, unless they reach it by the violence of revolution, or touch it gently with its own consent, and in the manner which itself prescribes. This supremacy of the Constitution can not be too much insisted on. The popular sentiment should confess and vindicate it. The nation's heart should feel it, and the nation's pulse should quicken with jealous indignation at the least approach towards it infringement.

The administration must be beneficent as well as constitutional. It must promote the interests of the people, which it does when it places them in the best possible circumstances to acquire wealth, knowledge, and virtue. To secure such an administration, honest and wise men must be placed at its head—men whose patriotism will prompt them to seek the public good, and whose skill will devise the proper means to promote it. Intimately connected, therefore, with the character of the administration is the power of election to office. Sometimes the Constitution elects, as in hereditary monarchies and aristocracies. But in our Government the elections are mostly democratic. They depend upon the people. Consequently, another element of prosperity is,

3. *Popular intelligence and patriotism.* In the United States every man who has the right of suffrage is a sovereign. He is invested with some of the highest prerogatives that pertain to the British throne. In him are blended legislative, judicial, and executive functions. By representatives of his own selection he makes the law, interprets the law, and

administers the law. How dangerous it is to invest an ignorant and profligate man with such lofty powers! Every American citizen possesses them. In proportion, then, to the intelligence and moral integrity of our citizen population is our Government secure and the nation prospectively prosperous and happy.

4. A fourth blessing which we should earnestly crave for our country is *the prevalence of Christian principles* which, more than all other causes combined, contribute to the prosperity of nations. This they do, not merely for the conservative tendency of such principles, but because a religious veneration for God secures his friendship, and enlists the energies of Omnipotence to build up and to defend. To convince us of this we need only to consult the history of the Jews. Popular intelligence is no blessing to society without popular integrity, and incorruptible integrity can not exist without the precepts and practice of the Christian religion.

These are the moral and political elements of national prosperity. It will be seen that they are of domestic growth. They arise from internal development. There are others, external or foreign, depending on the civil or militant acts of surrounding nations. But I shall not discuss them. I think, with Mr. Randolph, that "so long as all is well at home, nothing can be dangerously wrong abroad." And what seems wrong, as something often does, might generally be reached and remedied by prayer.

Another class of inherent elements of prosperity may be denominated *natural* or *physical*. They are, extent of territory, amount of population and wealth, climate, soil, and productions; and mercantile facilities, such as sea-coast, harbors, lakes, and navigable streams. But these are familiar statistics; and as they are mostly independent of moral influence, I merely enumerate and pass them by.

Having briefly noticed the elements of national prosperity, or the blessings which we should crave for our country, I proceed,

II. To show why we should seek them by prayer. We should thus seek them,

1. *Because these elements of prosperity, and the agents who control them, are at God's disposal.* This will be admitted. At least, to deny it requires a great stretch of infidelity. What does it imply? It implies that the minds of public men can be so controlled by Jehovah, that in constructing a government they shall prefer an aristocracy to a monarchy, or a republic to both. It implies that executive officers can be so influenced by the fear of God, or by moral preferences, that they shall be faithful and just. It implies that Providence can direct the attention of nations to the pursuit of truth, and can dispose them to successful efforts for mental and religious improvement. And, lastly, it implies that he can control the policy of other nations toward *this*, and incline them to be at peace with us; or by withdrawing his merciful restraints, can leave them to turn their wrath and weapons against us. Will any deny that God *can* do these things? Whether he does them is hereafter to be inquired. At present I only affirm that he *can* do them; although by "*can*," I mean not an

ability of power, but an ability of right; that is, he may do them consistently with his moral rectitude. But,

2. We should seek these blessings by prayer, *because national interests are affected by Divine providence.* To the believer in revelation the proof is direct and conclusive. Let us advert to Scripture examples. Consider the chain of events which planted the Jews in Palestine, and made them the wonder of nations. When Abraham was called into covenant with God—when Joseph was sold into Egypt, and made its lord, and became the savior of his brethren—when Moses was rescued from the Nile, adopted by the princess, taught in the wisdom of the Egyptians, fled to Jethro, and returned as the minister of God's mercy to his countrymen, and of God's wrath to their oppressors, was not Providence preparing to build up Jerusalem? When the dust, and the waters, and the cattle, and the first-born of Egypt were cursed by the newly commissioned prophet, did not *God* curse? When the sea was divided asunder, and the rock poured out water, and the heavens rained manna, and the tables of the law were delivered at Sinai, was it not by God's own providence? When, with so many and great miracles, Joshua, at the head of the tribes, entered the promised land, had the Lord nothing to do with it? When David went, with stone and sling, against the proud Philistine, and returned with trophies of victory—when Samuel anointed and Jonathan protected him, till at last he ascended the vacant throne, was God a mere spectator? When he sinned, and his enemies became strong—when his own house was against him—when

he fled from the fury of Absalom, and the nation was humbled in the dust, was God afar off? Had he no hand in the death of the rebel, in the return of David, and in the restoration of peace to distracted Jerusalem? Had he none in the destruction of the Assyrian hosts, in the captivities of his people, and in the marvelous proceedings of Cyrus to rebuild Jerusalem and restore the tribes? And, finally, had he none in those incidents of prophesied vengeance which brought on Jerusalem her ultimate doom, and has made her peeled and scattered children a by-word and a hissing to this very day?

You may say the Jews were God's people, and Jerusalem was the place of his rest—the city which he had chosen to place his name there. I answer, under the Gospel dispensation, every nation that fears God is his peculiar people. Let us, then, turn to our own country, and see if neither the past nor the present supplies any tokens of God's gracious interference. In the events which preceded and attended the settlement of these States are there no certain indications of a Divine purpose to rear the American colonies and establish them a nation? I appeal to those who have read the history, and can call to mind its wonders. Had Providence nothing to do with the glorious Revolution? Who provided the men and the muscle—the minds and the means—the national repulsions and the political affiliations for that period of trials, and treacheries, and tragedies? Were no ministers of Providence hovering over Braddock's Field, to guard the youthful hero, in whose life were garnered the interests of unborn nations—the franchises of a continent, if not of a world? Was that life the sport of fortune through years of peril, in which the sword cut down his fellows on his right and on his left? Turn from this grateful theme to the city of brotherly love. Fancy yourself, on the Fourth of July, '76, in that venerable edifice where the charter of our freedom, framed without the leave of masters, received the pledges of our Hancocks, and Jeffersons, and Harrisons, who devoted life, property, and honor for its defense. Was no God there? Was there none to guard the ark which contained that sacred covenant, during eight years of assault, pursuit, and slaughter? Was there none to control those deliberations that gave to this nation a Constitution, which, amidst severe conflicts of opinion, was scarcely adopted by the members of this confederation? Let Franklin, standing among his peers, and urging them to pause and implore Jehovah's blessing, answer.

But in later times were there no tokens that God cared for us? Let land and sea bear testimony. Lakes and oceans are God's speaking witnesses. Go to Tippecanoe, to Fort Meigs, to the Thames, and to New Orleans, and you will light upon the monuments of Jehovah's care for this rising nation. Go any where within our borders; for almost every stream, forest, and prairie within the broad circumference of the land records some gracious deliverance from open assault or covert mischief, which, except for God's timely mercy, had betrayed us or ours to ruin. In sanguinary conflicts where thousands fought, how often was the battle ours because Heaven made it ours! In those border struggles, kept up, with slight intermissions, since the settlement of Jamestown and Plymouth, the traces of which have not yet faded from our Western fields and habitations, what sanguinary horrors have our fathers escaped by the watchful providence of Jehovah!

God was with our ancestors beyond the sea; and he moved them to adventure hither, and dwell in this vast wilderness. He made for them a highway of waters, guided them and brought them to these shores. Where they pitched their tents he erected his pavilion. He saved them from famine and the tomahawk. In peace he blessed them with harmony and increase. When necessary, he taught their hands to war and their fingers to fight, and covered their heads in the day of battle. He inspired their hearts with the love of holy freedom. He controlled the minds which framed our excellent Constitution, and gave that sacred instrument the impress of his wisdom. To say nothing of the living, he bestowed on us a civic Washington and a Harrison, to bear the burdens of Government and defend our Constitution. And in view of these facts, infidel he is—infidel in its grossest name and measure—who denies that we, as well as Israel, have had our Moses and our Joshua—our rod of miracles and angel savior. Looking back, Christian citizens, and reviewing the merciful ways of Jehovah, we should be ready to exclaim as with one voice, "The Lord of hosts is with us; the God of Jacob is *our* refuge!" And let me ask if these gracious interpositions of Providence do not infer prayer for our country? That they do will be more evident,

3. From the fact *that such interpositions of Provi-*

dence in behalf of nations are known to have occurred in answer to prayer. Not to linger on this head, were not Moses, and Hezekiah, and Daniel men of prayer? Did they not supplicate blessings on their country? Did not God regard them? Was not their country blessed, and blessed *in answer* to their prayers? Has not God *commanded* us to pray for all men, especially for all that are in authority? Surely he would not command it unless he were resolved to hear; for he has never said, "Seek ye my face in vain."

Our Pilgrim fathers were men of prayer. With prayer they journeyed to these shores, and raised their Ebenezer. With prayer they met their savage enemies, and found them as stubble beneath their feet. With prayer they subdued the wilderness, and turned it into a fruitful field. With prayer the children of Robinson, Winthrop, and Penn breasted the storm of Revolution, and secured to us freedom and happiness.

Prayer, then, for our country is reasonable; and it is the most efficient act of patriotism. Every thing else may fail. Counsel may fail—combinations of virtuous citizens may fail—the ballot-box may fail—officers of the Government may desert their principles, and become recreant to the Constitution, and to the rights of their constituents. Thus all earthly policies and struggles may be in vain. If there be any thing that can not fail to right public wrongs and correct public abuses, it is prayer. Prayer offered by one man has done more for a nation than the best appointed armies. When the wisdom of senators and the prowess of heroes have failed, prayer has done the work. It has turned the counsel of the enemy into foolishness, and slain thousands in a night. No wonder; for where the faithful pray, there are the counsel and the sword of Jehovah.

But prayer is a *catholic* mode of procuring blessings for our country. It can be practiced by all. "I can not argue for my blessed Savior," said an unlearned, pious martyr, "but I can die for him." Some of you may say, "We can not fight or make laws for our country, but we can pray for her prosperity." Old age, leaning on its staff, can cry to God for his blessing on the nation. And this is almost the only proper sphere of direct effort for female patriotism. The mothers and daughters of the land can in this way wield an influence far-reaching as the presence, and strong as the omnipotence of Jehovah. Little do we know how much the supplications of our Revolutionary mothers contributed to the acquisition of our independence. Then, woman was a patriot. She did not mount the rostrum nor the war-horse; but she threw away her luxuries; and while her warrior husband grappled with the foe, she was shut in to plead with God. Washington prayed; and he defended a praying people, and led praying hosts to battle, or we should have been, this day, the vassals of our foe—the victims of unsuccessful revolution.

Christian citizens, you must be aware that this land is full of patriotism. If all that boast their love of country should come by any means to love God, who gave that country being and is the source of all its blessings, this would be a pious as well as a patriotic people. But while you hear so much from men of all sorts, about the love of country, look a little at their conduct. Does their patriotism mix its breathings with frequent oaths and blasphemies? They love their country as Satan loved the Savior when they stood together on a pinnacle of the temple. When such men talk about their love of country, the good may blush to be called patriots. Such patriotism is cheap. It costs little, and yet it always passes for its value.

If we love our country, let us publish it by our deeds, not by sounding a trumpet before us. As Christians, let us never display our patriotism by assuming the air of the demagogue, and contributing to the tumult of popular conventions. Let us not dishonor God's holy religion by public or private orations, made up of strange admixtures of eulogy and slander, both as vulgar as can well be invented, and expressed in terms better suited to the genius of Robespierre than to the temper of a lowly Christian. Railing is not a Christian service, even though it be at unworthy public officers. We may assail them in our closets with far better success, and this will be religious opposition. A *Christian demagogue* is next to Satan in uncomeliness of character. His deformity defies description. If we will abandon ourselves to this earthly drudgery, let us throw off our religious garb, and not involve Christ and the Church. The Christian who thus seeks to benefit his country has lost sight of his calling, or never understood it. He has laid aside spiritual for carnal weapons. However good his cause, he does neither guard nor grace it. He is as much out of character as Gabriel would be, bearing about with him the weapons of an assassin. An angel of light, disrobed of his celestial and Divinely appointed panoply, represents the Christian who, in attempting to serve his country, forgets to pray for its prosperity but yields himself up to partisan affiliations and rash political enterprise. Such professors of religion are a scourge to any country.

I rejoice that prayer still ascends to God in behalf of this republic. Happy for us that the altars on which our fathers offered incense are not all fallen down. Happy, that a few of them remain in high places. I rejoice to remind you that Harrison prayed. Among the virtues which the nation unitedly accord him, let this be placed foremost. I confess my admiration for his patriotism, his heroism, and his unostentatious benevolence in private life. But while I cheerfully acknowledge these, most of all I venerate his *efforts at devotion.* I regret his death for many reasons, but chiefly because in him we had a praying President, who, each morning and each evening, commenced and closed his public labors, by imploring God's assistance in the execution of his trusts and pleading for the Divine benediction upon his country. As a nation we needed this example. Let it not be lost upon us. While we treasure in our memories his dying words, let us be mindful of his manner of life during his brief Executive career. It silently invokes us, in the language of David, to "pray for the peace of Jerusalem." It testifies that he deemed the supreme Governor of nations worthy to be sought unto by subordinate rulers. Let us imitate his confessions of dependence on Jehovah.

We may watchfully regard the institutions of the land, but without God's aid we can not defend them. We may strive to resist assaults upon our civil Constitution; but without his aid our strength shall be as chaff. We may aim to heal the breaches in that sacred instrument; but unless God undertake for us, they will not be healed. We may boldly offer to withstand the shock of battle when it comes; but unless he defend, we perish in the conflict. In all things we are dependent upon Him who setteth up one and pulleth down another, and who as easily controls nations as he does men.

Finally, there is no hope for this nation but in prayer. When we become undevout, we shall be scattered and peeled. Nations originally ungodly may, for a season, survive a state of profligate infidelity and depravity; but a nation originally devout, can not part with its religion and retain its national honor and prosperity. Greece and Rome, with all their foul idolatries, were not quickly destroyed; but Jerusalem was suddenly and fearfully overwhelmed. So will it be with us. Surrounding nations may sin and survive. But if *we* turn to idols, we rush to fearful ruin. The foundations of this Government were laid with pious hands. It was reared with solemn invocations to Jehovah, and was defended by the supplications of devout, warring hosts. When it shall come to shelter the prayerless and profane, its office will cease. Then God will blot it from the earth, and commission holier men to rear up millennial institutions in its place. Let us not suppose that the piety of our ancestors will save their degenerate children from this deserved doom. Remember the Savior's warning to the Jews, "Think not to say within yourselves, 'We have Abraham to our father;' for God is able of these stones to raise up children unto Abraham." No wrath is so consuming as that which falls on a people whom God has blessed in vain. The Jews are an example. Like them we are blessed—in mercy may we never share their withering curse!

XXIII.

THE INCARNATION.

"*The Word was made flesh and dwelt among us.*" John i, 14.

THE incarnation is the first among the series of wonders in redemption. Whoever seeks to know the Gospel, must, as a learner, commence here. The first lesson must be the nativity. Let us, then, compose our thoughts to meditation on the origin, the mode, the mystery, the motive, and the beneficence of the incarnation.

I. Its *origin* is the love of God. Not the love of the Father only, but the love of Father, Son, and Spirit. An affection of the Trinity moved Christ's incarnation. It will mar and quench the beauty and the fire of our devotions to trace this gift exclusively to either divine person. It is true that "God gave the Son to be the Savior of the world;" and it is equally true that the Son gave himself. The several persons of Jehovah were consenting, and it was a common sacrifice—a sacrifice not only on the part of the Son who was crucified, but also on the part of the ever-blessed Trinity, who gave him to be crucified.

It is usually understood that Deity is impassive; or, in other words, is unsusceptible of suffering. This doctrine may be taught in the Bible, and may be confirmed by reason; but I suppose it does not imply that God can not exercise compassion. If so, I, for one, reject it. I know that the lament of Jesus over Jerusalem, and his tears at the grave of Lazarus, are ascribed to his humanity; and that may be according to truth—but certainly his language and behavior on those occasions scarcely equal in pathos the following exclamation of Jehovah over his ancient people: "How shall I give thee up, Ephraim? how shall I deliver thee, Israel? how shall I make thee as Admah? how shall I set thee as Zeboim? My heart is turned within me, my repentings are kindled together." Hosea xi, 8.

Is not this the language of compassion? It may be said that "it is accommodated to our conceptions." Then it surely teaches us that God is not all intellect; for it expresses "to our conceptions" the most benevolent and intense sympathies. If he is susceptible of no such emotions, how are our conceptions aided by language which indicates them? I feel warranted by this and many similar texts to maintain, as an article of my creed, that the infinite God is susceptible of compassion; or at least of a sentiment which can be designated by no better word in our language. I mean by compassion, in this instance, *a benevolent state* of the divine affections, under the *hinderance of God's charity or mercy*, through the *perverse tempers of free moral agents.* To speak of "the hinderance of God's mercy" may startle some, but not if they will study and fairly interpret such language as, "How often would I have gathered thy children together as a hen gathereth her brood under her wings, and ye would not!" Surely, if words can unequivocally indicate the "hinderance of mercy by perverse tempers," here is an example. I conclude, therefore, that they who inculcate the impassive nature of Deity do not thereby exclude him from compassion. But if God exercises compassion, when, in the progress of his universal government, was there the greatest occasion for its exercise? Doubtless when he gave his only begotten and well-beloved Son to bear the sin of a reprobated world.

Though the Father, Son, and Spirit are one divine essence, yet they are three divine persons; and the persons as well as the essence are eternal. The plurality of this Unity is such that it forms society. Of course, God is not solitary; nor was he before he commenced his creation. As far back as when no creature existed, God enjoyed fellowships infinitely blissful. This is an argument in the mouth of philosophy, to confirm the Scriptural testimony in favor of the Trinity. To suppose that before his first act of creation God had existed in a state of eternal solitude, is exceedingly repulsive to reason; and those who hold the doctrine of a Trinity need not suppose it. They may claim that there was always communion on the throne of God, and to corroborate the sentiment, may refer to Christ's words in John xvii, 5: "And now, O Father, glorify thou me with thine own self, with the glory which *I had with thee before the world was.*" And again, in verse 24: "Father, I will that they also whom thou hast given me, be with me where I am; that they may behold my glory which thou hast given me; for thou *lovedst me before the foundation of the world.*"

These texts unfold interesting particulars in regard to Christ's preëxistence. They not only confirm the fact that he did exist before his incarnation, that is, from eternity, but they teach us that such was the distinction (of persons) between the Father and the Son, that the Son could be the object of the Father's love. They teach us also that such was the exalted equality of these two persons, that the divine glory was common to both.

The second particular is what immediately concerns us. The Father loved the Son before the foundation of the world; that is, eternally. Mutual love constitutes fellowship. Parental and filial love form the most blissful of all fellowships. Such love there was between the Father and the Son. And it was eternal. O, then, what oceans of bliss must have attended these eternal fellowships between the persons of the Trinity! The Father loved the Son with a *parental* love, and, of course, with affections as intense as was possible to the Infinite Mind; for the Divine perfections of the Son warranted such an intense love.

But, in compassion to our race, the Father "gives his Son," "delivers him up," "spares him not," "bruises him," "puts him to grief," "makes his soul an offering for sin." Here is a sacrifice (not in the sense of penal sufferings, like those of the cross) on the part of the Father. The Son consents to be "delivered," "bruised," "put to grief," and suffer the hidings of his Father's face for a season. Here is a preliminary sacrifice on the part of the Son. And doubtless the Holy Ghost shares in these counsels of pity. That the gift of Jesus was a sacrifice on the part of the Father, we can not but infer from the language of Scripture: "He that *spared* not his own Son, but freely gave him up for us all, how shall he not with him also freely give us all things?" That it was a sacrifice on the part of the Son we learn from the agony in the garden, and from the expiring cry, "My God! my God! why hast thou forsaken me?" That the Holy Spirit joined in this sacrifice we may infer from the fact that God, in all his sacred persons, consented to the incarnation—the Holy Spirit, especially, having "prepared a body for the Son."

From all this I would conduct you to a conclusion which I conceive to be of practical importance. It is that the three persons of the Godhead, moved by one common affection, namely, compassion for our fallen race, made a common effort to restore us to purity and happiness. The Son is the atoning victim, and the formal sacrifice is made by him. Yet his chief agony did not consist in overt persecutions, or in pains inflicted by mortal hands, but in the hidings of his Father's face; and this last was a deprivation to the Father who inflicted, as well as to the Son who endured it. The Father "*spared*" the Son to be thus "*bruised*" by the Almighty Hand. Those infinitely blessed fellowships which had eternally subsisted between the persons of the Trinity, were now, as to their usual form, interrupted; and mingled in their felicities were the agonies of the filial and the compassions of the paternal God. It follows that, so far as tokens of compassion for our fallen state may provoke our penitence and adoration, we should worship not merely *one* but the three persons of Deity with equal ardors of gratitude and praise. We owe our redemption to God—to Father, Son, and Spirit. It is true that in Jesus we see "the fullness of the Godhead"—the fullness of the Divine compassion for our race. And it is not to be wondered at that when we adore, our grateful hearts should be turned to the cross, and should yearn over the victim of our transgressions. But enlightened devotion, such as the holy on earth and in heaven experience, recognizes the overwhelming presence and mercy and power of the Father, Son, and Holy Spirit.

Having thus considered the origin of the incarnation, and traced it by the Scriptures to the compassion of the Trinity, let us,

II. Contemplate its *mode.* First, it was a *real* incarnation. There was nothing illusory or merely apparent in Christ's humanity. His physical sensibilities and wants were strictly those of flesh and blood—were such as all men experience, except as sin and habit may have modified them. The Scriptures testify that Jesus Christ was made of a woman; that there is one God and one Mediator between God and men, the *man* Christ Jesus; that, as by man came death, by man also shall come the resurrection of the dead. To become man he is represented as having "emptied himself" of the form of God. All these hints and declarations are in direct opposition to a sentiment which early obtained among certain heretics who taught that Christ was not born of a woman, nor was in reality man; but that his birth, and sufferings, and death were illusory—in a word, that all pertaining to his earthly state was a mere apparition from heaven. It was necessary, if we credit the Scriptures, that the Redeemer should partake of the nature of the redeemed. Jesus therefore became man. He assumed not only a body, but a human soul, with its proper susceptibilities and infirmities. He became familiar with all the innocent weaknesses and woes of our nature ; and purposely so, for to feel and suffer like us were essential to the perfect fulfillment of the mediatorship which he had assumed. "We have not an high priest who can not be touched with the feeling of our infirmities ; but was in all points tempted as we are, yet without sin ;" "wherefore, in all things it behooved him to be made like unto his brethren, that he might be a merciful and faithful high priest in things pertaining to God. For in that he himself hath suffered, being tempted, he is able to succor them that are tempted." Heb. ii, iv.

Second, the incarnation was attended with circumstances of deep *humiliation.* Our Savior was born in an insignificant town ; and yet it seems to have contained no solitary dwelling mean enough to suit his poverty and obscurity. Mary, therefore, in the hour of her extremity, was expelled all human habitation, and in the rudest, vilest spot in its suburbs, gave birth to the Prince of glory. Among all the millions of mankind, history records the birth of *one* in a stable—that one is the Son of God. Who would have thought that she whom the angel pronounced "blessed among women," being driven out from human to brute habitations, should suffer unattended, and in the solitude of her strange exile and desertion, should mingle the notes of her first faint eucharist with the bleatings of the flock, and the lowings of the herd? The poverty of his parents, with their unseasonable but necessary journeying and absence from home, rendered the circumstances of the Savior's birth extremely humiliating. But the Holy One elected his own states, and was willing, it would seem, by his meek example, to teach us lightly to esteem the world, and to behave as pilgrims on earth. Thus does he admonish the rich of their nothingness, and the poor to take contentment and heaven as their portion. From the manger and the chill Winter night of the nativity, penury, in the midst of its sorest deprivations, may seek a gracious relief.

Third, this event was attended with tokens of *heavenly gratulation.* Those holy beings who had worshiped Christ in heaven, followed the descending train of his glory, that they might also worship him on earth. And though they found him humbled to the fashion of a man, it but served to inflame their seraphic ardors, and feed the fire of their devotion. Moreover, they had been used to approach him with loud-swelling anthems, and they could not then pay him a silent homage. They had been wont also to see every member of the celestial hierarchies join to fall prostrate in his presence; and then they would fain behold every thing on earth that had life join in holy raptures to offer him praise; and scarcely did they seem to be aware that simply to proclaim the presence of the Son of God on earth would not secure to him its universal homage. They burned, therefore, with such ardors to announce his gracious advent, and rouse the world to transports, that they could not wait on the shepherds' dreams. Impatient of their slumber, the joy burst forth, and heaven and earth were filled with halleluiahs. Dreary ages had passed since, at sight of this creation, "the morning stars sang together, and all the sons of God shouted for joy;" but then the sad silence was broken, and a "multitude of the heavenly host sang, Glory to God in the highest, on earth peace, good-will toward men."

These events, like the former, afford us instruction and admonition. Among other things they teach us that poverty is not always an infliction of God's wrath, and indicative of his displeasure; but that it sometimes attaches to the heavenly minded, as a certain badge of honor, indicating that the soul is too celestial in its relishes and joys to find any satisfaction in earthly goods and riches. Surely, this is not the only instance in which heavenly ministers have honored the meanest states of mortals with their attendance and commendation. The unheralded by earth are sometimes the heralded of heaven. How many who were born, and lived, and died, like Jesus reprobated and distressed, have also like him been the beloved of God—have been overshadowed by the dove-like Spirit, and are now watched and guarded in the sepulcher, that they may rise and "sit down with him on his throne!" For their comfort and joy let the obscure worshipers of Christ come, like the wise men, to the manger, and behold in the feeble embraces of the virgin, the despised of mortals, but the adored of angels—the scorn of earth, but the supreme beauty and glory of heaven. But,

III. Let us turn to the *mysteries* of the incarnation. It contains a series, and I will begin with the least, if least may be applied to what is infinite and overwhelming.

It is a great mystery that God should assume the nature of any creature. To say nothing of the comparative dignity of that creature, or the object to be gained in assuming its nature, it is an insolvable mystery that Deity would assume any finite nature for any object whatever. He could not do it *for his own sake.* He was infinitely satisfied with himself, and needed not the addition of creature attributes for self-fruition. Indeed, it is an interesting speculation that all unsinning intelligences are doubtless happy in their own constitutional attributes and prerogatives. It is safe to go a step further and say that all thinking, holy beings are so satisfied with their own natures that they would elect to be what they are, rather than any other order of intelligences. Angels do not wish to be men; and but for their sin and depravity, men would not wish to be angels. For the full contentment of his unoffending creatures, God has doubtless imparted to every order a just self-complacency—an innate preference of its own nature above that of others; except it be the preference of adoration which flows toward the Supreme and Divine. The idea of a voluntary change of nature, for self-enjoyment or aggrandizement, could not arise among creatures. Above all it could not arise in relation to God, as though he who is infinitely blessed could find an increase of self-fruition by assuming another, an inferior nature.

As God could not assume another nature for his

own sake, so neither was he bound by any considerations of justice or of charity, to do it in behalf of his creatures. Without it he always was and would ever have remained perfectly just and infinitely benevolent. Benevolence demands no more of any being than that his existing powers be employed to the utmost in promoting happiness. From eternity all the powers of Deity had been thus unceasingly employed. His assumption of another nature, not divine, in order to enlarge the sphere or multiply the trophies of his benevolence, is what no finite mind could have conceived. It never occurred to man, amidst the ruins of his fall; and when the revelation came by the Divine Word, it was most difficult to be believed; and, indeed, to this very day, faith in so great a mystery stands not "in the wisdom of man, but in the power of God."

But there is another mystery in the incarnation, namely: That God should have assumed our nature, and not rather the nature of angels. So far as we can learn, angels are our superiors, either in nature or in station, or in both. They were the first-born; and if primogeniture gave them no claim to so great a heritage, they were also the first fallen. Why, then, did not Mercy first find them out? We have no Scripture answer, and of course have no grounds to prejudge why theirs was not a misery as moving and as attractive to Mercy as was the human, and as well calculated to clothe the eternal Word in their suffering nature as in ours. It is true that some would explain this mystery. They assure us that as angels fell without and man with external temptations, it is meet that redemption pass them by and come to us. This would be more satisfactory if it were a reason revealed. Others tell us that man was made in God's image, and hence the propriety of man's redemption. But though man bears the image of his Maker, it is not easy to prove that angels are not miniature likenesses of the same glorious original. Had we as minute a history of the angels as we have of man, we could better decide whether man is more or less like his Creator than they are. As it is, we have no means of ascertaining.

But there is a third mystery. Why did Deity assume our nature in its most *abject form?* For this who can discern a necessity? It does not harmonize with the views of mankind. The Church itself has contrary notions of what is proper and for the glory of God, if we may judge from the pomp and luxury with which she displaces all the insignia of Christ's humiliation and self-abasement. But our blessed Lord not only took on him the seed of Abraham, but assumed the form of a servant, and wedded himself to the most needy, suffering state of mortals. Without wealth, without friends, without family distinction, he was eminent principally for his homelessness, poverty, and worldly reproach. If flesh and blood for sufferings and atonement were necessary, why did he not appear as a prince among men and demand the respect and homage of the world? Why did he not appropriate the bounties of nature to relieve his hunger, and thirst, and weariness; and not, while he was Lord of worlds, pass from region to region of his own broad domains "without even a place to lay his head!"

The fourth mystery is, that Jesus should *retain* our nature when it was no more needed for the uses to which it was originally devoted. He became human that he might suffer and die, and thus atone for our sins. Having atoned, why did he not lay aside his humanity and be as he was before the incarnation? We can not answer. That an eternal union should be confirmed between the two natures, the human and divine, is almost too much for thought or utterance; and had not the Scriptures declared it, the bare conception would seem most profane. The human nature forever blended with the divine, in One who shall be adored by saints and angels as they cast their crowns at the feet of Jesus! This is a mystery indeed. We can not wonder that the prophet exclaims, "Great is the mystery," nor that the angels should ardently desire to look into these things.

I would further observe that the incarnation is among the greatest of all religious mysteries. That the incarnate Word should die for us is no more difficult to be believed than that for us he should be clothed with the attributes of humanity and appear in fashion as a man. Credit this first assumption of the Gospel, and all else can easily be believed. Some who profess faith in the incarnation stumble at the cross. But this is most unreasonable. Whoever will attentively consider, must perceive that the first scene in redemption is equal to any and all that follow; and that if we skeptically demur to the doctrine of vicarious atonement, it is madness to admit that the "Word became flesh." Grant that the Word was incarnate, and it is easy to believe that he died for the world. Well, therefore, does the apostle commence the recital of the mysteries of godliness, by saying, "God was *manifest in the flesh.*"

Let not the mysteries of the incarnation discourage our faith, and rob us of the sure foundation of our hopes. Creation is full of mystery. All that God is, and all that he does, involves countless wonders, each of which is as far beyond our comprehension as any fact revealed in the Gospel. Angels wondered at the nativity, but they did not pause to doubt and cavil. Transported at the scene of Christ's humiliation, in strains of irrepressible rapture, they published his advent to the world. Let us follow the example, and being assured of the incarnation by the testimony of God, who can not lie, the greater its mystery the more fervently let us adore. Let the wonders of redemption feed the flame of our devotion. Let the ardors of our gratitude and praise be suited, if that were possible, to "the length, and breadth, and height, and depth of the love of Jesus, which passeth knowledge."

IV. Let us consider the *motive* of our blessed Savior's incarnation. We have seen that its origin was the compassion of God; but what roused that compassion? Doubtless the misery of mankind. He who will take the Scriptures in their natural import may be easily convinced of this. The very titles of the Messiah indicate it. Redeemer, Savior, Deliverer, etc., are names which carry the mind, by direct association, to the ruined and distressed condition of our race. In the prophecies it is testified by one who personifies Jesus Christ, "He hath sent me to bind up the broken-hearted, to proclaim liberty to the captive, and the opening of the prison to them that are bound." Our Savior says, "I am come to seek and to save that which was lost."

My object in urging that the motive of Christ's incarnation was the relief of human misery, may be briefly set forth. It has been urged by some divines that the great aim of redemption and its economy is the *glory of God.* This I conceive to be wholly unscriptural, and calculated to diminish the power of the Gospel on the hearts of men. The divine glory is doubtless manifested by the humiliation and sufferings of Christ; but that is an incident, (a precious one indeed,) and not the chief object of redemption. The grand object was man's salvation. Compassion for our woes, not solicitude for his own glory, brought the Son of God to the manger and the cross. God "*so loved* [pitied] *the world,* that he gave his only begotten Son." If the divine glory were to have remained the same in its manifestations we have reason to believe that God would still have given his Son for the world.

In devising the scheme of redemption, a method was adopted which should not *impair* the Divine glory—that should even reveal it in new and attractive forms. The first was necessary, and the last was desirable. It was necessary that God should be just in justifying them that believe in Jesus. And in all atoning acts and sufferings the integrity of God's character was cautiously maintained, and, indeed, more than maintained. It was, as already said, illustrated in a manner most wonderful and overwhelming to his creatures. Moreover, the blessedness of the redeemed and the glory of the Redeemer are so blended in the salvation of man, that we can not, ought not, to separate them in our devotions; and in those states of mind which arise under the sanctifying, comforting influences of the Spirit, we can not separate them. In those blessed moments we invariably feel that while man is ineffably blest, God is ineffably glorified by the cross. But in stating doctrine it is profitable to distinguish them, and place them in a Scriptural relation to the sufferings of Christ. And without controversy, the great object of the incarnation was man's rescue from sin and its miseries, and his everlasting blessedness in heaven. This was what occupied the thoughts and the affections of the Trinity when Father, Son, and Spirit concerted our redemption—when the Father gave his well-beloved Son—when the Son said, "Lo, I come! I delight to do thy will, O God"—when the scenes of the manger, the temptation, the garden, and the cross were transpiring in the face of earth and heaven.

V. The *beneficence* of the incarnation is a boundless field; but we can only glance at some of its productions.

The first is *probation.* This is a great and gracious prerogative. Survey man as fallen and divested of this one mercy. Look at Adam after the trangression and previous to the first evangelical promise; look at Judas when the treason was executed, and the irrevocable curse of his Master was upon him; look at the son or daughter of perdition, who, in the midst of a revival, has scorned the last visit of grace, and, forsaken of God, is bound over to a fiery retribution. Inquire of reprobate angels sealed with the signet of God's wrath, what is the value of probation. In the light of such examples we may better comprehend the magnitude of this unspeakable mercy. The doomed murderer in the prison or on the scaffold would give worlds for so slighted a grace. Who, then, can estimate its value, when it is the boon of an immortal spirit, and takes hold on unending weal or woe? We enjoy it. Each moment of life is a moment of trial—each thought inclines us to heaven or to hell—and to this or that by our own free election.

And whence this probation? Was it an original condition of our being? Did the charter of our creation embrace the reserved privileges of repentance and pardon—of the recovery of purity, peace, and heaven, forfeited and spurned? Look and see. "In the day thou eatest thereof thou shalt surely die." This and the expulsion, and the flaming sword of the cherubim, were poor encouragements to the exiles from Eden and from the presence of God. But soon (so sudden was Mercy in her movements) a ray of light glimmered amid this horrible darkness. "Her seed shall bruise thy head." From that obscure dawn what a day of hope has risen upon a forlorn world! But while we walk in its light, let us never forget that each moment of our probation has cost a drop of Jesus' blood. If it is cheap to us, it is dear to the dying Lamb. The blessed Savior has endowed us with no months, days, hours, or moments to be squandered in idleness or profaned by crime. He bestowed on us the costly gift that we might run a race—might make an expiring struggle for a crown of life.

Another beneficent result of the incarnation is *light* to discern the uses of probation. Without light probation were no grace ; and yet they may be separated. By the willful blindness of mortals they *are* separated, but not by Divine providence. Partially by his Word, and universally by his Spirit, he scatters light throughout the nations ; so that even the pagans, being a law unto themselves, are without excuse. But the full-orbed luminary is the Bible, which minutely traces the line of our duty, and admonishes us of every lurking danger—of every earthly and Satanic device to betray us into sin and convert our probation into an aggravated curse. And this light is the purchase of the cross. Every admonition of the Bible and of the Spirit cost the blessed Jesus groans of agony and sweat of blood.

A third beneficent result of the incarnation is the *proffer of power* to every probationer, to secure the utmost benefits of probation. Light without strength would be unavailing ; therefore, "when we were without strength, in due time Christ died for the ungodly." That is, he died not only to save us from ungodliness, but from *weakness;* and now, by his death, we may have power as well as pardon. Seeking by prayer, the unpardoned may obtain the aid of the Spirit to produce in them conviction, godly sorrow, and regeneration. By the same gracious power the regenerated may "be strengthened with all might in the inner man." This power of the Holy Spirit, without which light would be no mercy, and probation would be a curse, comes to us only through the incarnate and crucified Jesus. These are the principal benefits of the incarnation. Are they not ineffably rich and glorious?

This is the season which, according to the usages of the Church, is especially devoted to pious meditations on the nativity of our blessed Lord. And now, reviewing the theme, and associating the origin, the mode, the mystery, the motive, and the beneficence of the incarnation, how can we refrain from yielding our souls, bodies, and spirits a willing sacrifice unto God? Is not this a *reasonable* service? If Christ did condescend to purchase us at so great expense, and God will condescend to accept us, shall we decline? God forbid! Let us hasten to his altar, and seal our vows. Then let us hold up before us perpetual monitors of our duty and our sacred obligations, the manger, the garden, the cross! These are never to be thought upon but with raptures of joy, nor mentioned but in hosannas to the dying Lamb.

THE END.

www.ingramcontent.com/pod-product-compliance
Lightning Source LLC
LaVergne TN
LVHW021147110826
845150LV00005B/1146

* 9 7 8 1 4 2 5 5 4 8 1 8 6 *